Discovering God is the greatest adventure one can go on! Lee Strobel brings together some of the best-of-the-best thinkers to shed light on some of our most pressing questions. His approach is simple: examine the evidence and be willing to follow wherever it leads. I'm confident this book will help you better know the love of God!

Tim Tebow

Whether you're a faithful believer or hardened skeptic, if you will join Lee Strobel on his truth-seeking adventure with an open mind, I promise you'll learn something new! If you struggle with questions about the existence of God, Lee's excellent research skills—and deep-dive interviews with a variety of experts—provide fascinating insights that will help you find the answers you're seeking.

Shannon Bream, anchor of *Fox News Sunday*

I can live without being omniscient. I don't need to know everything. But I can't live without knowing whether God is real. If God is not real, then ultimately *nothing* matters. If God is real, then *everything* matters. Every thought. Every word. Every action. Like a world-class defense attorney, Lee Strobel makes another solid case not only for the reality of God but also for how to become his friend. Don't miss these precise, succinct, and powerful proofs that demonstrate God is real!

Kirk Cameron

There are times in life when things happen to us that make no sense and cause us to wonder if God is even there. My friend Lee Strobel tackles this and many other questions in his newest book. I love his refreshing, down-to-earth approach in which he asks the hard questions and helps us realize there are answers. As a former atheist, he gets to the bottom of the big questions of life with both biblical and logical arguments. If you're a believer, *Is God Real?* will help you doubt your doubts and believe your beliefs. And if you're not yet a believer, it may well give you the answers you're searching for. I highly recommend it!

Greg Laurie, pastor and evangelist, Harvest Church

Is God Real? is profoundly edifying and encouraging! Lee Strobel's signature journalistic style shines as he interviews several experts in fields ranging from science to history to biblical scholarship. He covers some of the most difficult questions surrounding the existence of God and the truthfulness of Christianity with exceptional ease and accessibility. For a culture of doubt and deconstruction, this book is a breath of fresh air.

Alisa Childers, author, *Another Gospel* and *Live Your Truth and Other Lies*; host, the *Alisa Childers* podcast

Lee Strobel has encouraged and challenged skeptic and believer alike for years now through his intriguing and insightful books. In *Is God Real?* he's done it again. Believers will be encouraged in their faith, while skeptics will be invited into faith.

Dr. Derwin L. Gray, cofounder and lead pastor, Transformation Church; author, *Lit Up with Love* (forthcoming)

Lee Strobel has done it again. Through asking insightful questions and telling captivating stories, he takes readers through a step-by-step process of examining the evidence for Christianity. *Is God Real?* is perfect for both seekers willing to explore the big questions of life and believers wanting to understand the reasonable foundations of faith. Wherever you are in your faith journey, you won't want to put this book down.

Sean McDowell, PhD, professor of apologetics, Biola University; author or coauthor of more than twenty books, including *Evidence for Jesus*

One thing I appreciate about Lee Strobel's books is his combination of depth and accessibility. His latest work provides an all-around introduction to some of the most impactful reasons for belief in the existence of God. You'll begin an exploration of the scientific, philosophical, historical, and existential arguments that have provided not only answers but also hope to so many people on their own spiritual journey. And in his characteristically gracious approach, he invites you—not tells you—to consider whether God is real.

Mary Jo Sharp, assistant professor of apologetics, Houston Christian University; founder, Confident Christianity Ministries

As new technologies add to the general confusion over what's real and what's not, popular author Lee Strobel brings his journalistic expertise to eight of the most significant interviews of his life to date. From each distinguished scholar, Strobel draws a robust case for the reality of God and skillfully ensures that readers will be able to grasp the potency of the evidence presented. I highly recommend this book to all who wrestle with doubt—or who desire to be of help to those who do.

Hugh Ross, PhD, astrophysicist

Lee Strobel has done it again. This time, he turns his unparalleled journalistic talent toward one of the most pressing questions of our time. As one of the few people who have the expertise, interview skills, or access to the world's most renowned experts, Lee investigates in *Is God Real?* the existence of God as a true professional journalist, asking the toughest questions and documenting the evidence so his readers can make the final decision. If you've ever searched for an answer to this question or know someone who has, this book is for *you*.

J. Warner Wallace, *Dateline* featured cold-case detective; senior fellow at the Colson Center for Christian Worldview; adjunct professor of apologetics at Talbot School of Theology (Biola University), Southern Evangelical, and Gateway Seminary; author of *Cold-Case Christianity* and *Person of Interest*

Is God Real? is vintage Lee Strobel. His books are always clear, interesting, and chock-full of ideas, and they do not dodge the tough questions for which people need answers. *Is God Real?* may be his best book yet. It focuses on the most fundamental topics a human being can ask: Is there a God and a purpose to life? If so, what is God like? How do we really know that our answers to these questions are true and reasonable? Moreover, Strobel's selection of expert interviewees could not be improved on. I urge atheists, Christians, and members of other religions to read this book. It is so good that intellectual honesty requires it.

J. P. Moreland, distinguished professor of philosophy, Talbot School of Theology, Biola University; coauthor, *The Substance of Consciousness*

If you could have only one of Lee Strobel's wonderful Case books, this would be the one. Lee takes the best of all of those award-winning books, updates them, adds new material, and puts everything into one life-changing read. With evidence like this, there is little doubt that God is real and that there is eternal hope for you and me.

Frank Turek, president of CrossExamined.org and author of *I Don't Have Enough Faith to Be an Atheist*

The need for engaging, accessible treatment of the key arguments for God's existence, the truth of Christianity, and the rationality of hope in a broken world is more urgent than ever. Lee Strobel's characteristic wit and insightful interview techniques make *Is God Real?* a fantastic gateway resource both for those exploring the Christian faith and for believers seeking to strengthen their faith and beef up their evangelistic tool chest.

Melissa Cain Travis, PhD, author of *Thinking God's Thoughts* and *Science and the Mind of the Maker*

IS
GOD
REAL?

ALSO BY LEE STROBEL

IS GOD REAL?

EXPLORING THE ULTIMATE
QUESTION OF LIFE

LEE STROBEL

NEW YORK TIMES BESTSELLING AUTHOR

ZONDERVAN
BOOKS

ZONDERVAN BOOKS

Is God Real?
Copyright © 2023 by Lee Strobel

Requests for information should be addressed to:
Zondervan, *3900 Sparks Dr. SE, Grand Rapids, Michigan 49546*

Zondervan titles may be purchased in bulk for educational, business, fundraising, or sales promotional use. For information, please email SpecialMarkets@Zondervan.com.

ISBN 978-0-310-36823-6 (international trade paper edition)
ISBN 978-0-310-36852-6 (special edition)
ISBN 978-0-310-36789-5 (audio)

Library of Congress Cataloging-in-Publication Data

Names: Strobel, Lee, 1952- author.
Title: Is God real? : exploring the ultimate question of life / Lee Strobel.
Description: Grand Rapids : Zondervan, 2023. | Includes bibliographical references.
Identifiers: LCCN 2023031050 (print) | LCCN 2023031051 (ebook) | ISBN 9780310367871 (hardcover) | ISBN 9780310367888 (ebook)
Subjects: LCSH: God—Proof. | Apologetics. | BISAC: RELIGION / Christian Theology / Apologetics | RELIGION / Christian Living / Personal Growth
Classification: LCC BT103 .S775 2023 (print) | LCC BT103 (ebook) | DDC 231—dc23/eng/20230807
LC record available at https://lccn.loc.gov/2023031050
LC ebook record available at https://lccn.loc.gov/2023031051

Selected interviews were edited from some of Lee Strobel's earlier books, including *The Case for a Creator*, *The Case for Miracles*, *The Case for Heaven*, *The Case for Faith*, and *In Defense of Jesus*.

Author is represented by the literary agent Don Gates @ THE GATES GROUP, www.the-gates-group.com.

Cover design: James W. Hall IV
Cover photo: Stocktrek Images, Inc. / Alamy Stock Photo
Interior design: Denise Froehlich

Printed in the United States of America

23 24 25 26 27 LBC 5 4 3 2 1

To Tony and Debbie Ferguson—
encouragers

CONTENTS

INTRODUCTION

Exploring Whether God Is Real

Believing in something doesn't make it true. Hoping that something is true doesn't make it true. The existence of God is not subjective. He either exists or he doesn't. It's not a matter of opinion. You can have your own opinions. But you can't have your own facts.

Ricky Gervais, "Why I'm an Atheist," *Wall Street Journal*, December 9, 2010

More than two hundred times a second, around the clock, someone is asking an online search engine about God—often with the simple inquiry, "Is God real?" If you type that question into Google, you'll get 3.7 billion results in two-thirds of a second—a digital tidal wave that generates more confusion than enlightenment.[1]

As for those who seek wisdom from the disembodied voice of Siri, there's only disappointment. Asked if God is real, she replies with a seeming shrug: "It's all a mystery to me." Even Artificial Intelligence comes up short. When ChatGPT is asked whether God exists, it offers a shallow overview of competing perspectives before concluding, "I cannot give a personal opinion on this matter."

Indeed, the question of whether God is real is the most

consequential issue of all because so much hangs on the answer. What exactly is at stake? As evolutionary biologist and atheist William Provine said, if there is no creator, then these are the inescapable implications:

- There's no evidence for God.
- There's no life after death.
- There's no absolute foundation for right and wrong.
- There's no absolute meaning for life.
- People don't really have free will.[2]

In recent years, the percentage of Americans who believe in God has been declining. According to Gallup, 87 percent said they believed in God in 2017, but that number dropped to 81 percent by 2022—the lowest in American history. In contrast, the number was 98 percent in 1967. When pressed about whether they are *certain* that God exists, only 64 percent of US adults now say yes.[3]

"The question of whether God is real is the most consequential issue of all because so much hangs on the answer."

Still, there are some positive spiritual signs as well. A survey in late 2022 showed that three out of four US adults said they want to grow spiritually, and nearly half (44 percent) said they are more open to God today than before the COVID-19 pandemic.[4] Three-quarters of Millennials say they're "searching for a sense of purpose in life."[5]

The numbers are starker for younger Americans. Generation Z (those born between 1999 and 2015) has been called the first post-Christian generation. For them, said Barna Research, "'atheist' is no longer a dirty word." They are twice as likely to call themselves atheist as older adults (13 percent versus 6 percent).[6]

At the same time, rates of depression and anxiety are soaring among young people. According to a 2023 report by the Centers for Disease Control, "almost 60 percent of female students experienced persistent feelings of sadness or hopelessness during the past year and nearly 25 percent made a suicide plan."[7]

"The bad news is that Gen Z is flat on its back, knocked down by sadness, loneliness, and anxiety," said youth ministry expert Greg Stier. The good news, he said, is that this sense of hopelessness is resulting in an increased openness to seeking spiritual answers.[8]

Shane Pruitt, who travels the country to speak with young people about faith, said in 2023, "I've personally seen more college students and teens start following Jesus in the last three years than in the previous eighteen years of ministry combined."[9]

Pollster David Kinnaman put it this way: "The rumors of Christianity's demise among younger people are greatly exaggerated."[10] In fact, predictions about the death of Christianity in America date back two hundred years, with Thomas Jefferson claiming in the 1820s that Christianity would soon give way to a more modern faith that eschewed miracles. Yet these prognostications have failed to materialize.[11]

I've spoken with a lot of people from various generations and found that so many of them are sincerely interested in exploring faith, with quite a few genuinely intrigued and even enthralled by Jesus. In my view, it's difficult not to have a sense of spiritual optimism, despite some of the troubling trends.

Right now, where do you stand on the question of whether God is real? Does the needle on your spiritual gauge point more toward skepticism or belief? Or would you say you're somewhere in the middle, not hostile toward faith but honestly interested in following the evidence wherever it leads?

Rejecting Belief in God

Among those who are convinced that God doesn't exist is British comedian and armchair philosopher Ricky Gervais. In an essay titled "Why I'm an Atheist," he explained that when he was about eight years old, Jesus was his hero. One day, he was at the kitchen table drawing a picture of Christ when his older brother Bob came in and asked, "Why do you believe in God?"

Said Gervais, "Just a simple question. But my mum panicked. 'Bob,' she said in a tone that I knew meant, 'Shut up!' Why was that a bad thing to ask? If there was a God and my faith was strong it didn't matter what people said. Oh . . . hang on. There is no God. He knows it, and she knows it deep down. It was as simple as that. I started thinking about it and asking more questions, and within an hour, I was an atheist."[12]

Others have reached a similar conclusion for varying reasons. The founding publisher of *Skeptic* magazine, Michael Shermer, told me he was led to Christ by his friend George when they were in high school, though Shermer admits he had mixed motives because he thought a conversion might help his odds of dating George's sister. Shermer lived as an evangelical Christian until he gradually lost his faith in college, where a professor attacked his beliefs and Shermer didn't find satisfying answers to some of his nettlesome theological questions.

Then his college sweetheart became paralyzed in a motor vehicle accident. Shermer asked God to heal her, and yet she remained disabled. I asked Shermer, "Was this the final nail in the coffin of your faith?" He replied, "Yeah, that pretty much did it. I was like, 'Ah, the heck with it.'"[13]

Can you relate to that? Has there been a time when you called out to God during a crisis but felt like you were only talking to yourself? For some people, God seems too hidden to be real.

Charles Templeton was the pastor of a burgeoning church in Toronto and pulpit partner of renowned evangelist Billy Graham before morphing into Canada's best-known spiritual skeptic. When I asked Templeton if there had been one thing in particular that caused him to lose his faith in God, he said it was a photograph in *Life* magazine many years earlier.

"It was a picture of a Black woman in northern Africa," he told me. "They were experiencing a devastating drought. And she was holding her dead baby in her arms and looking up to heaven with the most forlorn expression. I looked at it and I thought, *Is it possible to believe there is a loving or caring creator when all this woman needed was* rain?"

He shook his head. "I immediately knew it is not possible for this to happen and for there to be a loving God. There was no way."

Interestingly, though, Templeton broke down in tears during our interview because he said he missed Jesus—and there's reason to believe he did ultimately return to faith in God on his deathbed a few years later.[14]

Scholar Bart Ehrman said he left Christianity to become an agnostic partly because his research on the text of the New Testament cast doubt on the Bible's reliability—ironic because he dedicated his book on the topic to his mentor, Bruce Metzger, who told me that his own study of the matter only served to *deepen* his faith.[15]

Like Templeton, Ehrman also attributed his abandonment of Christianity to his inability to reconcile the existence of pain and anguish with a loving God. "For many people who inhabit this planet, life is a cesspool of misery and suffering," he wrote. "I came to a point where I simply could not believe that there is a good and kindly disposed Ruler who is in charge of it."[16]

Among evangelical Christians, a phenomenon called

deconstruction has been gaining notoriety in recent years. Some people have found that this systematic dissecting and reexamining of their beliefs has led to a stronger and more secure faith in the end. But Alisa Childers, author of *Another Gospel?*, has warned that "sometimes the Christian will deconstruct all the way into atheism."[17] In many instances, she said, the deconstructed faith fails to retain "any vestiges of actual Christianity."[18]

The size of the trend is uncertain, but by 2023, there were already nearly 350,000 posts on Instagram using the hashtag #deconstruction.[19] Said Sean McDowell and John Marriott in their book *Set Adrift: Deconstructing What You Believe without Sinking Your Faith*, "College students and young adults are finding it increasingly difficult to retain their faith and, as a result, are deconverting from it."[20]

As for me, however, I went in a far different direction. I deconstructed my atheism.[21]

From Skepticism to Belief

For years, I was a happy spiritual skeptic, with degrees in journalism and law and enjoying my career as a legal editor at the *Chicago Tribune*.[22] Then my agnostic wife's conversion to Christianity prompted me to spend nearly two years investigating whether God is real, focusing largely on the resurrection of Jesus.

Reluctantly, I became convinced that Jesus not only claimed to be the unique Son of God, but he also proved it by rising from the dead. I put my trust in Christ in 1981, and my life has never been the same—in a good way!

In fact, I've seen that kind of story again and again among people I've encountered down through the years. For example, just from within my sphere of relationships are these stories:

- J. Warner Wallace, a cold-case homicide detective, used his well-honed investigative skills to painstakingly analyze the historical reliability of the Gospels. He concluded that these written accounts "reliably and accurately described the resurrection of Jesus without ulterior motive." When he realized this, "everything changed for me."[23] He renounced his atheism and wrote the bestselling book *Cold-Case Christianity.*[24]
- Sarah Salviander, an astrophysicist raised by atheists, believed that Christianity was "philosophically trivial." But as she was studying deuterium abundances in relation to the big bang, she became "'completely and utterly awed' by the underlying order of the universe and the fact it could be explored scientifically"—and she became a Christian.[25] "I was awakened," she said, "to what Psalm 19 tells us so clearly: 'The heavens declare the glory of God, the skies proclaim the work of his hands.'"
- Stephen McWhirter, a musician, was a methamphetamine addict. The troubled son of a pastor, he hated Christianity and yet he inexplicably accepted a book from a friend about Jesus. As he read it at 3:00 a.m. amidst his drug paraphernalia, he encountered the presence of the living God. "I went from addiction to redemption," he said, "because God's real." Today he writes Christian worship songs.[26]
- Guillaume Bignon, a cynical software engineer, became a Christian after studying, among other topics, the nature of morality. Concerning his exploration of faith, he said, "I had to force myself to be open-minded because I really wanted everything to be false." But his skepticism withered the more he explored the evidence. He not only be-

came a Christian, but he went on to earn his doctorate in philosophical theology and write the memoir *Confessions of a French Atheist.*[27]

- Louis Lapides, a spiritually skeptical Vietnam veteran, examined the ancient messianic prophecies, prompting him to conclude that Jesus, and Jesus alone, is the divine Messiah sent to save Israel and the world. Lapides, raised Jewish, became a Christian and later a minister. "My friends knew my life had changed, and they couldn't understand it," he said. "I would say, 'Well, I can't explain what happened. All I know is that there's someone in my life, and it's someone who's holy, who's righteous, who's a source of positive thoughts about life—and I just feel whole.'"[28]

- Holly Ordway, an atheist professor of English literature, started to ask herself, *What if God is real?* Christian fiction planted seeds in her imagination; Christian philosophers provided a counterpoint to her naturalistic worldview; and her fencing coach turned out to be a Christian. "I realized that I could ask my coach questions and feel safe and respected while having a dialogue about these issues," she said. She ultimately found that the evidence of history "was best explained by concluding that the resurrection really happened." She became a Christian, a professor of apologetics, and author of the book *Not God's Type: A Rational Academic Finds a Radical Faith.*[29]

- Cody Huff, a drug addict and convicted burglar, was living on the streets of Las Vegas when he went to get a free shower at a church. A volunteer offered a hug and the words "Jesus loves you"—and it was the pivotal moment of his life. "Right away something was different," he told me. "The more I heard about Jesus, the more I wanted to hear. I couldn't get enough of the Bible." He came to faith, was ordained as a Baptist minister, and devoted the rest of his life to helping the homeless.[30]

- Michael Brown, a Jewish hippie with an insatiable appetite for illicit drugs, went to rescue two friends who were attending church in pursuit of girls. Brown got into discussions with Christians about why they believed that God is real. He became a follower of Christ, and now, with a doctorate in Near Eastern Languages, he is among the foremost defenders of Jesus being the Messiah.[31]
- Thomas Tarrants, a Ku Klux Klan terrorist, was wounded in a shoot-out with the FBI when he went to firebomb the home of a civil rights leader in Mississippi. Sentenced to prison, he escaped and survived another shoot-out in which an accomplice was killed. He then spent three years by himself in a six-by-nine-foot cell—with a Bible. He delved deeply into the Scriptures, eventually coming to a profound faith in Christ that liberated him from his racial hatred. Finally released, he earned his doctorate, was named president of the C. S. Lewis Institute, and became a champion of racial reconciliation.[32]

Again, these are just a few of the people I have personally known, and I could have added many others. All of them had some things in common. Despite their initial doubts about God, they kept an open mind and pursued the evidence and arguments wherever it took them. In the end, they were willing to reach an informed verdict in the case for God.

Yearning for the Transcendent

Let's face it, the question of whether God is real resonates deep inside all of us. Who doesn't want to know where we come from and where we're going after we die? Staring into the darkness in the middle of the night, we tend to wonder about the purpose of life.

Are we accidents of nature, destined to flourish for a brief moment and then wither and decay forever? Or are we the creation of a beneficent God who loves us and imbues meaning into our existence? Is there really hope after the grave, or is that merely wishful thinking from the only species that is able to recognize the horror of its inevitable demise?

From time to time, we feel an innate longing for God—which might actually be evidence that he is real. "One argument for God's existence regards the aching absence of God in human experience," said philosopher Douglas Groothuis. "There is, on the one hand, the pained longing for the transcendent and, on the other, the sense of the inadequacy of merely earthly goods to satisfy that longing. . . . We all experience a deep sense of yearning or longing for something that the present natural world cannot fulfill—something transcendently glorious."[33]

He pointed out that C. S. Lewis talked about several instances in which he sensed something wonderful beyond his grasp. "These were fleeting but invaluable moments, which he called the experience of 'joy,'" Groothuis said. "They were indicators that the everyday world was not a self-enclosed system; a light from beyond would sometimes peek through the 'shadow lands.' This thirst, which is intensified by small tastes of transcendence, indicates the possibility of fulfillment."[34]

Wrote Lewis in *Mere Christianity*, "Creatures are not born with desires unless satisfaction for those desires exists. A baby feels hunger: well, there is such a thing as food. A duckling wants to swim: well, there is such a thing as water. Men feel sexual desire: well, there is such a thing as sex. If I find in myself a desire which no experience in this world can satisfy, the most probable explanation is that I was made for another world. If none of my earthly pleasures satisfy it, that does not prove that the universe is a fraud. Probably earthly pleasures were never meant to satisfy it, but only to arouse it, to suggest the real thing."[35]

So perhaps our longing for the transcendent is a clue that it actually does exist. And yet there could be another explanation. Maybe our imagination conjures up the idea of God because we desperately want to be rescued from our fear of death. Could it be that we are so frightened by our own mortality that we subconsciously manufacture false ideas about a loving deity and eternity in heaven in order to ease our death anxiety?

One way or the other, our beliefs have very real consequences. How we live our lives and what we value the most inevitably flow from our convictions. The paramount question becomes whether our beliefs are based on fact or fantasy.

My motive has been to discover truth, regardless of what the implications might be. Maybe that's fueled by my investigative reporting at the *Chicago Tribune*, where I relentlessly followed the facts to make sure I was exposing the news as accurately as I could. Or maybe it's rooted in my law training, where I came to admire the beauty of a legal system designed to ferret out the truth. Regardless, I became obsessed with getting to the bottom of whether or not there's a God and then living with the consequences, one way or the other.

"Our beliefs have very real consequences. How we live our lives and what we value the most inevitably flow from our convictions."

If he was real, I wanted to know him personally. And if he wasn't, then I wasn't interested in playing any religious games.

Because truth matters.

"Now—Here Is My Secret"

Canadian writer Douglas Coupland, described as "possibly the most gifted exegete of North American mass culture,"[36] authored the book *Life after God* nearly three decades ago, and yet its themes remain hauntingly relevant even today.

The book tracks a young man through a troubled era. He's remorseful over his mistakes. His marriage has stagnated. He's ensnared in a meaningless job. Instead of deep friendships, he endures what he calls "halfway relationships." He's worried that he doesn't *feel* life the way he used to. But after 358 pages of aimlessness and frustration, this was his conclusion:

> "Now—here is my secret:
>   I tell it to you with an openness of heart that I doubt I shall ever achieve again, so I pray that you are in a quiet room as you read these words. My secret is that I need God—that I am sick and can no longer make it alone. I need God to help me give, because I no longer seem to be capable of giving; to help me be kind, as I no longer seem capable of kindness; to bring me love, as I seem beyond being able to love."[37]

Maybe you're a little like Coupland's character. Perhaps you have a secret too. It could be that your circumstances are causing you to conclude that maybe—*just maybe*—you need God to breathe new hope and life into your world. Or maybe you need him to chisel the crust off a heart that's corroded with self-interest and cynicism. Or maybe you need him because—well, to be honest, you're not sure why. You just sense that there's got to be more to your existence than a job, three meals a day, and the gnawing feeling that something's missing.

So you've started reading this book to see if it really makes sense to believe that God is real. Questions swirl in your mind. And maybe you're a little afraid of what you might find.

Or possibly you know a lot about the *idea* of God, but you're realizing that you don't really know God *personally*. You went to church as a kid or even went through some religious classes, but all of it has seemed to have numbed you toward God more than sensitized you to him. If someone asked, you'd say you were a spiritual person, although the truth is that a soul-satisfying faith has always eluded you.

Let me suggest this. Before you begin the first chapter of this book, pray a twenty-word prayer that can kindle a revolution in your soul. Pray it even though you may doubt that anyone is listening: *God, if you open my eyes to who you really are, then I will open my life fully to you.*

From your perspective, that prayer may seem peppered with risk. Because if you sincerely pray it, it catapults you from the status of an observer to someone who is intent on getting to the truth about God. You've entered unchartered territory. That old saying pops into your head: "Be careful what you ask for because you might get it."

You may be afraid that if you end up following Jesus, you'll find yourself stuffed inside a moral straitjacket that will suffocate you. Your freedom will be choked by restrictive regulations at a time when you see your life as needing fewer rules, not more.

Maybe you envision a risk of being turned into something you don't want to be—some kind of proselytizer who punctures every sentence with "Amen!" Or someone who forfeits fun in favor of faith.

Or it could be that you see a risk to your self-image if you're forced to concede some things about yourself that you'd rather not talk about. After all, isn't it healthier to focus on all the positive things you've done rather than dredge up your mistakes?

I prayed a prayer like this on January 20, 1980, even though those kinds of worries loomed large for me. I investigated God, encountered him, and then responded to him in a prayer of commitment and faith. Today, I can look back at the revolution that has happened with my life and say with complete candor that those initial risks I imagined were tremendously overblown. Personally, I found the Bible's promise to be true: "God rewards those who earnestly seek him."[38] Heb 11:6

Starting Your Journey of Discovery

What about you? Are you open to the idea of evaluating the evidence and coming to an informed conclusion about whether God is real? Imagine yourself as an umpire behind home plate in a baseball game, calling strikes and balls as you see them, without fear or favor. In other words, your task is to set aside bias and prejudice as best you can.

Will you find an ironclad case? Few things in life can be established without any doubt whatsoever. For instance, we can say with absolute certainty that $2 + 2 = 4$. Mostly, though, we make important decisions in our lives based on the preponderance of evidence. *Where do the facts point most convincingly? What is consistent with the evidence? What is more likely than not to be true? Does this case make sense?*

Look at it this way. Right now, I'm typing on a computer in my home office outside of Houston, Texas. Occasionally, I pause to sip from a bottle of water. But how do I know for sure that the water hasn't been poisoned?

Well, the water comes from a reputable supplier. The bottle was sealed when I got it. The water looks clear. There's no discoloration. It doesn't have an unusual odor. I haven't heard of anyone else getting sick from drinking water recently. My wife gave me the bottle, and she has no reason to hurt me.

And yet it *could* be poisoned. I don't have absolute proof that it's safe. But I do have sufficient evidence to warrant taking a step of faith by tasting it and finding that it's truly good.

Belief in God is similar. We evaluate the evidence and arguments; we test them with objections; we seek clarity; we pursue further answers. And if we end up with sufficient confidence, we take the advice of Psalm 34:8: "Taste and see that the LORD is good."

In fact, Jesus claimed to offer what he called "living water," saying, "Whoever drinks the water I give them will never thirst. Indeed, the water I give them will become in them a spring of water welling up to eternal life."[39]

So let me take you on a stimulating journey of discovery. Come with me as we travel around America—from Boston to Seattle, from Denver to Los Angeles, from Texas to Indiana—to meet some of the scholars I've interviewed about this foundational question of whether or not God is real. We'll look at science, philosophy, history, morality, and human nature.

And since 52 percent of Americans say they've experienced religious doubt in the past few years,[40] we'll examine two of the biggest obstacles to belief in God: (1) If he's real, why does he allow suffering in the world? And (2) if he's real, why does he seem so hidden from us?

Remember, much hangs in the balance. Beliefs have real-world consequences. Let these experts make their best case. Evaluate their insights and consider whether there is sufficient evidence to drink deeply from the living water that Jesus offers.

Then *you* decide. Is God real?

CHAPTER 1

THE COSMOS REQUIRES A CREATOR

*Perhaps the best argument . . . that
the Big Bang supports theism is
the obvious unease with which it is
greeted by some atheist physicists.*

**Astrophysicist C. J. Isham, "Creation of
the Universe as a Quantum Process"**

My eyes scanned the magazines at a newsstand near my home. A woman graced *Glamour*. Sleek cars streaked across *Motor Trend*. And there on the cover of *Discover* magazine, unadorned, floating in a sea of pure white background, was a simple red sphere. It was just three-quarters of an inch in diameter, not too much bigger than a marble.

As staggering as it seems, it represented the actual size of the entire universe when it was just an infinitesimal fraction of one second old. Cried out the headline, *Where Did Everything Come From?*[1]

Thousands of years ago, the Hebrews believed they had the answer: "In the beginning God created the heavens and the earth" are the Bible's opening words.[2] Everything began, they claimed, with the primordial *fiat lux*—the voice of God commanding light into existence.[3]

What's your view of that claim? Does it seem like a simplistic superstition? An unsupported theory? Or perhaps a divinely inspired insight? Does the beginning of the universe really point toward the existence of a divine creator?

For some people, the mere presence of the universe somehow explains itself. "It seems impossible that you could get something from nothing," Bill Bryson said in his book *A Short History of Nearly Everything*, "but the fact that once there was nothing and now there is a universe is evident proof that you can."[4]

But does that make sense? Maybe British astrophysicist Edward Milne was right when he capped a mathematical treatise by saying, "As to the first cause of the Universe . . . that is left for the reader to insert, but our picture is incomplete without Him."[5]

"I wasn't interested in unsupported conjecture or armchair musings. I wanted the hard facts of mathematics, the cold data of cosmology."

As for myself, I wasn't interested in unsupported conjecture or armchair musings. I wanted the hard facts of mathematics, the cold data of cosmology, and only the most reasonable inferences that can be drawn from them. That's what sent me to a suburb of Atlanta, Georgia, to visit a widely published scholar who has studied and debated these issues for decades.[6]

William Lane Craig, PhD, DTheol

As a college student who graduated in 1971, Bill Craig had been taught that various arguments for the existence of God were weak, outdated, and ultimately ineffective. And that's what he believed—until he happened upon philosopher Stuart C. Hackett's 1957 book *The Resurrection of Theism*.[1]

Hackett was a brilliant thinker who took these theistic arguments seriously, rigorously defending them from every objection he could find or imagine. One argument in the book was that the universe must have had a beginning and therefore a creator.

Craig was so intrigued that he decided to use his doctoral studies under British theologian John Hick to see if this argument could withstand scrutiny. He ended up writing his dissertation on the topic—an exercise that launched him into a lifetime of exploring cosmology.

Today, Craig has authored more than thirty books, including *The Kalam Cosmological Argument*; *Theism, Atheism, and Big Bang Cosmology*; and *Time and Eternity*, as well as scores of scholarly articles in professional journals of philosophy and theology. In 2016, he was named by *The Best Schools* as one of the fifty most influential living philosophers. He has spoken at major universities around the world, including Harvard, Yale, Stanford, Oxford, Cambridge, and Moscow.

Despite his lofty academic achievements, Craig has an uncanny ability to communicate complex concepts in accessible and yet technically accurate language—a rare skill I planned to put to the test with this challenging subject.

The *Kalam* Cosmological Argument

"You're a famous proponent of the *kalam* cosmological argument for God's existence," I said as we began our conversation. "Before you define what that is, though, give me some background. What does *kalam* mean?"

"Let me describe the origins of the argument," he said. "In ancient Greece, Aristotle believed that God isn't the creator of the universe, but that he simply imbues order into it. In his view, both God and the universe are eternal. Of course, that contradicted the Hebrew notion that God created the world out of nothing. So Christians later sought to refute Aristotle. One prominent Christian philosopher on the topic was John Philoponus of Alexandria, Egypt, who lived in the fourth century. He argued that the universe had a beginning.

"When Islam took over North Africa, Muslim theologians picked up these arguments because they also believed in creation. One of the most famous Muslim proponents was al-Ghazali, who lived from 1058 to 1111.

"Now, back to your question about the word *kalam*—it's Arabic for 'speech' or 'doctrine,' but it came to characterize the whole medieval movement of Islamic theology. That was called *kalam*—this highly academic theology of the Middle Ages, which later evaporated."

"How do you frame the *kalam* argument?"

"As formulated by al-Ghazali, the argument has three simple steps: 'Whatever begins to exist has a cause. The universe began to exist. Therefore, the universe has a cause.' Then you can do a conceptual analysis of what it means to be a cause of the universe, and a striking number of divine attributes can be identified."

I decided to work my way through all three steps of al-Ghazali's nearly millennium-old argument, starting with a point that—surprisingly—has become more and more disputed in recent years.

STEP #1: Whatever Begins to Exist Has a Cause

"When I first began to defend the *kalam* argument," Craig said, "I anticipated that its first premise—that whatever begins to exist has a cause—would be accepted by virtually everyone. I thought the second premise—that the universe began to exist—would be much more controversial. But the scientific evidence has accumulated to the extent that atheists are finding it difficult to deny that the universe had a beginning. So they've been forced to attack the first premise instead."

Craig shook his head. "To me, this is absolutely bewildering!" he said, his voice rising in dismay. "It seems metaphysically necessary that anything which begins to exist *has* to have a cause that brings it into being. Things don't just pop into existence, uncaused, out of nothing. Yet the atheist Quentin Smith concluded our book on the topic by claiming that 'the most reasonable belief is that we came from nothing, by nothing, and for nothing.'[2] That sounds like a good conclusion to the Gettysburg Address of Atheism! It simply amazes me that anyone can think this is the most rational view.

"Generally, people who take this position don't try to prove the premise is false because they can't do that. Instead, they fold their arms and play the skeptic by saying, 'You can't prove that's true.' They dial their degree of skepticism so high that nothing could possibly convince them."

I asked, "What positive proof can you offer?"

"This first premise is intuitively obvious once you clearly grasp the concept of absolute nothingness," he said. "You see, the idea that things can come into being uncaused out of nothing is worse than magic. At least when a magician pulls a rabbit out of a hat, there's the magician and the hat!

"But in atheism, the universe just pops into being out of nothing, with absolutely no explanation at all. I think once people understand the concept of absolute nothingness, it's simply obvious to them that if something has a beginning, it could not have popped into being out of nothing but must have a cause that brings it into existence."

Admittedly, that was difficult to dispute, but I needed something more substantial. "Can you offer anything harder than just intuition? What scientific evidence is there?"

"Well, we certainly have empirical evidence for the truth of this premise. This is a principle that is constantly confirmed and never falsified. We never see things coming into being uncaused out of nothing. Nobody worries that while they're away at work, say, a horse might pop into being, uncaused, out of nothing, in their living room, and be there defiling the carpet. We don't worry about those kinds of things because they never happen. So this is a principle that is constantly verified by science. At least, Lee, you have to admit we have better reason to think it's true than it's false."

Still, my research had yielded at least one substantive objection to *kalam*'s first premise. It emanates from the wacky world of quantum physics, where all kinds of strange, unexpected things happen at the subatomic level—a level, by the way, at which the entire universe existed in its very earliest stages, when electrons, protons, and neutrinos were bursting forth in the big bang.

Maybe our commonplace understanding of cause and effect doesn't apply in this circus-mirror environment of "quantum weirdness," a place where, as science writer Timothy Ferris writes, "the logical foundations of classical science are violated."[3]

IS THE UNIVERSE A FREE LUNCH?

I pulled out the copy of the *Discover* magazine with the marble-sized universe on its cover. The article, I said to Craig, says that according to quantum theory, things can materialize out of a vacuum, even though it's generally pairs of short-lived subatomic particles. In fact, said the article, "the spontaneous, persistent creation of something even as large as a molecule is profoundly unlikely." Yet in 1973, an assistant professor at Columbia University suggested that the entire universe might have come into existence this way. The whole universe might be, to use MIT physicist Alan Guth's phrase, "a free lunch."[4]

"These subatomic particles the article talks about are called 'virtual particles,'" Craig said. "They are theoretical entities, and it's not even clear that they actually exist as opposed to being merely theoretical constructs.

"However, there's a much more important point. You see, these particles, if they are real, do *not* come out of nothing. The quantum vacuum is not what most people envision when they think of a vacuum—that is, absolutely nothing. On the contrary, it's a sea of fluctuating energy, an arena of violent activity that has a rich physical structure and can be described by physical laws. These particles are thought to originate by fluctuations of the energy in the vacuum.

"So it's not an example of something coming into being out of nothing or something coming into being without a cause. The quantum vacuum and the energy locked up in the vacuum are the cause of these particles. And then we have to ask, 'Well, what is the origin of the whole quantum vacuum itself? Where does *it* come from?'"

He let that question linger before continuing. "You've simply pushed back the issue of creation. Now you've got to account for how this very active ocean of fluctuating energy came into being. Suddenly, we're back to the origins question."

Craig's answer satisfied me. In fact, there didn't seem to be any rational objection that could seriously jeopardize the initial assertion of the *kalam* argument—and it has been that way since the early philosophers began to use it centuries ago.

STEP #2: The Universe Had a Beginning

Turning to the second premise of the *kalam* argument, I said to Craig, "If we were sitting here a hundred years ago, the idea that the universe began to exist at a specific point in the past would have been very controversial, wouldn't it?"

"No question about it," replied Craig. "The assumption ever since the ancient Greeks has been that the material world is eternal. Christians have denied this on the basis of biblical revelation, but secular science always assumed the universe's eternality. So the discovery in the twentieth century that the universe is not an unchanging, eternal entity was a complete shock to secular minds."

"How do we really know that the universe started at some point in the past?" I asked.

"Essentially," said Craig, "there are two pathways toward establishing it. One could be called either mathematical or philosophical, while the other is scientific. Let's begin with the mathematical argument, which, incidentally, picks up on the thinking of Philoponus and the medieval Islamic theologians I mentioned earlier."

THE PATHWAY OF MATHEMATICS

The early Christian and Muslim scholars, Craig explained, used mathematical reasoning to demonstrate that it was impossible to have an infinite past. Their conclusion, therefore, was that the universe's age must be finite—that is, it must have had a beginning.

"They pointed out that counterintuitive absurdities would result if you were to have an actually infinite number of things," he said. "Since an infinite past would involve an actually infinite number of events, then the past simply can't be infinite.

"Let's use an example involving marbles," he continued. "Imagine I had an infinite number of marbles in my possession and that I wanted to give you an infinite number of marbles. One way I could do that would be to give you the entire pile of marbles. In that case, I would have zero marbles left for myself.

"However, another way to do it would be to give you all of the odd-numbered marbles. Then I would still have an infinity left over for myself, and you would have an infinity too. You'd have just as many as I would—and, in fact, each of us would have just as many as I originally had before we divided into odd and even! Or another approach would be for me to give you all of the marbles numbered four and higher. That way, you would have an infinity of marbles, but I would have only three marbles left.

"What these illustrations demonstrate is that the notion of an actual infinite number of things leads to contradictory results. In the first case, infinity minus infinity is zero; in the second case, infinity minus infinity is infinity; and in the third case, infinity minus infinity is three. In each case, we have subtracted the identical number from the identical number, but we have come up with nonidentical results.

"For that reason, mathematicians are forbidden from doing subtraction and division in transfinite arithmetic because this would lead to contradictions. You see, the idea of an actual infinity is just conceptual; it exists only in our minds. Working within certain rules, mathematicians can deal with infinite quantities and infinite numbers in the conceptual realm. However—and here's the point—it's not descriptive of what can happen in the real world."

I was following Craig so far. "You're saying, then, that you couldn't have an infinite number of events in the past."

"Exactly, because you would run into similar paradoxes," he said. "Substitute 'past events' for 'marbles,' and you can see the absurdities that would result. So the universe can't have an infinite number of events in its past. It must have had a beginning."

However, I spotted an inconsistency. "Then what about the idea of God being infinitely old?" I asked. "Doesn't your reasoning also rule out the idea of an eternal deity?"

"It rules out the concept of a God who has endured through an infinite past time. But that's not the classic idea of God," he said. "Time and space are creations of God that began at the big bang. If you go back beyond the beginning of time itself, there is simply eternity. By that, I mean eternity in the sense of time-lessness. God, the eternal, is timeless in his being. God did not endure through an infinite amount of time up to the moment of creation; that would be absurd. God transcends time. He's beyond time. Once God creates the universe, he could enter time, but that's a different topic altogether."

I quickly reviewed in my mind what Craig had said so far, concluding that it seemed logically coherent. "How convincing do you think the mathematical pathway is?" I asked.

"Well, *I'm* convinced of it!" he replied with a chuckle. "In fact, this is such a good argument that even if I had lived in the nineteenth century, when there was little scientific evidence for the beginning of the universe, I would still believe that the universe is finite in the past on the basis of these arguments."

We turned the corner to begin discussing the scientific evidence for the universe being created in the big bang billions of years ago.[5] "What discoveries began pointing scientists toward this model?" I asked.

"When Albert Einstein developed his general theory of relativity in 1915 and started applying it to the universe as a whole, he was shocked to discover it didn't allow for a static universe. According to his equations, the universe should either be exploding or imploding. In order to make the universe static, he had to fudge his equations by putting in a factor that would hold the universe steady.

"In the 1920s, the Russian mathematician Alexander Friedman and the Belgium astronomer George Lemaître developed models based on Einstein's theory. They predicted the universe was expanding. Of course, this meant that if you went backward in time, the universe would go back to a single origin before which it didn't exist. Astronomer Fred Hoyle derisively called this the 'big bang'—and the name stuck!

"Starting in the 1920s, scientists began to find empirical evidence that supported these purely mathematical models. For instance, in 1929, the American astronomer Edwin Hubble discovered that the light coming to us from distant galaxies appeared to be redder than it should be, and that this was a universal feature of galaxies in all parts of the sky. Hubble explained this red shift as the result of the fact that the galaxies are moving away from us. He concluded that the universe is literally flying apart at enormous velocities.

"Then in the 1940s, George Gamow predicted that if the big bang really happened, then the background temperature of the universe should be just a few degrees above absolute zero. He said this would be a relic from a very early stage of the universe. Sure enough, in 1965, two scientists accidentally discovered the universe's background radiation—and it was only about 3.7 degrees above absolute zero. There's no explanation for this apart from the fact that it is a vestige of a very early and a very dense state of the universe, which was predicted by the big bang model.

"The third main piece of evidence for the big bang is the origin of light elements. Heavy elements, like carbon and iron, are synthesized in the interior of stars and then exploded through supernovae into space. But the very, very light elements, like deuterium and helium, cannot have been synthesized in the interior of stars because you would need an even more powerful furnace to create them. These elements must have been forged in the furnace of the big bang itself at temperatures that were billions of degrees.

"So predictions about the big bang have been consistently verified by scientific data. Moreover, they have been corroborated by the failure of every attempt to falsify them by alternative models. Unquestionably, the big bang model has impressive scientific credentials."

I knew, however, that there have been more recent refinements of the standard big bang model. "How would you assess the health of the big bang model today?" I asked.

"It's the standard paradigm of contemporary cosmology," he answered. "I would say that its broad framework is very securely established as a scientific fact. Stephen Hawking has said, 'Almost everyone now believes that the universe, and time itself, had a beginning at the Big Bang.'"[6]

By this point in our discussion, Craig had provided compelling facts to support the two premises of the *kalam* argument. All that remained was its conclusion—and the absolutely staggering implications that logically flow from it.

STEP #3: Therefore the Universe Has a Cause

"Given that whatever begins to exist has a cause and that the universe began to exist, there *must* be some sort of transcendent cause for the origin of the universe," Craig told me.

"Even atheist Kai Nielsen said, 'Suppose you suddenly hear a loud bang . . . and you ask me, "What made that bang?" and I reply, "Nothing, it just happened." You would not accept that.'[7] He's right, of course. And if a cause is needed for a small bang like that, then it's needed for the big bang as well. This is an inescapable conclusion—and it's a stunning confirmation of the millennia-old Judeo-Christian doctrine of creation out of nothing."

> "Given that whatever begins to exist has a cause and that the universe began to exist, there must be some sort of transcendent cause for the origin of the universe."

But although logic dictates that a cause sparked the big bang, I wondered how much logic can also tell us about its identity. "What specifically can you deduce about this cause?" I asked Craig.

"There are several qualities we can identify," he replied. "A cause of space and time must be an uncaused, beginningless, timeless, spaceless, immaterial, personal being endowed with freedom of will and enormous power," he said. "And that is a core concept of God."

"Hold on!" I insisted. "Many atheists see a fatal inconsistency. They don't see how you can say the creator could be 'uncaused.' One of them, George Smith, says, 'If *everything* must have a cause, how did god become exempt?'"[8]

Craig's eyebrows shot up. "Well, that just misses the point!" he exclaimed. "Obviously, they're not dealing with the first premise of the *kalam* argument, which is *not* that *everything* has a cause, but that *whatever begins to exist* has a cause. I don't know of any reputable philosopher who would say *everything* has a cause. So they're simply not dealing with a correct formulation of the *kalam* argument.

"And this is not special pleading in the case of God. After all, atheists have long maintained that the universe doesn't need a cause because it's eternal. How can they possibly maintain that the universe can be eternal and uncaused, yet God cannot be timeless and uncaused?"

At that point, another objection popped into my mind. "Why does it have to be one creator?" I asked. "Why couldn't multiple creators have been involved?"

"My opinion," Craig answered, "is that Occam's razor would shave away any additional creators."

"What's Occam's razor?"

"It's a scientific principle that says we should not multiply causes beyond what's necessary to explain the effect. Since one creator is sufficient to explain the effect, you would be unwarranted in going beyond the evidence to posit a plurality."

"That seems a little soft to me," I said.

"Well, it's a universally accepted principle of scientific methodology," he replied. "And besides, the *kalam* argument can't prove everything about the creator. Nothing restricts us from looking at wider considerations. For instance, Jesus of Nazareth proclaimed the truth of monotheism, and he was vindicated by his resurrection from the dead, for which we have convincing historical evidence.[9] Consequently, we have good grounds for believing that what he said was true."

I conceded the point, but at the same time, my mind began to fill with other objections about the identity of the universe's cause. Among the most troubling was whether the *kalam* argument can tell us if the creator is personal, as Christians believe, or merely an impersonal force, as many New Age adherents maintain.

The Personal Creator

"One of the most remarkable features of the *kalam* argument is that it gives us more than just a transcendent cause of the universe, but it also implies a personal creator," Craig said.

"How so?"

"There are two types of explanations—scientific and personal," he began, adopting a professorial tone. "Scientific explanations explain a phenomenon in terms of certain initial conditions and natural laws, which explain how those initial conditions evolved to produce the phenomenon under consideration. By contrast, personal explanations explain things by means of an agent and that agent's volition or will."

I interrupted to ask Craig for an illustration. He obliged by saying, "Imagine you walked into the kitchen and saw a kettle boiling on the stove. You ask, 'Why is the kettle boiling?' Your wife might say, 'Well, because the kinetic energy of the flame is conducted by the metal bottom of the kettle to the water, causing the water molecules to vibrate faster and faster until they're thrown off in the form of steam.' That would be a scientific explanation. Or she might say, 'I put it on to make a cup of tea.' That would be a personal explanation. Both are legitimate, but they explain the phenomenon in different ways."

So far, so good. "But how does this relate to cosmology?"

"You see, there cannot be a scientific explanation of the first state of the universe. Since it's the first state, it simply cannot be explained in terms of earlier initial conditions and natural laws leading up to it. So if there is an explanation of the first state of the universe, it *has* to be a personal explanation—that is, an agent who has volition to create it. That would be the first reason that the cause of the universe must be personal.

"A second reason is that because the cause of the universe

transcends time and space, it cannot be a physical reality. Instead, it must be nonphysical or immaterial. Well, there are only two types of things that can be timeless and immaterial. One would be abstract objects, like numbers or mathematical entities. However, abstract objects can't cause anything to happen. The second kind of immaterial reality would be a mind. A mind can be a cause, and so it makes sense that the universe is the product of an unembodied mind that brought it into existence.

"Finally, let me give you an analogy that will help explain a third reason for why the first cause is personal. Water freezes at zero degrees centigrade. If the temperature were below zero degrees from eternity past, then any water that was around would be frozen from eternity past. It would be impossible for the water to just begin to freeze a finite time ago. In other words, once the sufficient conditions were met—that is, the temperature was low enough—then the consequence would be that water would automatically freeze.

"So if the universe were just a mechanical consequence that would occur whenever sufficient conditions were met, and the sufficient conditions were met eternally, then it would exist from eternity past. The effect would be co-eternal with the cause.

"How do you explain, then, the origin of a finite universe from a timeless cause? I can only think of one explanation: the cause of the universe is a personal agent who has freedom of will. He can create a new effect without any antecedent determining conditions. He could decide to say, 'Let there be light,' and the universe would spring into existence. I've never seen a good response to this argument on the part of any atheist."

Alternatives to the Big Bang

Efforts to come up with alternatives to the standard big bang model have intensified in recent years. Some scientists are troubled by the fact that the beginning of the universe necessitates a creator. Others are perturbed because the laws of physics can't account for the creation event. "Has this kind of attitude," I asked Craig, "fueled efforts to circumvent the idea of the big bang?"

"I believe it has. A good example is the steady state theory proposed in 1948," he replied. "It said that the universe was expanding, all right, but claimed that as galaxies retreat from each other, new matter comes into being out of nothing and fills the void. So in contradiction to the first law of thermodynamics, which says that matter is neither created nor destroyed, the universe is supposedly being continually replenished with new stuff."

"What was the evidence for it?"

"There was none!" Craig declared. "It never secured a single piece of experimental verification. It was motivated purely by a desire to avoid the absolute beginning of the universe predicted by the big bang model—in fact, one of its originators, Sir Fred Hoyle, was quite overt about this."

Over the next several hours, I peppered Craig with various exotic theories that attempt to eliminate the need for a beginning of the universe. One by one, he was able to explain why they fall short, either because they violate the laws of physics or lack any scientific verification.

One challenge came from the late J. Howard Sobel, a professor at the University of Toronto, who was among the world's leading defenders of atheism. He devoted seventy pages in his magnum opus to critiquing the cosmological argument, though he focused primarily on a version advanced by Gottfried Wilhelm Leibniz and only secondarily addressed the *kalam* formulation popularized by Craig.

Responding in the *Canadian Journal of Philosophy*, Craig was able to demonstrate that Sobel's rebuttal of the philosophical arguments against the infinitude of the past are "fallacious" and that Sobel's response to the evidence for the beginning of the universe "involves a gratuitous and radical revision of contemporary astrophysical cosmogony."[10]

"What's important to understand, Lee, is how reversed the situation is from, say, a hundred years ago," Craig said to me. "Back then, Christians had to maintain by faith in the Bible that despite all appearances to the contrary, the universe was not eternal but was created out of nothing a finite time ago. Now, the situation is exactly the opposite.

"It is the atheist who has to maintain, by faith, despite all of the evidence to the contrary, that the universe did not have a beginning a finite time ago but is in some inexplicable way eternal after all. So the shoe is on the other foot. It's the atheist who feels very uncomfortable and marginalized today."

As I sat there in Craig's office, my mind could conjure up no rational scenario that could derail the inexorable logic of the *kalam* argument. The philosophical and scientific evidence of contemporary cosmology was pointing persuasively toward the conclusion that a personal creator of the universe does exist.

In other words, God is real.

> *"The philosophical and scientific evidence of contemporary cosmology was pointing persuasively toward the conclusion that a personal creator of the universe does exist. In other words, God is real."*

Now it was time to consider the laws and parameters of physics. Is there any credibility to the claim that they have been tuned to an incomprehensible precision in order to create a livable habitat for humankind—another category of evidence that, indeed, points toward the existence of God?

CHAPTER 2

The Universe Needs a Fine-Tuner

Here is the cosmological proof of the existence of God. The fine-tuning of the universe provides prima facie evidence of deistic design.

British cosmologist Edward Harrison,
Masks of the Universe

Geraint F. Lewis creates universes for a living.

That is, he uses supercomputers to tinker with leptons, quarks, and the four fundamental forces of nature to build exotic simulations of what alternate worlds might look like. He has discovered that it's daunting to pose as a creator, even for someone with a doctorate in astrophysics from the world-renowned Institute of Astronomy at the University of Cambridge.

"Playing with the laws of physics, it turns out, can be catastrophic for life," he said. "Often . . . the periodic table disappears, and all the astonishing beauty and utility of chemistry desert us. The galaxies, stars, and planets that host and energize life are replaced by lethal black holes or just a thin hydrogen soup. . . . These are . . . not the kind of place that you'd expect to encounter complex, thinking beings like us."[1]

On the other hand, creating an actual universe from nothing, while carefully fine-tuning a flourishing habitat for human beings, is a primary job description of God. "<u>The heavens declare the glory of God</u>," reads Psalm 19:1. "<u>The skies proclaim the work of his hands.</u>"

In fact, "fine-tuning" is one of the most compelling arguments for God's existence. The numbers that govern the operation of our universe are calibrated with <u>mind-boggling precision so that life can exist. In other words, the very physics of the universe are so precisely tuned that they defy the explanation that the universe is merely the result of chance.</u>

> "The very physics of the universe are so precisely tuned that they defy the explanation that the universe is merely the result of chance."

When asked which argument for God's existence he and other skeptics consider the strongest, the late atheist Christopher Hitchens replied, "I think every one of us picks the fine-tuning one as the most intriguing."[2]

In his book *God: The Evidence*, the Harvard-educated former atheist Patrick Glynn credits the fine-tuning of the cosmos as being among the key reasons for his conclusion that the universe is the handiwork of a master designer.

He said that, as recently as the 1960s, a reasonable person weighing the scientific evidence would likely come down on the side of skepticism, but that's no longer the case. "Today," he concluded, "the concrete data point strongly in the direction of the God hypothesis. It is the simplest and most obvious solution to the [fine-tuning] puzzle."[3]

Indeed, the once-skeptical Paul Davies, former professor of theoretical physics at the University of Adelaide, is now convinced that there must be a purpose behind the universe.

"Through my scientific work I have come to believe more and more strongly that the physical universe is put together with an ingenuity so astounding that I can't accept it merely as a brute fact," he wrote in his book *The Mind of God*. "I cannot believe that our existence in the universe is a mere quirk of fate, an accident of history, an incidental blip in the great cosmic drama."[4]

That's a staggering statement from an eminent scientist. To check into the evidence for the universe's uncanny precision, I arranged a sit-down interview with an accomplished professor of physics at his home in Oklahoma.

INTERVIEW WITH

Michael G. Strauss, PhD

After earning his doctorate in Experimental High Energy Physics at UCLA, Michael George Strauss joined the faculty of the University of Oklahoma in 1995. He lectures around the world and has written an astonishing nine hundred scholarly articles on elementary particle physics. He also performs research at CERN's Large Hadron Collider in Switzerland, smashing protons together to understand, among other things, the properties of the top quark, the fundamental particle with the highest mass.

Interestingly, Strauss's study of the world's tiniest particles has become more and more relevant to understanding the origin and order of the universe. This is because when the collider hurls protons together, the resulting energy density is so high that it simulates what the universe was like a trillionth of a second after the big bang, helping lead to new insights into the study of cosmology.

In the previous chapter, William Lane Craig made a

compelling case that the big bang points to the existence of God. Now I wanted to see if Strauss could marshal convincing evidence that the actual operation of our universe reflects the mind of God. We sat down to chat in the front room of his house.

The Problem of a Cosmic Beginning

I told Strauss about an interview I once conducted with Michael Shermer, editor of *Skeptic* magazine, in which he claimed that the best answer to how the universe originated is simply this: "We don't know." He suggested there might be other possible explanations than "God did it."

"Look," replied Strauss, "we don't live our lives based on obscure possibilities; we live our lives based on probabilities. Is it possible my wife poisoned my cereal this morning? Anything is possible, but not everything is probable. The real question is this: Given what we observe with the universe, what's the highest probability? Everything tells us there was a real beginning. Everything else is a mere possibility, with no observational or experimental evidence to back it up."

When I turned to the issue of the incredible fine-tuning of the universe, Strauss initially offered this illustration: "Picture a control board with a hundred different dials and knobs, each representing a different parameter of physics. If you turn any of them just slightly to the left or right—*poof!* Intelligent life becomes impossible anywhere in the universe."

To make matters even more challenging, one scholar explained that "it's not just each constant or quantity that must be exquisitely finely tuned; their ratios to one another must also be finely tuned. So improbability is multiplied by improbability by improbability until our minds are reeling in incomprehensible numbers."[1]

This is the reality Geraint Lewis faces when he tries to create computer simulations of universes by manipulating the laws and constants of physics, yielding only catastrophic results.

Said Strauss, "Even just mistakenly bumping into one of those dials could make the world sterile and barren—or even nonexistent. And that's not only the opinion of Christian scientists. Virtually every scientist agrees the universe is finely tuned. The question is, how did it get this way? I think the most plausible explanation is that the universe was designed by a creator."

"Can you give me a few examples of the fine-tuning?" I asked him.

"Sure," he answered. "One parameter is the amount of matter in the universe. As the universe expands, all matter is attracted to other matter by gravity. If there were too much matter, then the universe would collapse on itself before stars and planets could form. If there were too little matter, then stars and planets could never coalesce."

"How finely tuned is the amount of matter?"

"It turns out that shortly after the big bang, the amount of matter in the universe was precisely tuned to one part in a trillion, trillion trillion trillion trillion," he replied. "That's a ten with sixty zeroes after it! In other words, throw in a dime's worth of extra matter and the universe wouldn't exist."

A calculation puts the number in perspective. The visible universe is 27.6 billion light years in diameter. A single millimeter compared to the diameter of the universe would still be incomprehensibly larger than this one finely tuned parameter![2]

Strauss continued. "British physicist Paul Davies—who is an agnostic—said, 'Such stunning accuracy is surely one of the great mysteries of cosmology.'"[3]

"How does he try to explain it away?"

"He said cosmic inflation might force the universe to have

exactly the right amount of matter." Inflation refers to a period of super-rapid expansion in the universe's very early history, which settled down to a more "leisurely" expansion since then.

"Does that make sense?"

"Even if you assume cosmic inflation is a mechanism that works, it doesn't make the fine-tuning problem go away."

"Why not?"

"Here's an illustration. If I tried to pour gasoline into my lawn mower through a really small hole, it would be very difficult. Why? Because the hole is finely tuned. But if I take the same fuel and pour it into a funnel, then I can easily fill the gas tank. Now, does the fact that I have a funnel—a mechanism that works—mean that I've eliminated the fine-tuning problem? No, of course not. If I have a mechanism that works, it also points to a designer."

"So," I summarized, "even if cosmic inflation is true, it merely moves the design issue back one stage."

"Right," Strauss said.

Putting a Zero on Every Particle

Then Strauss offered another fine-tuning example from something he studies in his research—the strength of the strong nuclear force. "This is what holds together the nucleus of atoms," he explained. "Ultimately, it's the strength of this force that produces the periodic table of elements."

"What happens if you manipulate the strong nuclear force?" I asked.

"If you were to make it just 2 percent stronger while all the other constants stayed the same, you'd add a lot more elements to the periodic table, but they would be radioactive and life-destroying. Plus, you'd have very little hydrogen in the universe—and no hydrogen, no water, no life."

"What if you turned the knob the other way?"

"Decrease the force by a mere 5 percent, and all you'd have would be hydrogen. Again, a dead universe. Another area of my research involves quarks, which make up neutrons and protons. If we change the light quark mass just 2 or 3 percent, there would be no carbon in the universe."

"And no carbon means—what?" I asked.

Strauss gestured at the two of us. "That you and I wouldn't be sitting here."

The examples could go on and on. In fact, entire books have been written about them. Here's another one: the ratio of the electromagnetic force to the gravitational force is fine-tuned to one part in ten thousand trillion trillion trillion.

To understand that number, said astrophysicist Hugh Ross, imagine covering a *billion* North American continents with dimes up to the moon—238,000 miles high. Choose one dime at random, paint it red, and put it somewhere in the piles. Blindfold a friend and have him pick out one dime from the billion continents. What are the odds he'd choose the red dime? One in ten thousand trillion trillion trillion.[4]

But the most extreme example I've seen comes from Oxford mathematical physicist Roger Penrose, who partnered with Stephen Hawking to write *The Nature of Space and Time*. His calculations show that in order to start the universe so it would have the required state of low entropy, the setting would need to be accurate to a precision of one part in ten to the power 10^{125}.

This mind-blowing number, Penrose said, "would be impossible to write out in the usual decimal way because even if you were able to put a zero on every particle in the universe, there would not even be enough particles to do the job."[5]

The implications aren't lost on secular scientists. "It is hard to resist the impression that the present structure of the universe, apparently so sensitive to minor alterations in numbers, has been rather carefully thought out," said Paul Davies. "The seemingly miraculous occurrence of these numerical values must remain the most compelling evidence for cosmic design."[6]

Building a Life-Sustaining Planet

Strauss wasn't done yet. "Not only is our universe precisely calibrated to a breathtaking degree, but our planet is also remarkably and fortuitously situated so life would be possible."

"In what way?" I asked.

"To have a planet like ours where life exists, first you need to be in the right kind of galaxy. There are three types of galaxies: elliptical, spiral, and irregular. You need to be in a spiral galaxy like we are because it's the only kind that produces the right heavy elements and has the right radiation levels.

"But you can't live just anywhere in the galaxy," he continued. "If you're too close to the center, there's too much radiation and there's also a black hole, which you want to avoid. If you're too far from the center, you won't have the right heavy elements. You'd lack the oxygen and carbon you'd need. You have to live in the so-called 'Goldilocks Zone,' or the galactic habitable zone, where life could exist."

"Are you referring to intelligent life?" I asked.

"Anything more complex than bacteria," he said.

Then he continued. "To have life, you need a star like our sun. Our sun is a Class G star that has supported stable planet orbits in the right location for a long time. The star must be in its middle age, so its luminosity is stabilized. It has to be a bachelor star—many stars in the universe are binary, which means two stars orbiting each other, which is bad for stable planetary orbits. Plus, the star should be a third-generation star, like our sun."

"What does that mean?"

"The first generation of stars were made of hydrogen and helium from the big bang. They only lasted a relatively short time. The second generation created heavy elements like carbon, oxygen, silicon, iron, and other things we need. The third generation is made up of stars that have enough material to create rocky planets like Earth and carbon-based life forms."

Strauss paused, but I could tell he wasn't done yet. "There are so many parameters that have to be just right for our planet to support life," he said. "The distance from the sun, the rotation rate, the amount of water, the tilt, the right size so gravity lets gases like methane escape but allows oxygen to stay.

"You need a moon like ours—it's very rare to have just one large moon—in order to stabilize the Earth's tilt. As counterintuitive as it sounds, you even need to have tectonic activity, which experts said could be 'the central requirement for life on a planet.'[7] Plate tectonics drives biodiversity, helps avoid a water world without continents, and helps generate the magnetic field. Also, it's nice to have a huge planet like Jupiter nearby to act like a vacuum cleaner by attracting potentially devastating comets and meteors away from you."

I said, "Periodically, newspapers tout the discovery of what astronomers call an 'Earthlike planet,'" I said.

"Yes, but generally all they mean is that it has a similar size as Earth or that it might be positioned to allow surface water. But there's so much more to Earth than those two factors."

"How many conditions have to be met to create an Earthlike planet?" I asked.

"Hugh Ross sets the number at 322," he replied.[8] "So if you run probability calculations, you find that there's a 10^{-304} chance you're going to find another planet that's truly like Earth."[9]

"Still, there are lots of potential candidates out there," I pointed out. "One estimate is there could be more than a billion trillion planets."

"Granted," he said. "So let's factor that number into our probability equation. That still means the odds of having any higher life-supporting planet would be one in a million trillion."

He let that astonishing number sink in. "In science," he said, "we have a phrase for probabilities like that."

"Really? What is it?"

There came a grin. "Ain't gonna happen."

Testing Alternative Theories

Some scientists, recognizing the obvious fine-tuning of the universe, have manufactured bizarre explanations for how this uncanny precision could have occurred in a purely naturalistic way.

For instance, John Barrow and Frank Tipler, in their book *The Anthropic Cosmological Principle*, said the universe is clearly designed, which requires intelligence, and intelligence is only possessed by humans. So they hypothesize that humans will continue to evolve until someday they become like gods—*at which point they reach back in time and create the universe themselves!*[10]

"These are two bright scientists, and it's the best they can come up with," Strauss said, shaking his head. "Needless to say, this concept hasn't gained traction."

Neither has the idea that our universe is actually a *Matrix*-like simulation being run on a massive computer by some super-programmer. After all, that still raises the problem of how *his* universe came into existence.

Then there's the idea—mentioned to me by Michael Shermer—that black holes lead to creation of baby universes, which then create more universes through black holes, and so on for eternity. But that leaves open the question of where the first black hole–producing universe came from. Said scholar Luke Barnes scoffingly, "The physics underlying the idea is speculative, to say the least."[11]

Another hypothesis that quickly evaporated is that the fine-tuning is the result of random happenstance. The odds of that, scientists say, are functionally equivalent to zero. "The precision is so utterly fantastic, so mathematically breathtaking, that it's just plain silly to think it could have been an accident," William Lane Craig said.[12]

As physicist Robin Collins told me, "If I bet you a thousand dollars that I could flip a coin and get heads fifty times in a row, and then I proceeded to do it, you wouldn't accept that. You'd know that the odds against that are so improbable—about one chance in a million billion—that it's extraordinarily unlikely to happen. The fact that I was able to do it against such monumental odds would be strong evidence to you that the game had been rigged.

"And the same is true for the fine-tuning of the universe," he continued. "Before you'd conclude that random chance was responsible, you'd conclude that there is strong evidence that the universe was rigged. That is, designed."[13]

Collins also addressed the idea that perhaps some as-yet-undiscovered Theory of Everything could somehow require the parameters of physics to have exactly the values they do.

"It wouldn't bother me a bit," he said to me. "It simply moves the improbability of the fine-tuning up one level."

He explained by saying, "It would really be amazing if this Grand Unified Theory—out of the incredible range of possibilities—managed to force all the fine-tuning dials to where they just happened to create a life-sustaining universe. . . . It would show that the designer was even more ingenious than we first thought. As difficult as it would be to fine-tune the universe by adjusting all of the individual dials, it would be even more difficult to create an underlying law of nature that then forced all the dials into those specific positions. All that would do would be to make me even more in awe of the Creator."[14]

The Multiverse Option

What are the most likely explanations for the fine-tuning? Science philosopher Tim W. E. Maudlin, author of *Metaphysics within Physics*, said in his endorsement in the front of *A Fortunate Universe* that there are just two plausible alternatives: "a multiverse or a designer."[15]

"Let's talk about the multiverse option," I said to Strauss. "Stephen Hawking talks about M-theory, which would allow for a nearly infinite number of other universes. If the dials of physics were twirled at random in all of those, sooner or later, one universe is going to hit the jackpot and get the right conditions for life."

"First of all," Strauss said, "we don't know if M-theory is correct. It's based on string theory, which is an esoteric concept for which all the equations haven't even been worked out yet. The theory may be untestable and nonfalsifiable, and there's no observational evidence for it, so is it really science?"

Strauss noted that when Hawking proposed the M-theory, renowned science writer John Horgan wrote in *Scientific American*, "M-theory, theorists now realize, comes in an almost infinite number of versions. . . . Of course, a theory that predicts everything really doesn't predict anything." The title of Horgan's blog on the topic said it all: "Cosmic Clowning: Stephen Hawking's 'New' Theory of Everything Is the Same Old Crap."[16]

Strauss continued, "Physicists have come up with various ideas for how multiverses could be birthed, but again, there's no observational or experimental evidence for it. In fact, there is likely no way for us to discover something that's beyond our universe. And even if there were multiple universes, the Borde-Guth-Vilenkin theorem says they all must go back to one beginning point, so now we return to the question of who or what created the universe in the first place."

His conclusion? "If you want to believe in one of the multiverse theories, you basically need blind faith."[17]

Similar comments came from John Polkinghorne, former professor of mathematical physics at Cambridge University: "The many-universes account is sometimes presented as if it were purely scientific, but in fact a sufficient portfolio of different universes could only be generated by speculative processes that go well beyond what sober science can honestly endorse."[18]

Oxford philosopher Richard Swinburne was blunt. "To postulate a trillion-trillion other universes, rather than one God, in order to explain the orderliness of our universe, seems the height of irrationality."[19]

More recently, German theoretical physicist Sabine Hossenfelder, who studies quantum gravity at the Frankfurt Institute for Advanced Studies, criticized the multiverse idea as "a waste of time." Hossenfelder, the agnostic author of *Existential Physics*, added that the popular press overstates the number of scientists who endorse the multiverse theory. "It's very niche, actually, this whole multiverse thing," she said.[20]

In their book *A Fortunate Universe*, Geraint Lewis and Luke A. Barnes denied that any scientist has managed to debunk the universe's fine-tuning. They summarized the conclusions of more than two hundred published papers in the field.

"On balance, the fine-tuning of the Universe for life has stood up well under the scrutiny of physicists," they wrote.[21] They added that it's "not the case" that fine-tuning is the invention of a bunch of religious believers who hijacked physics to their own ends. Rather, they said, "physics has tended to consolidate our understanding of fine-tuning."[22]

Fine-Tuned for Life

Oxford-educated physicist John Leslie, author of the influential book *Universes*, believes that if ours is the only universe—and, again, there's no scientific evidence that any others exist—then the fine-tuning is "genuine evidence . . . that God is real."[23]

"I agree," said Strauss. "Let's go back to what I know for a fact as a scientist. I know there's one universe that appears to have a beginning, which is incredibly calibrated in a way that defies naturalistic explanations, and there's a highly improbable planet whose unlikely conditions allow us to exist. To me, all of that begs for a divine explanation."

I raised my hand. "Hold on," I said. "Maybe our universe *isn't* so finely tuned. For instance, why would a creator waste so much space if he wanted to create a habitat for humankind? The universe is unimaginably huge, but it's largely a wasteland that's inhospitable to life."

"Actually, the universe is the smallest it could possibly be and still have life," Strauss replied.

That statement shocked me. "I'd like to hear you explain *that* one," I said.

"If you start with the big bang and your goal is to make a solar system like ours, you have to go through two previous generations of stars. The first generation left behind some of the elements of the periodic table but lacked the right amounts of carbon, oxygen, and nitrogen to make rocky planets and complex life. Then the second generation of stars formed from the debris of the first generation. When these burned out, they made more heavy elements and scattered them throughout the universe. Our sun coalesced from that debris.

"Now here's my point: this third generation of stars is the first possibility for a solar system like ours to exist. So if you start with the big bang, it takes nine billion years to create a solar system like ours—which is approximately when our solar system formed, 4.5 billion years ago. So if you're God and your purpose is to create Earth suitable for people and you use these processes, it would take about 13.5 billion years. And during that time, what is the universe doing?"

"Expanding."

"Right, it's getting bigger and bigger. So even though it's incredibly large, this is the youngest, and therefore the smallest, that the universe can be if you want to create one planet that's hospitable for life."

"Okay," I replied, "now I get it."

The God Hypothesis

I asked Strauss, "If God is the most likely explanation for our universe and planet, then what can we logically deduce about him from the scientific evidence?"

"Several things. First," he said, grabbing a finger as he went through each point, "he must be transcendent, since he exists apart from his creation. Second, he must be immaterial or spirit, since he existed before the physical world. Third, he must be timeless or eternal, since he existed before physical time was created. Fourth, he must be powerful, given the immense energy of the big bang.

"Fifth, he must be smart, given the fact that the big bang was not some chaotic event but was masterfully finely tuned. Sixth, he must be personal, since a decision had to be made to create. Seventh, he must be creative—I mean, just look at the wonders of the universe. And eighth, he must be caring, since he so purposefully crafted a habitat for us."

> "All the qualities we've elicited from the scientific evidence are consistent with the God of the Bible."

"Still, how do we know this creator is the God of Christianity?" I asked.

"All the qualities we've elicited from the evidence are consistent with the God of the Bible," he replied. "If there's just one creator, that rules out polytheism. Since he's outside of creation, this rules out pantheism. The universe is not cyclical, which violates the tenets of Eastern religions. And the big bang contradicts ancient religious assumptions that the universe is static."

Hugh Ross, who earned his doctorate at the University of Toronto, points to several ways in which the ancient writings in the Bible reflect the findings of contemporary cosmology.

"It is worth noting," Ross wrote, "that Scripture speaks about the transcendent beginning of physical reality, including time itself (Genesis 1:1; John 1:3; Colossians 1:15–17; Hebrews 11:3); about continual cosmic expansion, or 'stretching out' (Job 9:8; Psalm 104:2; Isaiah 40:22, 45:12; Jeremiah 10:12); about unchanging physical laws (Jeremiah 33:25), one of which is the pervasive law of decay (Ecclesiastes 1:3–11; Romans 8:20–22). These descriptions fly in the face of ancient, enduring, and prevailing assumptions about an eternal, static universe—until the twentieth century."[24]

Strauss glanced briefly out the window, turning philosophical in our last moments together.

"You know," he said, taking a sip of water, "I'm friends with an artist who says he can look at a piece of art and see the soul of the artist. I can't do that, but I'm a scientist. I can look deeply into the universe and the subatomic world and see the soul of *the* Artist.

"Then I look at the bizarre world of quantum mechanics. Lee, it's so different from anything you and I can imagine. To me, that's a reflection of Isaiah 55, which says that God's ways are different than our ways. His thoughts are greater than our thoughts.[25]

"The artist looks at a painting and says, 'These brushstrokes tell me about the mood of the painter.' As a physicist, I know that virtual particles inside of protons have a mass that's finely tuned so that I can exist. That tells me something about the mood of the creator—he's both ingenious and caring. Why else would he cause all of creation to accrue to our benefit?

"Frankly, I look at a painting and say, 'Huh, that's nice.' To me, it's just color on canvas. But I'm privileged to be a scientist. I can see the nuances and subtleties and intricacies of nature in a way that others can't. And invariably, they point me toward one conclusion: *the God hypothesis has no competitors.*"

That rang true to me. Honestly, just these first two categories of evidence—cosmology and physics—were sufficient to establish for me that God is real. Would you say that might be true for you?

Still, there's another area that buttresses this case even more—the biological information found inside each cell of our body. Where did that come from? Was it mere evolutionary processes or a superintelligence? Answering that question necessitated a plane ticket to the Pacific Northwest.

CHAPTER 3

OUR DNA DEMANDS
A DESIGNER

*Human DNA contains more organized
information than the Encyclopedia Britannica.
If the full text of the encyclopedia were to
arrive in computer code from outer space,
most people would regard this as proof of
the existence of extraterrestrial intelligence.
But when seen in nature, it is explained [by
Darwinists] as the workings of random forces.*

**Science writer George Sim Johnson,
"Did Darwin Get It Right?"**

In 1953, when Francis Crick told his wife, Odile, that he and a colleague had discovered the secret of life—the chemical structure of DNA in which the instructions for building proteins are encoded—she didn't believe him. Years later, she confessed to her husband, "You were always coming home and saying things like that, so naturally I thought nothing of it."[1]

This time, he wasn't exaggerating. He and James D. Watson would receive the Nobel Prize for discovering the now-famous double helix of deoxyribonucleic acid, where the "language of life" is stored.

As scientists have studied the six feet of DNA tightly coiled inside every one of our bodies' one hundred trillion cells, they have marveled at how it provides the genetic information necessary to create all the proteins out of which our bodies are built. In fact, each one of the thirty thousand genes that are embedded in our twenty-three pairs of chromosomes can yield as many as 20,500 different kinds of proteins.[2]

The astounding capacity of microscopic DNA to harbor this mountain of information, carefully spelled out in a four-letter chemical alphabet, "vastly exceeds that of any other known system," said geneticist Michael Denton.

In fact, he said the information needed to build the proteins for all the species of organisms that have ever lived—a number estimated to be approximately one thousand million—"could be held in a teaspoon [of DNA] and there would still be room left for all the information in every book ever written."[3]

DNA serves as the information storehouse for a finely choreographed manufacturing process in which the right amino acids are linked together with the right bonds in the right sequence to produce the right kind of proteins that fold in the right way to build biological systems.

"This new realm of molecular genetics [is] where we see the most compelling evidence of design on the Earth," said once-skeptical biology professor Dean Kenyon.[4]

It seemed fitting that when scientists announced they had finally mapped the three billion codes of the human genome—a project that filled the equivalent of 75,490 pages of *The New York Times*—divine references abounded. President Bill Clinton said scientists were "learning the language in which God created life," while geneticist Francis Collins said DNA is "our own instruction book, previously known only to God."[5]

Does that seem hyperbolic to you? Are such public bows

to a creator merely a polite social custom, meant only as a nodding courtesy to a predominantly theistic country? Or does the bounty of information in DNA really warrant the conclusion that an intelligent designer must have infused genetic material with its protein-building instructions? In short, does the existence of biological information in our cells provide persuasive evidence that God is real?

Looking for solid answers, I flew to Seattle to sit down with one of the country's foremost experts on origin-of-life issues.

INTERVIEW WITH

Stephen C. Meyer, PhD

After earning degrees in physics and geology, Stephen Meyer went on to receive his master's degree in the history and philosophy of science at Cambridge University. He later obtained his doctorate from Cambridge, with a dissertation that analyzed the scientific and methodological issues in origin-of-life biology.

Since then, he has become one of the most compelling voices in the intelligent design movement. He left his career as a professor at Whitworth College in 2002 to become director of the Discovery Institute's Center for Science and Culture. His books include *Signature in the Cell*, which was named a Book of the Year by the *Times* [of London] *Literary Supplement*, and *The Return of the God Hypothesis*.

As for me, I was seeking straightforward answers to an issue that has befuddled origin-of-life scientists for the last several decades: How did DNA and life itself come into existence? Could it be evidence that God is real? Or might there be a more prosaic materialistic explanation?

The DNA-to-Design Argument

I began our discussion by reading Meyer a quote I had scribbled in my notes: "According to Bernd-Olaf Küppers, the author of *Information and the Origin of Life*, 'the question of the origin of life is thus equivalent to the problem of the origin of biological information,'"[1] I said. "Do you agree with him?"

"Oh, absolutely, yes," Meyer replied. "When I ask students what they would need to get their computer to perform a new function, they reply, 'You have to give it new lines of code.' The same principle is true in living organisms.

"If you want an organism to acquire a new function or structure, you have to provide information somewhere in the cell. You need instructions for how to build the cell's important components, which are mostly proteins. And we know that DNA is the repository for a digital code containing the instructions for telling the cell's machinery how to build proteins. Küppers recognized that this was a critical hurdle in explaining how life began: where did this genetic information come from?

"Think of making soup from a recipe. You can have all the ingredients on hand, but if you don't know the proper proportions or which items to add in what order or how long to cook the concoction, you won't get a soup that tastes very good.

"Well, a lot of people talk about the 'prebiotic soup'—the chemicals that supposedly existed on the primitive Earth prior to life. Even if you had the right chemicals to create a living cell, you would also need information about how to arrange them in very specific configurations in order to perform biological functions. Ever since the 1950s and 1960s, biologists have recognized that the cell's critical functions are usually performed by proteins, and proteins are the product of assembly instructions stored in DNA."

"Let's talk about DNA then," I said. "You've written that there's a 'DNA to design argument.' What do you mean by that?"

"Very simply," he said, "I mean that the origin of information in DNA—which is necessary for life to begin—is best explained by an intelligent cause rather than by any of the types of naturalistic causes that scientists typically use to explain biological phenomena."

"When you talk about 'information' in DNA, what exactly do you mean?" I asked.

"We know from our experience that we can convey information with a twenty-six-letter alphabet or even just two characters, like the zeros and ones used in the binary code in computers. One of the most extraordinary discoveries of the twentieth century was that DNA actually stores information—the detailed instructions for assembling proteins—in the form of a four-character digital code.

"The characters happen to be chemicals called adenine, guanine, cytosine, and thymine. Scientists represent them with the letters A, G, C, and T, and that's appropriate because they function as alphabetic characters in the genetic text. Properly arranging those four 'bases,' as they're called, will instruct the cell to build different sequences of amino acids, which are the building blocks of proteins. Different arrangements of characters yield different sequences of amino acids."

With that, Meyer showed me an illustration he often uses with college students. Reaching over to a desk drawer, he took out several oversized plastic snap-lock beads of the sort that young children play with. He held up orange, green, blue, red, and purple beads of different shapes.

"These represent the structure of a protein. Essentially, a protein is a long linear array of amino acids," he said, snapping the beads together in a line. "Because of the forces between the amino acids, the proteins fold into very particular three-dimensional shapes," he added as he bent and twisted the line of beads.

"These three-dimensional shapes are highly irregular, sort of like the teeth in a key, and they have a lock-key fit with other molecules in the cell. Often, the proteins will catalyze reactions, or they'll form structural molecules or linkers or parts of molecular machines. This specific three-dimensional shape that allows proteins to perform a function derives directly from the one-dimensional sequencing of amino acids."

Then he pulled some of the beads apart and began to rearrange their order. "If I were to switch a red one and a blue one, I'd be setting up a different combination of force interactions, and the protein would fold completely differently. So the sequence of the amino acids is critical to getting the long chain to fold properly to form an actual functional protein. Wrong sequence, no folding—and the sequence of amino acids is unable to serve its function.

"Proteins, of course, are the key functional molecule in the cell; you can't have life without them. Where do they come from? Well, that question forces a deeper issue—what's the source of the assembly instructions in DNA that are responsible for the one-dimensional sequential arrangements of amino acids that create the three-dimensional shapes of proteins? Ultimately," he emphasized, "the functional attributes of proteins derive from information stored in the DNA molecule."

The Library of Life

I was fascinated by the process Meyer had described. "What you're saying is that DNA would be like a blueprint for how to build proteins," I said, using an analogy I had heard many times before.

Meyer hesitated. "Actually, I don't like the blueprint metaphor," he said. "You see, there are probably other sources of information in the cell and in organisms. As important as DNA is, it doesn't build everything. All it builds are the protein molecules, but they are only subunits of larger structures that themselves are informatively arranged."

"Then what's a better analogy?"

"DNA is more like a library," he said. "The organism accesses the information it needs from DNA so it can build some of its critical components. And the library analogy is better because of its alphabetic nature. In DNA, there are long lines of A, C, G, and Ts that are precisely arranged in order to create protein structure and folding. To build one protein, you typically need 1,200 to 2,000 letters or bases—which is a lot of information."

"And this raises the question again of the origin of that information," I said.

"It's not just that a question has been raised," he insisted. "It's *the* critical and foundational question. If you can't explain where the information comes from, you haven't explained life, because it's the information that makes the molecules into something that actually functions."

I asked, "What does the presence of information tell you?"

"I believe the presence of information in the cell is best explained by the activity of an intelligent agent," he replied. "Bill Gates said that DNA is like a software program, only much more complex than anything we've ever devised. That's highly suggestive, because we know that at Microsoft, Gates used intelligent programmers to produce software. Information theorist Henry Quastler said as far back as the 1960s that the 'creation of new information is habitually associated with conscious activity.'[2]

"Even the very simplest cell we study today or find evidence of in the fossil record requires information that is stored in DNA or some other information carrier. And we know from our experience that information is habitually associated with conscious activity. Using uniformitarian logic, we can reconstruct the cause of that ancient information in the first cell as being the product of intelligence."

As my mind tracked his line of reasoning, everything seemed to click into place—except one thing. "However," I said, "there's a caveat."

Meyer cocked an eyebrow. "Like what?"

"All of that is true—unless you can find some better explanation."

"Yes, of course," he said. "You have to rule out other causes of the same effect. Origin-of-life scientists have looked at other possibilities for decades, and frankly, they've come up dry."

Before we went any further, though, I needed to satisfy myself that the other possible scenarios fall short of the intelligent design theory.

The Missing Soup

In 1871, Charles Darwin wrote a letter in which he speculated that life might have originated when "a protein compound was chemically formed . . . in some warm little pond, with all sorts of ammonia and phosphoric salts, light, heat, electricity, etc. present."[3]

"I hear scientists talk a lot about this prebiotic soup," I said to Meyer, referring to the idea that the basic organic compounds necessary for forming cells accumulated in oceans on the primate Earth. Over millions of years, macromolecules, proteins, and nucleic acids supposedly formed and eventually developed the ability to reproduce. Natural selection drove more complexity until the first simple cell system emerged.[4]

"How much evidence is there that this nutrient broth, or prebiotic soup, actually existed?" I asked.

"The answer is there isn't any evidence," came his reply. "If this prebiotic soup had really existed, it would have been rich in amino acids. And therefore there would have been a lot of nitrogen because amino acids are nitrogenous. So when we examine the earliest sediments of the Earth, we should find large deposits of nitrogen-rich minerals."

"What have scientists found?"

"Those deposits have never been located," he said.

In fact, he said that Jim Brooks wrote in *Origins of Life* as far back as 1985 that "we can be reasonably certain that there never was any substantial amount of 'primitive soup' on Earth when ancient PreCambrian sediments were formed; if such a soup ever existed it was only for a brief period of time."[5]

This was astounding. "Don't you find that surprising, since scientists routinely talk about the prebiotic soup as if it were a given?" I asked.

"Yes, certainly it's surprising," he replied. "Michael Denton wrote, 'Considering the way the prebiotic soup is referred to in so many discussions of the origin of life as an already established reality, it comes as something of a shock to realize that there is absolutely no positive evidence for its existence.'[6] And even if we were to assume that the prebiotic soup did exist, there would have been significant problems with cross-reactions."

"What do you mean?"

"Even if amino acids existed in the theoretical prebiotic soup, they would have readily reacted with other chemicals. This would have been another tremendous barrier to the formation of life."

Undoubtedly, obstacles to the formation of life on the primitive Earth would have been formidable, even if the world were awash with an ocean of biological precursors. Still, is there *any* reasonable naturalistic route to life? Like a homicide detective rounding up the usual suspects, I decided to run down the various scenarios to see if any of them made sense.

SCENARIO #1: Random Chance

I began with an observation. "I know that the idea of life forming by random chance is out of vogue among scientists," I said.

Meyer agreed. "Virtually all origin-of-life experts have utterly rejected that approach," he said with a wave of his hand.

"Even so, the idea is still very much alive at the popular level," I pointed out. "For many college students who speculate about these things, chance is still the hero. They think if you let amino acids randomly interact over millions of years, life is somehow going to emerge."

"But there's no merit to it," Meyer replied. "Imagine trying to generate even a simple book by throwing Scrabble letters onto the floor. Even a simple protein molecule, or the gene to build that molecule, is so rich in information that the entire time since the big bang would not give you the probabilistic resources you would need to generate that molecule by chance."

"Even if the first molecule had been much simpler than those today?" I asked.

"There's a minimal complexity threshold," Meyer said. "There's a certain level of folding that a protein has to have, called tertiary structure, that is necessary for it to perform a function. You don't get tertiary structure in a protein unless you have at least seventy-five amino acids or so. That may be conservative. Now consider what you'd need for a protein molecule to form by chance.

"First, you need the right bonds between the amino acids. Second, amino acids come in right-handed and left-handed versions, and you've got to get only left-handed ones. Third, the amino acids must link up in a specified sequence, like letters in a sentence.

"Run the odds of these things falling into place on their own and you find that the probabilities of forming a rather short functional protein at random would be one chance in a hundred thousand trillion trillion trillion trillion trillion trillion trillion trillion trillion trillion. That's a ten with 125 zeroes after it!

"And that would only be one protein molecule—a minimally complex cell would need between three hundred and five hundred protein molecules. Plus, all of this would have to be accomplished in a mere 100 million years, which is the approximate window of time between the Earth cooling and the first microfossils we've found.

"To suggest chance against those odds is really to invoke a naturalistic miracle," he concluded. "It's a confession of ignorance."

SCENARIO #2: Natural Selection

Random chance might not account for the origin of life, but evolutionary biologist Richard Dawkins said that when natural selection acts on chance variations, then evolution is capable of accomplishing seemingly impossible tasks.[7]

"Can natural selection explain how evolution managed to scale the mountain of building the first living cell?" I asked Meyer.

"Whether natural selection really works at the level of biological evolution is open to debate, but it most certainly does not work at the level of *chemical* evolution, which tries to explain the origin of the first life from simpler chemicals," Meyer replied. "As

Theodosius Dobzhansky said, 'Prebiological natural selection is a contradiction in terms.'"[8]

"How so?"

"Darwinists admit that natural selection requires a self-replicating organism to work," Meyer explained. "Organisms reproduce, their offspring have variations, the ones that are better adapted to their environment survive better, and so those adaptations are preserved and passed on to the next generation.

"However, in order to have reproduction, there has to be cell division. And that presupposes the existence of information-rich DNA and proteins. But that's the problem—those are the very things they're trying to explain!

"In other words, you've got to have a self-replicating organism for Darwinian evolution to take place, but you can't have a self-replicating organism until you have the information necessary in DNA, which is what you're trying to explain in the first place. It's like the guy who falls into a deep hole and realizes he needs a ladder to get out. So he climbs out, goes home, gets a ladder, jumps back into the hole, and climbs out. It begs the question."

I raised another possibility. "Maybe replication first began in a much simpler way and then natural selection was able to take over," I said. "For example, some small viruses use RNA as their genetic material. RNA molecules are simpler than DNA, and they can also store information and even replicate. What about the 'RNA first hypothesis' that says reproductive life originated in a realm that's much less complex than DNA?"

"There's a mountain of problems with that," Meyer said. "Just to cite a couple of them—the RNA molecule would need information to function, just as DNA would, and so we're right back to the same problem of where the information came from. Also, for a single strand of RNA to replicate, there must be an identical RNA molecule close by. To have a reasonable chance of having two identical RNA molecules of the right length would require a library of ten billion billion billion billion billion billion RNA molecules—and that effectively rules out any chance origin of a primitive replicating system."[9]

Although popular for a while, the RNA theory has generated its share of skeptics. Origin-of-life researcher Graham Cairns-Smith said, "The many interesting and detailed experiments in this area" have shown that the theory is "highly implausible."[10] Biochemist Gerald Joyce of the Scripps Research Center was even more blunt: "You have to build straw man upon straw man to get to the point where RNA is a viable first biomolecule."[11]

SCENARIO #3: Chemical Affinities and Self-Ordering

Meyer pointed out that by the early 1970s, most origin-of-life scientists had become disenchanted with the options of random chance and natural selection. As a result, some explored a third possibility—various self-organizational theories for the origin of the information-bearing macromolecules DNA and proteins.

For example, scientists theorized that chemical attractions may have caused DNA's four-letter alphabet to self-assemble or that the natural affinities between amino acids prompted them to link together by themselves to create protein.

"One of the first advocates of this approach was Dean Kenyon, who coauthored the textbook *Biochemical Predestination*," Meyer said. "The title tells it all. The idea was that the development of life was inevitable because the amino acids in proteins and the bases, or letters, in the DNA alphabet had self-ordering capacities that accounted for the origin of the information in these molecules."

However, I already knew that Kenyon later repudiated the conclusions of his book, declaring that "we have not the slightest chance of a chemical evolutionary origin for even the simplest of cells" and that intelligent design "made a great deal of sense, as it very closely matched the multiple discoveries in molecular biology."[12]

It's true, said Meyer, that there are examples in nature where chemical attractions do result in a kind of self-ordering. Salt crystals are a good illustration. Chemical forces of attraction cause sodium ions, Na+, to bond with chloride ions, Cl-, in order to form highly ordered patterns within a crystal of salt. You get a sequence of Na and Cl repeating over and over.

But he said that when scientists did experiments, they found that amino acids didn't demonstrate these same bonding affinities. While there were some very slight affinities, they didn't correlate to any of the known patterns of sequencing that are found in functional proteins.

Besides, information theorist Hubert Yockey and chemist Michael Polanyi raised a deeper issue: "What would happen if we *could* explain the sequencing in DNA and proteins as a result of self-organization properties? Wouldn't we end up with something like a crystal of salt, where there's merely a repetitive sequence?"[13]

Explained Meyer, "If all you had were repeating characters in DNA, the assembly instructions would merely tell amino acids to assemble in the same way over and over. You wouldn't be able to build all the many different kinds of protein molecules you need for a living cell to function. It would be like handing a person an instruction book for how to build an automobile, but all the book said was 'the-the-the-the-the-the.' You couldn't hope to convey all the necessary information with that one-word vocabulary.

"Whereas information requires variability, irregularity, and unpredictability—which is what information theorists call complexity—self-organization gives you repetitive, redundant structure, which is known as simple order. And complexity and order are categorical opposites. Chemical evolutionary theorists are not going to escape this," he said.

"Almost a Miracle"

Like a skillful boxer picking apart the defenses of his opponent, Meyer had adroitly dismantled the three categories of naturalistic explanations for the origin of life and information in DNA. In short, no hypothesis has come close to explaining how information necessary to life's origin arose by naturalistic means.

As Francis Crick, a philosophical materialist, has conceded, "An honest man, armed with all the knowledge available to us now, could only state that in some sense, the origin of life appears at the moment to be almost a miracle, so many are the conditions which would have had to have been satisfied to get it going."[14]

For many researchers, the only recourse has been to continue to have faith that, as one scientist put it, some previously unknown "magic mineral" will be discovered to have had "exactly the right properties to cause the necessary reactions to occur to create a nucleic acid."[15]

"Maybe someday," I said to Meyer, "scientists will come up with another hypothesis."

"Maybe they will," he replied. "You can't prove something like this with 100 percent certainty because you don't know what new evidence will show. That's why all scientists reason in a way that's provisional. Having said that, though, we do know that some possibilities can be excluded categorically. They're dead ends."

"Some skeptics would claim you're arguing from ignorance," I pointed out. "Scientists admit they don't know how life started, so you conclude there must have been an intelligent designer."

"No, not at all. I'm not saying intelligence design makes sense simply because other theories fail," he insisted. "Instead, I'm making an inference to the best explanation, which is how scientists reason in historical matters. Based on the evidence, the scientist assesses each hypothesis on the basis of its ability to explain the evidence at hand. Typically, the key criterion is whether the explanation has 'causal power,' which is the ability to produce the effect in question.

"In this case, the effect in question is information. We've seen that neither chance, nor chance combined with natural selection, nor self-organizational processes have the causal power to produce information. But we do know of one entity that does have the required causal powers to produce information, and that's intelligence. We're not inferring to that entity on the basis of what we *don't* know, but rather on the basis of what we *do* know. That's not an argument from ignorance."

"Isn't there a fundamental weakness to your argument though?" I asked. "You're arguing by analogy, comparing the information in DNA to information we find in language. Arguments based on analogies are notoriously weak. Advocates might emphasize the similarities between two things, but opponents will stress the differences."

Replied Meyer, "I'm not arguing by analogy. The coding regions of DNA have *exactly* the same relevant properties as a computer code or language. We know books and computer codes are designed by intelligence, and the presence of this type of information in DNA also implies an intelligent source.

"Scientists in many fields recognize this connection between information and intelligence. When archaeologists discovered the Rosetta stone, they didn't think its inscriptions were the product of random chance or self-organizational processes. Obviously, the sequential arrangement of symbols was conveying information, and it was a reasonable assumption that intelligence created it. The same principle is true for DNA."

More scientists are coming to agree. "Origin-of-life researchers have failed to generate any tangible progress toward a strictly materialistic explanation for life's inception," said Fazale Rana, who earned his doctorate in chemistry with an emphasis in biochemistry and has done postdoctoral studies in the biophysics of cell membranes. "The harmony between the Bible's account of the origin of life and nature's record provides powerful evidence for the validity of the Christian faith."[16]

As for Meyer, he had made a convincing case that intelligence—and intelligence alone—can explain the presence of precise information within genetic material. By itself, this was compelling evidence for the existence of a designer of life. When taken together with the origin of the universe and its fine-tuning, the case for God being real becomes powerful and persuasive.

> "Intelligence—and intelligence alone—can explain the presence of precise information within genetic material. When taken together with the origin of the universe and its fine-tuning, the case for God being real becomes powerful and persuasive."

However, while these scientific findings make theism the best possible explanation for our world, they fall short of establishing the overall credibility of Christianity. For that, I knew I would need to turn to history in order to investigate the pivotal claim of the Christian faith—that Jesus of Nazareth proved his divinity by returning from the dead.

CHAPTER 4

Easter Showed That Jesus Is God

If Jesus rose from the dead, then you have to
accept all that he said; if he didn't rise from
the dead, then why worry about any of what
he said? The issue on which everything hangs
is not whether or not you like his teaching
but whether or not he rose from the dead.

Pastor and author Timothy Keller,
Twitter post, April 5, 2022

There I was in the most unlikely place for a Christian author—sitting in the living room of the opulent Playboy Mansion in Los Angeles as I conducted a television interview with *Playboy* founder Hugh Hefner, who was clad in his customary pajamas and silk smoking jacket.

When I asked about his spiritual beliefs, this quintessential hedonist professed a minimal belief in God, as a word for "the beginning of it all" and the "great unknown," but not in the God of Christianity, which he called "a little too childlike for me."

Then I brought up Jesus' resurrection—and suddenly his eyes grew wide. "Oh," he said in a tone of wonder, "if one had any real evidence that, indeed, Jesus did return from the dead, then that is the beginning of a dropping of a series of dominoes that takes us to all kinds of wonderful things," he told me. "It assures an afterlife and all kinds of things that we would all hope are true."

Though he admitted he never explored the historical evidence for Jesus returning to life, Hefner remained a doubter. "Do I think that Jesus was the Son of God?" he asked. "I don't think that he is any more the Son of God than we are."[1]

That is, unless the resurrection is true. Everything comes down to that. "If Christ has not been raised," wrote the apostle Paul, "your faith is futile."[2] That's because the cross either unmasked Jesus as a pretender or opened the door to a supernatural resurrection that has irrevocably confirmed his divinity.

> "The cross either unmasked Jesus as a pretender or opened the door to a supernatural resurrection that has irrevocably confirmed his divinity."

After all, Jesus did make divine claims about himself through both words and deeds.[3] Among the examples are these: he forgave sins, which only God can do (Matthew 9:1–3); he called himself the Son of Man, a reference to the divine figure in Daniel 7:13–14, who is sovereign, eternal, and worshiped; he demonstrated divine control over nature (Matthew 14:30–33); he said he would sit at God's right hand and exercise divine judgment (Mark 14:61–64), which was considered by Jewish leaders to be an assertion of deity; he received worship (Matthew 28:17); he claimed to have all authority over heaven and earth (Matthew 28:18); he exhibited divine attributes, including omnipresence (Matthew 28:20) and omniscience (Matthew 9:4); and he claimed that he deserves the same honor as the Father (John 5:22–23).

At one point, Jesus declared, "I and the Father are one."[4] The Greek for *one* is not masculine but neuter, which means

Jesus was *not* saying, "I and the Father are the *same person*," but he was saying, "I and the Father are the *same thing*"—that is, one in nature or essence.[5] His opponents picked up rocks to stone him "for blasphemy, because you, a mere man, claim to be God."[6] No wonder the Jewish authorities said, "We have a law, and according to that law he must die, *because he claimed to be the Son of God.*"[7]

Of course, anyone can assert that they're divine. But if Jesus claimed to be God, died, and then returned from the dead—well, that's convincing evidence that he was telling the truth.

Have you ever delved into the historical evidence for the resurrection? It's a fascinating experience! I spent nearly two years doing this in response to my wife's conversion to Christianity—and that's what transformed me from skeptic to believer.

To help analyze the historical data, I called one of the leading scholars on the resurrection, whose 718-page tome *The Resurrection of Jesus: A New Historiographical Approach* is a landmark work on the topic. He agreed to come over to my house to discuss this cornerstone doctrine.

INTERVIEW WITH

Michael Licona, PhD

Michael Licona, who earned his doctorate on the resurrection from the University of Pretoria in South Africa, was mentored by Gary Habermas, one of the world's leading resurrection authorities. Together, they wrote the award-winning book *The Case for the Resurrection of Jesus.* Historian Paul Maier said that book's responses to naturalistic explanations for the resurrection "are the most comprehensive treatment of the subject anywhere."[1]

In recent years, Licona has debated such formidable opponents as Shabir Ally, the fierce defender of Islam; spiritual street fighter Dan Barker; skeptic Richard Carrier; liberal professor Elaine Pagels; and agnostic scholar Bart Ehrman.

Licona's own faith was sharpened by the period of doubt he went through at the end of his graduate studies in 1985. His questions about the veracity of Christianity nearly prompted him to jettison the beliefs he had held since the age of ten. Instead, his renewed investigation into Christianity and other major world religions, as well as his in-depth study of atheism, ended up solidifying his conviction that Christianity rests on a firm historical foundation.

The Historian's Three *R*s

After we settled into adjacent couches in my family room, I asked Licona, "How would a historian begin investigating something like the resurrection?"

"You've heard of the three *R*s of an elementary education—reading, 'riting, and 'rithmetic?" he asked. "Well, there are also three *R*s for doing good history: relevant sources, responsible method, and restrained results. First, historians must identify all the relevant sources."

"What would those be in the case of Jesus?"

"There are the New Testament writings; a few secular sources who mention Jesus, such as Josephus, Tacitus, and Pliny the Younger; the apologists, who were early defenders of Christianity; and even the Gnostic writings. We also want to examine the apostolic fathers, who were the next generation after the apostles."

"Which of the apostolic fathers are the most significant?"

"Clement of Rome is believed to have been a disciple of the apostle Peter, and Polycarp was probably a disciple of John, so their writings can give us a window into what those apostles taught," he said. "Then once all of the relevant sources have been identified, we have to apply responsible method. This means assigning the greatest weight to reports that are early, eyewitness, enemy, embarrassing, and corroborated by others."

"And what do you mean by restrained results?"

"This means that historians should not claim more than the evidence warrants."

"What about biases?" I asked. "You can't deny that you see the historical evidence through the lenses of your own prejudices."

"Absolutely. Nobody is exempt, including theists, deists, atheists, or whatever—we all have our biases," Licona said. "That's why you have to put certain checks and balances in place. This is what historian Gary Habermas did in creating the 'minimal facts approach' to the resurrection."

"How does this keep biases in check?"

"Under this approach, we only consider facts that meet two criteria. First, there must be very strong historical evidence supporting them. And second, the evidence must be so strong that the vast majority of today's scholars on the subject—including skeptical ones—accept these as historical facts. Let's face it, there's a greater likelihood that a purported historical fact is true when someone accepts it, even though they're not in agreement with your metaphysical beliefs."

"How do you know what all these scholars believe about the resurrection?"

"Habermas has compiled a list of more than 2,200 sources in French, German, and English in which experts have written on the resurrection from 1975 to the present. He has identified minimal facts that are strongly evidenced and are regarded as historical by the large majority of scholars, including skeptics. We try to come up with the best historical explanation to account for these facts.

"It's like putting together a jigsaw puzzle. Each piece represents a historical fact, and we want to put them together in a way that doesn't leave out any pieces and doesn't require us to force any of the pieces to make them fit. In the end, the puzzle creates a picture that's based on the best explanation for the facts we have."

With that background in place, I issued Licona a challenge. "Use only the minimal facts," I said, "and let's see how strong of a case you can build for Jesus rising from the dead."

Licona moved to the edge of the couch. "I'll use just five minimal facts—and you can decide for yourself how persuasive the case is."

FACT #1: Jesus Was Killed by Crucifixion

"The first fact is Jesus' crucifixion," he began. "Even an extreme liberal like John Dominic Crossan says, 'That he was crucified is as sure as anything historical ever can be.'[2] Skeptic James Tabor says, 'I think we need have no doubt that given Jesus' execution by Roman crucifixion he was truly *dead*.'[3] Both Gerd Lüdemann, who's an atheistic New Testament critic, and Bart Ehrman, who's an agnostic, call the crucifixion an indisputable fact. Why? First of all, because all four gospels report it."

I put up my hand. "Whoa!" I said. "Are you assuming that the Bible is the inspired word of God?"

Licona seemed glad I had brought up the issue. "Let me clarify something: for the purposes of examining the evidence, I'm not considering the Bible to be inerrant, inspired, or Scripture of any kind. I'm simply accepting it for what it unquestionably is—a set of ancient documents that can be subjected to historical scrutiny like any other accounts from antiquity."

With that clarification, he went on with his case. "Now, beyond the four gospels, we also have a number of non-Christian sources that corroborate the crucifixion. For instance, the historian Tacitus said Jesus 'suffered the extreme penalty during the reign of Tiberius.' The Jewish historian Josephus reports that Pilate 'condemned him to be crucified.' Lucian of Samosata, who was a Greek satirist, mentions the crucifixion, and Mara Bar-Serapion, who was a pagan, confirms Jesus was executed. Even the Jewish Talmud reports that 'Yeshu was hanged.'"

"Yeshu? Hanged?"

"Yes, *Yeshu* is *Joshua* in Hebrew; the Greek equivalent is translated as *Jesus*. And in the ancient world, to be hung on a tree referred oftentimes to a crucifixion."[4]

"Were the executioners competent enough to be sure that Jesus was really dead?"

"I'm confident they were. You've got Roman soldiers carrying out executions all the time. It was their job. They were very good at it. Besides, death by crucifixion was basically a slow and agonizing demise by asphyxiation because of the difficulty in breathing created by the victim's position on the cross. And that's something you can't fake.

"This fact is as solid as anything in ancient history: Jesus was crucified and died as a result. The scholarly consensus is absolutely overwhelming."

"Lee, this first fact is as solid as anything in ancient history: Jesus was crucified and died as a result. The scholarly consensus is absolutely overwhelming."

I agreed that Jesus' death by crucifixion is indisputable. Even the secular, peer-reviewed *Journal of the American Medical Association* carried an analysis of the crucifixion that concluded,

"Clearly, the weight of the historical and medical evidence indicates that Jesus was dead [even] before the wound to his side was inflicted."[5]

With that firmly established, Licona moved on to his next minimal fact.

FACT #2: Jesus' Disciples Believed That He Rose and Appeared to Them

"The second fact is the disciples' beliefs that Jesus had actually returned from the dead and had appeared to them," Licona said. "There are three strands of evidence for this: (1) Paul's testimony about the disciples, (2) oral traditions that passed through the early church, and (3) the written works of the early church.

"First, *Paul's testimony.* He's important because he reports knowing some of the disciples personally, including Peter, James, and John.[6] And Paul says in 1 Corinthians 15:11 that whether 'it was I or they, this is what we preach,' referring to the resurrection of Jesus. In other words, Paul knew the apostles and reports that they claimed—just as he did—that Jesus had returned from the dead.

"Then we have *oral tradition.* Obviously, people in those days didn't have tape recorders and few people could read, so they relied on verbal transmission for passing along what happened until it was later written down. Scholars have identified several places in which this oral tradition has been copied into the New Testament in the form of creeds, hymns, and sermon summations. This is really significant because the oral tradition must have existed prior to the New Testament writings for the New Testament authors to have included them."

"So it's early."

"Very early, which weighs heavily in their favor, as any historian will tell you. For example, we have creeds that laid out basic doctrines in a form that was easily memorized. One of the earliest and most important creeds was relayed by Paul in his first letter to the Corinthian church, which was written about AD 55," he said.

"It says: 'For what I received I passed on to you as of first importance: that Christ died for our sins according to the Scriptures, that he was buried, and that he was raised on the third day according to the Scriptures, and that he appeared to Cephas [Peter], and then to the Twelve. After that, he appeared to more than five hundred of the brothers and sisters at the same time, most of whom are still living, though some have fallen asleep. Then he appeared to James, then to all the apostles.'[7]

"Many scholars believe Paul received this creed from Peter and James while visiting with them in Jerusalem three years after his conversion.[8] That would be within five years of the crucifixion."

Licona's eyes got wide. "Think about that—it's really amazing!" he said, his voice rising. "As one expert said, 'This is the sort of data that historians of antiquity drool over.'[9] Not only is it extremely early, but it was apparently given to Paul by eyewitnesses or others he deemed reliable, which heightens its credibility even more."

"How important is this creed, in your opinion?"

"It's powerful," he declared. "Although early dating does not totally rule out the possibility of invention or deceit on the part of Jesus' followers, it is much too early to be the result of legendary development over time, since it can practically be traced to the original disciples of Jesus. In fact, this creed has been one of the most formidable obstacles to critics who try to shoot down the resurrection. It's simply gold for a historian."

I was familiar with this creed. The eminent historian James D. G. Dunn of the University of Durham, a Fellow of the British

Academy, concluded, "This tradition, we can be entirely confident, *was formulated as tradition within months of Jesus' death.*"[10] That's like a news flash in ancient history, not some legend that morphed over the many decades since Jesus' death.

Licona continued, "And we've got even more oral tradition. For instance, the New Testament preserves several sermons of the apostles. At a minimum, we can say that the vast majority of historians believe that the early apostolic teachings are enshrined in these sermon summaries in Acts—and they're not at all ambiguous. They declare that Jesus rose bodily from the dead.[11]

"Finally, we have written sources, such as Matthew, Mark, Luke, and John.[12] It's widely accepted, even among skeptical historians, that the Gospels were written in the first century. Even very liberal scholars will concede that we have four biographies written within seventy years of Jesus' life that unambiguously report the disciples' claims that Jesus rose from the dead."

I knew there were good reasons for dating the Gospels much closer to the life of Jesus. Because Acts doesn't record important events that happened in the AD 60s, it should be dated before 62. Since Acts is the second of a two-part work, we know that the first part—Luke's gospel—must have been written before that. And Luke incorporates parts of the gospel of Mark, which means Mark is even earlier. Jesus was crucified in AD 30 or 33, meaning a maximum gap of about thirty years.[13]

Licona went on, "I think an excellent case can be made for dating the Gospels earlier," he said, "but let's go with the more generous estimations. That's still extremely close to the events themselves, especially compared to many other ancient historical writings. Our two best sources on Alexander the Great, for instance, weren't written until at least four hundred years after his life.[14]

"Then we have the writings of the apostolic fathers, who

were said to have known the apostles or were close to others who did. There's a strong likelihood that their writings reflect the teachings of the apostles themselves—and what do they say? That the apostles were dramatically impacted by Jesus' resurrection.

"Consider Clement, for example. The early church father Irenaeus reports that Clement had conversed with the apostles—in fact, Irenaeus commented that he 'might be said to have the preaching of the apostles still echoing, and their traditions before his eyes.' Tertullian, the African church father, said Clement was ordained by Peter himself."

"So what does Clement report about the beliefs of the disciples?" I asked.

"In his letter to the Corinthian church, written in the first century, he writes, 'Therefore, having received orders and complete certainty caused by the resurrection of our Lord Jesus Christ and believing in the Word of God, they went with the Holy Spirit's certainty, preaching the good news that the kingdom of God is about to come.'[15]

"Then we have Polycarp. Irenaeus says that Polycarp was 'instructed by the apostles, and conversed with many who had seen Christ,' including John; that he 'recalled their very words'; and that he 'always taught the things which he had learned from the apostles.' Tertullian confirms that John appointed Polycarp as bishop of the church in Smyrna.

"Around AD 110, Polycarp wrote a letter to the Philippian church in which he mentions the resurrection of Jesus no fewer than five times. He was referring to Paul and the other apostles when he said, 'For they did not love the present age, but him who died for our benefit and for our sake was raised by God.'[16]

"So think about the depth of evidence we have in these three categories: Paul, oral tradition, and written reports. In all, we've got nine sources that reflect multiple, very early, and eyewitness testimonies to the disciples' claims that they had seen the risen Jesus. This is something the disciples believed to the core of their being."

"How do you know that?"

"Because we have evidence that the disciples had been transformed to the point where they were willing to endure persecution and even martyrdom. We find this in multiple accounts inside and outside the New Testament.

"Just read through Acts, and you'll see how the disciples were willing to suffer for their conviction that Jesus rose from the dead. The church fathers Clement, Polycarp, Ignatius, Tertullian, and Origen—they all confirm this. In fact, we've got at least seven early sources testifying that the disciples willingly suffered in defense of their beliefs—and if we include the martyrdoms of Paul and Jesus' half brother James, we have eleven sources."

"But," I objected, "people of other faiths have been willing to die for their beliefs through the ages. So what does the suffering of the disciples really prove?"

"First, it means that they certainly regarded their beliefs to be true. They didn't willfully lie about this. Liars make poor martyrs," he said. "Second, the disciples didn't just *believe* Jesus rose from the dead, but they knew for a fact whether he did. They were on the scene and able to ascertain for sure that he had been resurrected. So it was for the *truth* of the resurrection that they were willing to die.

"This is totally different than a modern-day Islamic terrorist or others willing to die for their beliefs. These people can only have faith that their beliefs are true, but they aren't in a position to know for sure. The disciples, on the other hand, knew for a *fact* whether the resurrection had truly occurred—and knowing the *truth*, they were willing to die for the belief that they had."

"Then what's the bottom line?" I asked.

Licona pointed out that even the liberal scholar Paula Fredriksen believes that "the disciples' conviction that they had seen the risen Christ . . . is [part of] historical bedrock, facts known past doubting."[17]

"I think that's pretty much undeniable—and I believe the evidence is clear and convincing that what they saw was the return of Jesus from the dead," Licona said. "And we're not done yet—we've got three more minimal facts to consider."

FACT #3: The Conversion of the Church Persecutor Paul

"We know from multiple sources that Paul—then known as Saul of Tarsus—was an enemy of the church and committed to persecuting the faithful," Licona continued. "But Paul himself says that he was converted to a follower of Jesus because he had personally encountered the resurrected Jesus.[18] So we have Jesus' resurrection attested by friend and foe alike, which is very significant.

"Then we have six ancient sources in addition to Paul—such as Luke, Clement of Rome, Polycarp, Tertullian, Dionysius of Corinth, and Origen—reporting that Paul was willing to suffer continuously and even die for his beliefs. Again, liars make poor martyrs. We can be confident that Paul not only claimed the risen Jesus appeared to him, but that he really believed it."

I couldn't let this point slip by without an objection. "People convert to other religions all the time," I said. "What's so special about Paul?"

"When virtually all people convert, it's because they've heard the message of that religion from *secondary* sources—that is, what other people tell them," Licona explained. "Yet that's not the case with Paul. He says he was transformed by a personal encounter with the risen Christ. His conversion is based in *primary* evidence—Jesus directly appeared to him. That's a big difference.

"You can't claim that Paul was a friend of Jesus who was primed to see a vision of him due to wishful thinking or grief after his crucifixion. Saul was a most unlikely candidate for conversion. His mindset was to oppose the Christian movement he believed was following a false Messiah. His radical transformation from persecutor to missionary demands an explanation—and I think the best explanation is that he told the truth when he said he met the risen Jesus on the road to Damascus.

"He had nothing to gain in this world—except his own suffering and martyrdom—for making this up."

FACT #4: The Conversion of the Skeptic James, Jesus' Half Brother

"The next minimal fact involves James, the half brother of Jesus," Licona said. "We have good evidence that James was not a follower of Jesus during Jesus' lifetime. Mark and John both report that none of Jesus' brothers believed in him."[19]

"Why do you consider their reports to be authentic?" I asked.

"Because of the principle of embarrassment. People are not going to invent a story that's going to be embarrassing or potentially discrediting to them, and it would be particularly humiliating for a first-century rabbi not to have his own family as his followers.[20]

"Then, however, the pivotal moment occurs. The ancient creedal material in 1 Corinthians 15 tells us that the risen Jesus appeared to James. Again, this is an extremely early account that has all the earmarks of reliability.[21]

"As a result of his encounter, James doesn't just become a Christian, but he later becomes leader of the Jerusalem church. We know this from Acts and Galatians.[22] Actually, James was so thoroughly convinced of Jesus' messiahship because of the resurrection that he died as a martyr, as both Christian and non-Christian sources attest.[23] So here we have another example of a skeptic who was converted because of a personal encounter with the resurrected Lord and was willing to die for his convictions."

With that, Licona advanced to the last of his minimal facts.

FACT #5: Jesus' Tomb Was Empty

"Although the fifth fact—that the tomb of Jesus was empty—is part of the minimal case for the resurrection, it doesn't enjoy the nearly universal consensus among scholars that the first four do," Licona began. "Still, there's strong evidence in its favor."[24]

"How strong?"

"Gary Habermas determined that about 75 percent of scholars on the subject regard it as a historical fact. That's quite a large majority. Personally, I think the empty tomb is very well-supported if the historical data is assessed without preconceptions. Basically, there are three strands of evidence: the Jerusalem factor, enemy attestation, and the testimony of women."

"Jerusalem factor?" I asked.

"This refers to the fact that Jesus was publicly executed and buried in Jerusalem, and then his resurrection was proclaimed in the very same city. In fact, several weeks after the crucifixion, Peter declares to a crowd right there in Jerusalem, 'God has raised this Jesus to life, and we are all witnesses of it.'[25]

"Frankly, it would have been impossible for Christianity to get off the ground in Jerusalem if Jesus' body were still in the tomb. The Roman or Jewish authorities could have simply gone over to his tomb and viewed his corpse, and the misunderstanding would have been over. But there's no indication that this occurred.

"Instead, what we do hear is enemy attestation to the empty tomb. In other words, what were the enemies of Jesus saying?

That the disciples stole the body. This is reported not only by Matthew but also by Justin Martyr and Tertullian. Here's the thing: Why would you say someone stole the body if it were still in the tomb? This is an implicit admission that the tomb was empty.

"On top of that, the idea that the disciples stole the body is a lame explanation. Are we supposed to believe they conspired to steal the body and pulled it off, and then they were willing to suffer continuously and even die for what they knew was a lie? That's such an absurd idea that scholars universally reject it today.

"In addition, we have the testimony of women that the tomb was empty. Not only were women the first to discover the vacant grave, but they are mentioned in all four gospels, whereas male witnesses appear only later and in two of them."

"Why is this important?"

"Because in both first-century Jewish and Roman cultures, women were lowly esteemed and their testimony was considered very questionable. They were certainly considered less credible than men. For example, the Jewish Talmud says, 'Any evidence which a woman [gives] is not valid (to offer).' Josephus said, 'But let not the testimony of women be admitted, on account of the levity and boldness of their sex.'

"My point is this. If you were going to concoct a story in an effort to fool others, you would never in that day have hurt your own credibility by saying that women discovered the empty tomb. If [the gospel writers] had felt the freedom simply to make things up, surely they'd claim that men—maybe Peter or John or even Joseph of Arimathea—were the first to find the tomb empty."

> "When we consider the Jerusalem factor, the enemy attestation, and the testimony of women, there are good historical reasons for concluding Jesus' tomb was empty."

"So this is another example of the criterion of embarrassment."

"Precisely. The best theory for why the gospel writers would include such an embarrassing detail is because it was what actually happened, and they were committed to recording it accurately, regardless of the credibility problem it created in that culture.

"So when we consider the Jerusalem factor, the enemy attestation, and the testimony of women, there are good historical reasons for concluding Jesus' tomb was empty. William Ward of Oxford University put it this way: 'All the strictly historical evidence we have is in favor [of the empty tomb], and those scholars who reject it ought to recognize that they do so on some other ground than that of scientific history.'"[26]

"Okay, you've laid out your minimal facts," I said. "How would you summarize your case?"

"Shortly after Jesus died from crucifixion, his disciples believed they saw him risen from the dead. They said he appeared not only to individuals but in several group settings—and the disciples were so convinced and transformed by the experience that they were willing to suffer and even die for their conviction that they had encountered him.

"Then we have two skeptics who regarded Jesus as a false prophet—Paul, the persecutor of the church, and James, who was Jesus' half brother. They completely changed their opinions 180 degrees after encountering the risen Jesus. Like the disciples, they were willing to endure hardship, persecution, and even death rather than disavow their testimony that Jesus' resurrection occurred.

"Thus we have compelling testimony about the resurrection from friends of Jesus, an enemy of Christianity, and a skeptic. Finally, we have strong historical evidence that Jesus' tomb was empty. In fact, even enemies of Christianity implicitly admitted it was vacant. Where did the body go? If you were to ask the disciples, they would have told you they personally saw Jesus after he returned to life.

"So we've looked at relevant sources, and we've applied responsible historical methodology. Now we need restrained results. We have to ask ourselves, *What's the best explanation for the evidence—the explanation that doesn't leave out any of the facts or strains to make anything fit?* My conclusion, based on the evidence, is that Jesus did return from the dead."

"You personally think the case is strong?"

"Oh, absolutely, because it outdistances the competing hypotheses by such a large margin. No other explanation comes close to accounting for all the facts. That makes future disconfirmation unlikely. Historically speaking, I think we've got a cogent and convincing case."

Fielding Objections

A common challenge to Michael Licona's case is that the disciples didn't really encounter the resurrected Jesus, but instead they were hallucinating. "Doesn't this account for the appearances of Jesus?" I asked.

He replied by saying that hallucinations can't be shared by multiple people, and yet scholars have at least three instances when the risen Jesus appeared to groups.

"You see, hallucinations aren't contagious. They're personal. They're like dreams," Licona said. "I couldn't wake up my wife in the middle of the night and say, 'Honey, I'm dreaming of being in Hawaii. Quick, go back to sleep, join me in my dream, and we'll have a free vacation.' You can't do that. Scientists will tell you that hallucinations are the same way.

"On top of that, hallucinations can't account for the empty

tomb. They can't account for the appearance to Paul, because he wasn't grieving—he was occupied with trying to destroy the church. And in the midst of that, he believes he sees the risen Jesus. James was a skeptic. He wasn't in the frame of mind for hallucinations to occur either."[27]

I moved on to another popular objection.[28] "Why," I asked Licona, "should the story of Jesus' resurrection have any more credibility than pagan stories of dying and rising gods—such as Osiris, Adonis, Attis, and Marduk—that are so obviously mythological? Some critics say Christianity is merely a copycat religion that took the idea of the resurrection from these earlier myths."

Licona was well-versed on this controversy. "First of all, it's important to understand that these claims don't in any way negate the good historical evidence we have for Jesus' resurrection that I've spelled out," he replied.

"Second, T. N. D. Mettinger—a senior Swedish scholar, professor at Lund University, and member of the Royal Academy of Letters, History, and Antiquities of Stockholm—wrote one of the most recent academic treatments of dying and rising gods in antiquity. He admits in his book *The Riddle of Resurrection* that the consensus among modern scholars—*nearly universal*—is that there were no dying and rising gods that preceded Christianity. They all postdated the first century."

Obviously, that timing is crucial. Christianity couldn't have borrowed the idea of the resurrection if myths about dying and rising gods weren't even circulating when Christianity was birthed in the first century AD.

"Then Mettinger takes a decidedly minority position and claims that there are at least three and possibly as many as five dying and rising gods that predate Christianity. But the key question is this: Are there any actual parallels between these myths and Jesus' resurrection?"

"What did he conclude?" I asked.

"After combing through all of these accounts and critically analyzing them, Mettinger states that none of these serve as parallels to Jesus. *None* of them," Licona emphasized.

"They are far different from the reports of Jesus rising from the dead. They occurred in the unspecified and distant past and were usually related to the seasonal life-and-death cycle of vegetation. In contrast, Jesus' resurrection wasn't repeated, wasn't related to changes in the seasons, and was sincerely believed to be an actual event by those who lived in the same generation of the historical Jesus. In addition, Mettinger concludes that 'there is no evidence for the death of the dying and rising gods as vicarious suffering for sins.'"[29]

I later obtained Mettinger's book to double-check Licona's account. Sure enough, Mettinger caps his study with this stunning statement: "There is, as far as I am aware, no prima facie evidence that the death and resurrection of Jesus is a mythological construct, drawing on the myths and rites of the dying and rising gods of the surrounding world."[30]

In short, this leading scholar's analysis is a sharp rebuke to popular-level authors and internet bloggers who make grand claims about the pagan origins of Jesus' return from the dead. Ultimately, Mettinger affirmed, "the faith in the death and resurrection of Jesus retains its unique character in the history of religions."[31]

The Rest of the Story

Licona could have presented all kinds of other historical evidence for the resurrection, but he limited himself to only five facts that are well-attested historically and that the vast majority of scholars—including skeptics—concede are trustworthy. Making his case even from the lips of liberal and disbelieving scholars served to greatly heighten the credibility of the Easter event.

I was reminded of the conclusions of prominent historian N. T. Wright, who has taught at both Oxford and Cambridge Universities and authored the 817-page book *The Resurrection of the Son of God*. "It is no good falling back on 'science' as having disproved the possibility of resurrection. Any real scientist will tell you that science observes what normally happens; the Christian case is precisely that what happened to Jesus is not what normally happens," he said.

"For my part, as a historian I prefer the elegant, essentially simple solution rather than the one that fails to include all the data: to say that the early Christians believed that Jesus had been bodily raised from the dead, and to account for this belief by saying that they were telling the truth," he said.[32] "The proposal that Jesus was bodily raised from the dead possesses unrivaled power to explain the historical data at the heart of early Christianity."[33]

For me, the verdict in the case for the resurrection is clear. Jesus did, indeed, return from the dead and thus vindicated his claim to being divine.

Yes, God is real—and Jesus is his unique Son.

CHAPTER 5

EXPERIENCING GOD

*There is a sense in which Christians can
legitimately claim to know the reality of
God because of their experiences of God.*

**Philosopher Harold A. Netland, *Religious
Experience and the Knowledge of God***

The daredevil motorcyclist Evel Knievel, a womanizer and
drunkard who once went to prison for beating up a business
partner with a baseball bat, was on the beach in Florida when he
felt God "speak" to him on the inside: "Robert, I've saved you
more times than you'll ever know. Now I need you to come to
me through my Son Jesus."

Knievel was stunned! He sought out a book on the historical
evidence for Jesus and ended up experiencing a radical conversion to Christ. When he told his story at his baptism, seven
hundred people responded by receiving Jesus as their forgiver
and leader. Knievel died about a year later, and at his request his
tombstone is etched with the words "Believe in Jesus Christ."[1]

Bob Passantino was a spiritual skeptic who loved to embarrass
Christians by asking tough questions about faith. Then he met

a seminary student who finally began to give him some good answers.

One day, Bob and his friend Bruce were in a car, discussing their concerns about the dangerous direction of the world and how they could be prepared for what might happen next. Suddenly, Bob felt the unmistakable presence of the Holy Spirit fill the vehicle. Without sound or words, he clearly heard Jesus say to him, "None of that matters. You are putting your trust in yourselves instead of in me. All that matters is that I love you. Follow me. . . . Follow me. . . . Follow me."

Shocked, Bob said to Bruce, "None of this matters! Jesus is real!" To Bob's surprise, Bruce blurted out, "Don't you feel the Holy Spirit? We have to follow Jesus! He's calling us!" Bob ended up becoming an accomplished Christian apologist who would spend the rest of his life helping others who were on the same search for truth.[2]

Nabeel Qureshi was a devout Muslim who began to investigate Christianity after getting into debates with a Christian friend. At one point, Nabeel asked God for a clear vision—and then he had a vivid and chilling dream of a banquet where he was being excluded because he had rejected the invitation.

When he asked his friend about the dream, he was told it was an uncanny depiction of what Jesus described in the gospel of Luke[3]—even though Nabeel had never opened a Bible.

"I'm a man of science. A medical doctor. I deal with flesh and bones, with evidence and facts and logic. But *this*," he said to me, searching for the right words, "this was the exact vision I needed. It was a miracle. A miracle that opened the door for me."

Ultimately, Nabeel became a renowned Christian speaker who wrote a bestselling book about his story and traveled the world to tell people about his Savior until his untimely death in 2017.[4]

Not all the evidence for God's existence is based on the hard data of physics or the cold calculations of a philosophical syllogism. For some people, such as with my friends Evel, Bob, and Nabeel, it was a profound spiritual experience that dramatically opened their eyes to the fact that God is real. What's more, just hearing about their credible stories can influence others toward the conclusion that God exists.

For many others, it's their experience with God *after* their conversion—a profound sense of community with him and the transformation he brings into their lives—that confirms the truth that God really does exist.

We're seeing spiritual experiences proliferate throughout the Middle East, in countries that have been closed to the gospel but where many Muslims are having life-changing "Jesus dreams." In fact, more Muslims have become Christians in the last few decades than the previous fourteen hundred years since Muhammad, and it's estimated that one-quarter to one-third of them experienced a dream or vision of Jesus before their salvation experience.[5]

> "For some people, a profound spiritual experience dramatically opened their eyes to the fact that God is real."

While these dreams are unique to each individual, in many cases corroboration shows these experiences aren't merely subjective but are actual spiritual encounters. For instance, in many dreams Jesus tells the person something they couldn't have otherwise known, or in some cases two people have an identical dream on the same night—corroboration that points toward the objective reality of these incidents.

The stunning consistency of these dreams across international boundaries suggests that they are more than merely the product of overactive imaginations. A devout Muslim would have no incentive to imagine such an encounter with the Jesus of Christianity that might lure them into Islamic apostasy and lead to a death sentence in certain countries.

Religious experiences vary widely, from dramatic visions to more subtle and inexplicable encounters that change lives. For example, the wildly successful British music star Mathangi "Maya" Arulpragasam, popularly known as M. I. A., named by *Esquire* as one of the seventy-five most influential people of the twenty-first century, was "100 percent comfortable with Hinduism" and thought that Jesus was just "a silly story."

Then in 2016, she was in an unspecified "place of need" when she had a supernatural vision of Jesus. "I wasn't asleep. It wasn't a dream. It wasn't a hallucination," she said. "My first reaction was to laugh. I couldn't believe what was happening. I always thought he was made up."

The vision was brief. No words were exchanged. Yet "within a split second" she went from disbelief to belief in Christianity. "In my time of need, the God who turned up to save me was not Shiva; it was Jesus," she said. "That is the truth. . . . This experience *happened*."[6]

Some of the most astounding experiences come in the form of miraculous answers to prayer. For example, a medical journal published the extraordinary case study of a woman who had been blind for more than a dozen years from an incurable condition. One night at bedtime, her husband, a Baptist pastor, prayed, "O God! You can restore . . . eyesight tonight, Lord. I know you can do it! And I pray you will do it tonight."

With that, his wife opened her eyes and saw her husband for the first time. "After years of darkness I could see perfectly," she said. And her eyesight has remained intact for more than forty-seven years.[7]

More Common Than Many Think

How widespread are these various kinds of spiritual experiences? I commissioned a scientific national survey, conducted by Barna Research, which disclosed that 38 percent of American adults have had at least one miraculous experience that could only have come from God. That's equivalent to more than 94 million spiritual encounters. Among evangelical Christians, that number soars to 78 percent.[8]

"Many might be surprised to discover what a high percentage of serious Christians—and even non-Christians—can tell of specific experiences in which they are sure God spoke to them," said influential philosopher Dallas Willard.[9]

Cambridge-educated anthropologist Tanya Marie Luhrmann researched the practices of evangelical and charismatic Christians for her book *When God Talks Back.* "Many Americans not only believe in God in some general way but experience God directly and report repeated contact with the supernatural," she wrote. "These evangelicals have sought out and cultivated concrete experiences of God's realness."[10]

According to a study, Luhrmann said, nearly one-quarter of all Americans embrace a Christian spirituality "in which congregants experience God immediately, directly, and personally."[11]

Philosopher Harold Netland, author of *Religious Experience and the Knowledge of God*, said, "Christians routinely speak of God's presence in their lives, God 'speaking' to them or guiding them, God convicting them of something sinful, God's special peace in the midst of trials—and all of this involves experience."[12]

He added that "a testimony—a personal account of how one's conversion to Jesus Christ through the supernatural work of the Holy Spirit results in a dramatically changed life—gives voice to an especially important kind of experience."[13]

Christians even talk about experiencing God more deeply in the midst of their struggles. "The cancer battle has been tough," wrote Nanci Alcorn, wife of bestselling author Randy Alcorn, during a four-year fight with the disease that eventually took her life. "However, my time with [God] has been epic! He has met me in ways I never knew were possible. I have *experienced* his sovereignty, mercy, and steadfast love in tangible ways. I now trust him at a level I never knew I could."[14]

Many theologians believe that the best explanation for these various religious experiences is that they reflect a genuine perception of a divine reality. Skeptics, however, tend to write off these phenomena as being unreliable or having some sort of naturalistic explanation.

Are you open to the possibility that religious experiences may provide meaningful evidence that God is real? Do you think it's possible to discern which experiences are authentic? Could someone else's spiritual encounter—one that's backed up by credible evidence—actually influence your beliefs about God? What about you personally? Have you ever had an experience that you're convinced came from a divine source?

Philosopher Douglas Groothuis is among the scholars who believe that certain religious experiences can provide "considerable evidence for the existence of a personal and relational being."[15]

If that's accurate, then religious experiences may be a compelling capstone to our examination of evidence for the existence of God. To check into this phenomenon further, I flew to Colorado, where Groothuis is a professor of philosophy, and drove to his office at Denver Seminary for an in-depth interview.

INTERVIEW WITH

Douglas Groothuis, PhD

The first time I ever interviewed Doug Groothuis (pronounced GRŌT-hice) was under difficult circumstances. At the time, his wife, Rebecca, was dying of a brain condition, and Groothuis spoke to me in a candid way about their emotional anguish.[1] Back then, Groothuis appeared haggard, his beard unruly and his brown hair seemingly combed with his fingers. His wife ended up dying shortly after our time together.[2]

Now, several years later, Groothuis was more animated and upbeat, leaner, clean-shaven, and more dapper in attire. He has married a high school acquaintance named Kathleen, and today, in his mid-sixties, he seems more engaged with his work than ever.

Groothuis became a serious Christian at age nineteen after forays into Eastern mysticism and atheism. He went on to earn his doctorate in philosophy at the University of Oregon. Since then he has taught at a secular college, debated atheists, written a slew of scholarly and popular articles, and authored sixteen books. My favorite is his hefty *Christian Apologetics: A Comprehensive Case for Biblical Faith.*

Groothuis greeted me and cleared a space at a small table

in his book-choked office. After updating each other on our personal lives, we began by talking about what makes experiences with God possible.

"Woe to Me! I Am Ruined!"

"Christian theology says people are rational creatures who are made in the image of God,"[3] I began as I opened my notebook. "Is that what makes experiences with God possible and natural?"

"Yes," said Groothuis. "As Francis Schaeffer pointed out, God is infinite and personal, and we are finite and personal.[4] Because of that, we have the potential of connecting on a personal, relational level. Being made in God's image opens the door to communion with him. We have affinity despite the fractures in our relationship caused by our sin. So we have the possibility of obtaining knowledge about God through general revelation, or nature; special revelation, or the Scriptures; and also through having personal experiences with the God who conceived us and created us."

"Can these experiences provide evidence that God exists?"

"Absolutely, yes, they can be part of a cumulative case for God. The key question is whether an experience is veridical."

"Veridical?" I asked. "What do you mean?"

"An experience is veridical if it conveys truth and is not deceptive. For example, a mirage of a pool of water that a thirsty person imagines in the desert isn't veridical. It's a false belief. A hallucinatory fantasy induced by drugs isn't veridical. But if an experience with God is authentic—if it's based on reality and conveys truth—then it's veridical."

I jotted the word in my notes as a reminder to ask Groothuis later about how an experience can be evaluated to make sure it's authentic.

"Let's talk about these experiences," I went on. "We tend to hear about the dramatic ones, but they really run the gamut, don't they?"

Groothuis leaned back. "Oh, there's so much," he said. "There are cases, for example, where people encounter a majestic, awe-inspiring, and compelling divine being."

"That's what the Old Testament prophet Isaiah wrote about, right?"

"Yes, he sees the Lord exalted, seated on a throne, with the train of his robe filling the temple, with angels calling out, 'Holy, holy, holy, is the Lord God Almighty; the whole earth is full of his glory!' Isaiah falls on his face and declares, 'Woe to me! I am ruined! For I am a man of unclean lips and I live among a people of unclean lips, and my eyes have seen the King, the Lord Almighty.'"[5]

"Are there any theological reasons why this kind of experience couldn't continue after biblical days?"

"No, and we see contemporary accounts of amazing experiences with God all around the world. For example, there are Jesus dreams occurring among Muslims in closed cultures—this is a well-documented phenomenon. We see God breaking into the lives of people in a dramatic manner—for example, Evel Knievel feeling God speaking to him in a manner that changed his entire life. And we see more subtle experiences of God. Christians talk all the time about how God encourages, convicts, or guides them, or he gives them courage or peace, or he otherwise manifests himself in their lives. In fact, Christians undergo what's called a 'transformational experience.'"

"You mean their moment of conversion?"

"Actually, I'm thinking of the personal transformation that accompanies Christian belief, repentance, and religious commitment. The Bible promises an 'abundant' life[6] in Christ, and Christians experience significant changes in their lives and attribute these changes to the influence of God. They typically report a new moral awareness and progress, a sense of guidance or calling, and a deep sense of belonging to God. The Bible says in Galatians that, over time, Christians will experience increased love, joy, peace, patience, kindness, goodness, faithfulness, gentleness, and self-control.[7] This kind of transformational experience is to be expected if the Christian message is true."

Peace That Passes Understanding

"What about you?" I asked. "Have you had personal experiences of God?"

"I've been a Christian since 1976, and I've been through my share of difficulties and challenges. Through it all, though, I've heard God speak to me through Scripture, through sermons, through the wisdom of godly friends. And at times the experience is more profound."

"Can you give me an example?"

"I remember a prayer meeting around 1990 when several of us were fasting and praying for a friend who was quite ill. I remember going home and waking up the next day and thinking, *Something's strange.*"

"What was it?"

"I've struggled with anxiety for much of my life, and at the time I was in a very stressful period as I worked on my doctorate. And yet starting that day and continuing for two weeks, I felt absolutely no worry or anxiety. There was such an incredible sense of freedom and joy in the Lord like I'd never known before. After two weeks, it was gone, but I attribute that experience to a special presence of the Holy Spirit in that prayer meeting."

"Did you find that this experience confirmed your faith in a sense?"

"Yes, in a way. I wasn't on an antidepressant; this wasn't the result of some meditative technique; it wasn't mental discipline. It just happened. These periodic visitations of the Holy Spirit can be quite moving, though I would caution that Christians shouldn't try to live off them. If they do, they might start pursuing spiritual highs and encounter counterfeits or stray outside of biblical doctrine."

"During the time when your wife's health was deteriorating, did you find moments of peace and strength in various ways?"

"I did, but not regularly and not in exceptional ways," he replied. "For us, it was the hope that God infused into our lives—a *rational* hope. The hope of the gospel, the hope of a resurrected body, the hope of a new heaven and a new earth. Hope was the experience for us, more than joy or even peace. And that hope sustained us in remarkable ways."

The Testing of Experiences

Next, I wanted to explore how we can evaluate other apparent experiences with God to see whether or not they are trustworthy.

"The Bible says we're supposed to test the spirits to determine whether they're really from God,"[8] I said. "How can we do that?"

"There are four ways to categorize claims of religious experiences," replied Groothuis. "First, someone may be lying. Second, a person may have an experience that's purely subjective, like a hallucination or mirage, and incorrectly think it's an encounter with God. Third, someone may experience something extraordinary but not divine and yet incorrectly attribute it to God. And fourth, a person may experience an actual divine reality, which philosophers consider 'numinous' experiences."

"Numinous experiences?"

"It's a term coined by German theologian Rudolf Otto.[9] It

means experiencing a transfixing or even frightening object that is distinct from the person experiencing it. In other words, there's the subject who has the experience; there's the conscious experience of the numinous; and then there's the numinous object itself. The key is that these are encounters with something that's objectively outside of the person. It's not just conjured up by someone's overactive imagination. A numinous experience can be a conduit for knowledge because there's a relationship between a subject and an object."

"How would this apply, say, to Isaiah's encounter with God?"

"There's Isaiah, who's distinct from God; there's his conscious experience of meeting God; and then there's God, who's objectively real and separate from Isaiah."

I pondered the concept for a moment. "This would mean that religious experiences of Hindus and Buddhists wouldn't qualify," I observed.

"That's right," said Groothuis. "In Eastern mysticism, the whole notion of self disappears, as does the knowable object. The subject-object relationship is swallowed up by the void. Mystics talk about pure consciousness and experiences that cannot be described. That's a million miles away from the kind of experience that Isaiah had."

The important distinction about Christian experiences, Groothuis stressed, is that "they involve an encounter with an external and personal being of transcendent significance."

"Should we be skeptical about a religious experience if we have one?" I asked.

"We can take that too far," he replied. "I like the 'principle of credulity' proposed by philosopher Richard Swinburne.[10] This says that unless there's good evidence to the contrary, if a person seems to experience something, they should believe it's probably authentic. So we should generally take our experiences to be truth-conveying unless there is a reason to think otherwise."

With that, Groothuis offered an illustration. "Right now I'm talking to Lee Strobel. What if in a minute or two, somebody who looks exactly like you appeared in the doorway and said, 'That's not the real Lee Strobel; *I'm* the real Lee Strobel.' Well, then I'd be thrown into an epistemic quandary. But unless something like that happens, it's rational for me to believe I'm talking to Lee Strobel. So in the case of a religious experience, if I believe I've encountered God in one way or the other, all things being equal, I should suppose that I probably did encounter God."

"But you might be mistaken."

"Sure. But we can't consider all truth claims and experiences to be guilty until proven innocent. We don't typically go through life treating every experience as if it's false until it's proven to be true. That's unworkable. Swinburne also proposed the 'principle of testimony,' which says, all things being equal, we don't assume that people are lying or are deceived."[11]

"But it may be that they're not telling the truth," I said.

"Maybe," he conceded, "but the burden of proof should be on establishing guilt, not assuming from the outset that a person's testimony is false. If someone says they experienced God in a particular way, we shouldn't assume they're deceived or lying unless we have indications that there's falsehood involved."

One test of whether an experience with God is authentic, added Groothuis, is to weigh it against the teachings of Scripture because we have solid reasons for trusting the Bible's reliability. "The Bible becomes *the* guide for testing the validity of an experience," he said. "Whatever experience occurs, if it's really from God, it will not contradict the Bible."

Then Groothuis added one other caveat: "Whenever we weigh the legitimacy of an experience, we need to do it against the background evidence for the existence of God," he said. "If the evidence were to point away from God being real, then obviously this would be a good reason to discount the authenticity of any religious experience. But the evidence does the opposite—we have multiple reasons for believing in God's existence."

"That means we shouldn't be surprised if we actually encounter him."

"Exactly. So many people of all backgrounds have reported experiences of God around the world and throughout history—and there are instances where there's external corroboration, as you know."

> *"One test of whether an experience with God is authentic is to weigh it against the teachings of Scripture because we have solid reasons for trusting the Bible's reliability."*

That brought to mind various cases I've written about through the years, such as the Muslim woman in Egypt who encountered Jesus in a supernatural dream. When she asked him to tell her more, he pointed to a man beside him and said, "Ask my friend tomorrow about me."

The next day in the crowded Cairo marketplace the woman saw the man from her dream, with the same clothes and glasses. She confronted him, exclaiming, "You're the one! You were in my dream last night!" It turned out he was a Christian missionary who instantly realized she had had a dream about Jesus. In fact, the only reason he was visiting the marketplace that day was because he felt God had a special assignment for him. In the end, he was able to share the gospel with the Muslim woman for three hours.

This is typical of the "Jesus dreams" happening in Islamic countries. People don't go to sleep as a Muslim and awaken as a Christian; rather, the dream points them toward somebody who subsequently teaches them from the Bible. This provides external corroboration of their personal experience in the dream.[12]

"How can skeptics get around this?" I asked Groothuis.

"For the unbeliever, that means they have to say that precisely none of these experiences are true. They would have to explain away *every single one of them* as a delusion or have to develop some model that captures all of these experiences and shows that none of them are of God for some reason or another."

"That's a hard case to make," I said.

"Especially," Groothuis added, "when we have so much evidence for the truth of Christianity."

Of Goats and Binoculars

Because religious experiences typically happen at an unpredictable time to one individual, this means they aren't repeatable, can't be measured, and can't be scientifically tested. "Doesn't that present a significant challenge in determining their validity?" I asked.

"Well, first, it's understandable that God would be difficult to quantify or measure. After all, he's an invisible personal being who chooses when and where he wants to reveal himself. We should expect that God wouldn't be verifiable the way that a physical object can be."

Groothuis offered an analogy. "Suppose you're looking through binoculars while hiking and you see a goat. You quickly hand the binoculars to your friend, but by the time he looks through them, he doesn't see the goat. Now, what's the more reasonable response: that you lied, or that the goat moved out of view?"

"That the goat moved."

"Right, and that's analogous to experiences of God. God manifests himself as God wills. We can't force him to repeat an experience for someone else. We can't put him under a microscope or in a test tube, and we can't measure him by empirical means."

I asked, "What are some steps we can take to examine religious experiences for their authenticity?"

"First, we can compare the experience to the long tradition of religious experiences within Christianity, going all the way back to the Bible. Is the experience at least consistent with this basic tradition, even though there might be differences? Second, we can investigate to see if there are any surrounding factors that would challenge the credibility of an experience."

"Such as—what?"

"Was the person under the influence of drugs? Does he or she have a history of deceiving people or having mental illness? Are peripheral details—like when and where the person had the experience—shown to be inaccurate? Does the individual have something to gain from sharing the experience? Obviously, these would cast doubt on their report."

Groothuis paused to give me time to scribble notes. "And then, third," he said, "we have to keep in mind that religious experiences are only one avenue of evidence for a religious worldview. We also have to pursue other lines of argumentation and evidence."

"Can you illustrate that?"

"Let's say a Mormon missionary encourages you to read the Book of Mormon and see whether you experience a 'burning in the bosom' that supposedly confirms its authenticity. Even if you felt a warming in your heart, that experience wouldn't be confirmation that Mormonism's polytheistic teachings and revision of Christian doctrines are true. It wouldn't overcome the lack of historical and archaeological support for the Book of Mormon. So religious experience needs to be weighed against other germane sources of evidence for or against a worldview."

"What about evaluating the validity of Eastern mystical experiences?"

"The enlightenment experiences of both *nirvana* in Buddhism and *moksha* in Hinduism require the negation of individuality, personality, and language. There's no personal encounter with another being of immense holiness and power. If a mystical experience is devoid of any intellectual content, it can't possibly serve as logical evidence for any worldview."

"And Christianity?"

"If you ask me why I believe Christianity is true, religious experiences are not the first evidence I'd mention. Initially, I'd talk about the kind of evidence that Christian philosophers typically offer—evidence about the origin and fine-tuning of the universe, the existence of objective morality, the resurrection, and so forth."

"That makes religious experiences—what?"

"Corroborative," he replied. "By themselves, they don't offer conclusive proof. They're *part* of the case, but they're not *the* case. Still, they're one more persuasive category of evidence which affirms that Christianity is true."

> "Religious experiences are one more persuasive category of evidence which affirms that Christianity is true."

The Psychology of Religious Experiences

Nevertheless, such figures throughout history such as Ludwig Feuerbach, Karl Marx, and Sigmund Freud have tried to undermine the legitimacy of religious experiences by saying they are the product of wish fulfillment or a projection of our psychological needs and desires. For instance, Freud said religious beliefs are an illusion, that "what is characteristic of illusions is that they are derived from human wishes."[13]

"Why can't we write off religious experiences as a psychological phenomenon in which people see what they want to see?" I asked.

A sour look spread across Groothuis's face. "That falls flat for a number of reasons," he replied.

"Such as?"

"Feuerbach, Freud, and Marx thought religious belief was based on superstition," he said. "They thought that because there's no evidential weight behind it, they could explain away faith as being purely psychological. But, Lee, you know that's not true. I've written an 846-page book on the historical, philosophical, and scientific reasons that support Christianity.

"Second," he added, "just because we have a strong wish for X doesn't mean that X isn't true. Even Hans Küng said that 'a real God may certainly correspond to the wish for God.'[14] That means it's possible for a person to come to God because of a deep psychological need, such as a quest for love or acceptance, and still hold a true belief. And finally, third, there are aspects of Christianity that are not good candidates for wish fulfillment."

I chuckled. "I'd agree with that," I said. "If I were going to make up a religion to fulfill my wishes, it would teach that we can do anything we want, whenever we want to do it, and I'd have godlike powers. No constraints!"

Groothuis nodded. "If I were creating a religion, there are a lot of features of Christianity I'd leave out. Like how strict Jesus is about our thoughts and our anger. He says that vicious thoughts are tantamount to vicious acts[15]—I'd jettison that! I certainly wouldn't invent a religion where some of my friends might end up in hell. But the Bible often goes against the grain of what we want, and numinous experiences are often a shock to the person experiencing them. You can't domesticate God."

I noted that psychologist Paul Vitz of New York University

has studied the lives of well-known atheists throughout history and concluded that they may have been motivated by psychological factors to *disbelieve* in God. Their problems with their earthly fathers may have turned them off to the idea of a heavenly Father.[16]

"Yes, the charge of psychological projection against Christians can be turned against the skeptic," agreed Groothuis. "Given the fact that the vast majority of humanity has believed in God and the supernatural, it seems more likely that it's the atheists who suffer from some psychological disorder that makes belief in God difficult for them."[17]

Groothuis had covered the topics I wanted to address—religious experiences, he made clear, are a legitimate component of the case for Christianity. I closed my notebook and clicked off my tape recorder. As we stood to shake hands, though, he turned the tables on me.

An Angel and a Prophecy

"What about you?" Groothuis asked. "Have you undergone a personal experience with God?"

I let out a laugh. "Hey, I'm the reporter here, not you."

"I'm a philosopher," he replied, "and you know that we love to ask our own questions. So—what about you?"

I shifted my feet and leaned against the back of the chair. "Well, there's no question God has transformed my life," I began. "And then there was the time when I was still an atheist and my infant daughter was healed after some Christians prayed for her."

What filled my mind, though, was the only religious experience I recall from my childhood. "I remember," I said to Groothuis, "the most vibrant dream of my life, when I spoke with an angel and received a prophecy that came true sixteen years later."

He gestured for us to sit back down. "Tell me."

With that, I unfolded the incident.

* * *

When I was about twelve years old, prior to my move into athe-ism, I dreamed I was making a sandwich in the kitchen when a luminous angel appeared and began to tell me—almost off-handedly—about how glorious heaven is. I listened for a while and then said matter-of-factly, "I'm going there"—meaning, of course, at the end of my life.

The angel's reply stunned me. "How do you know?"

How do I know? What kind of question is that? "Well, uh, I've tried to be a good kid," I stammered. "I've tried to do what my parents say. I've tried to behave. I've been to church."

Said the angel, "That doesn't matter."

Now I was astonished. How could that *not* matter—all my efforts to be compliant, to be dutiful, to live up to the expecta-tions and demands of my parents and teachers. Panic rose in me. I couldn't open my mouth to respond.

The angel let me stew for a few moments. Then he said, "Someday you'll understand." Instantly, he was gone—and I woke up in a sweat. It's the only dream I remember from my childhood.

Over the years, I came to reject the possibility of the super-natural and even God himself. But sixteen years after that dream, the angel's prophecy came true.

I went to church at the behest of my wife and heard the gos-pel and understood it for the first time. I learned that I couldn't earn my way to heaven through my behavior or good deeds; rather, entrance to paradise was a free gift of God's grace that I just needed to gratefully receive.

The moment this clicked for me, a vivid memory flooded my mind—the angel who had foretold that someday I would understand God's message of redemption. Ultimately, it was this Good News that went on to change my life and eternity.

"What do you think?" I asked Groothuis. "Was that a God-orchestrated experience, or something else?"

Groothuis's eyes narrowed as he considered the question. "It could very well have come from the Lord," he replied.

"Yeah," I said, "I think so too."

CHAPTER 6

WHICH GOD IS REAL?

*I want atheism to be true and am
made uneasy by the fact that some of
the most intelligent and well-informed
people I know are religious believers.*

Philosopher Thomas Nagel, *The Last Word*

Chad Meister, a young electromechanical engineer who had grown up questioning the reality of God, was sitting in his apartment in Tempe, Arizona. He was holding a gun. Mired in depression, he was on the verge of suicide.

Amid his anguish, he called out, "God, if you're there, please show me, because I don't want to live anymore. And if you're not there, life's not worth living." With that, he instantly had a vision. Everything went dark, and all he could see were black-and-white letters spelling out: "Acts 14:22."

"I had no idea what that was," he recalled later. "I thought maybe it had something to do with the Bible, but I'd never read the Bible, although I had heard of some of the books in it."

Putting down the gun, he went out, got a Bible, came back to his apartment, and searched until he found the chapter and verse, in which Paul and Barnabas told followers of Jesus, "We must go through many hardships to enter the kingdom of God."

That sentiment registered deeply with Chad. As he thought

back on the travails of his life, he realized for the first time that God had been there all along, pursuing him like the "hound of heaven," but Chad had repeatedly pushed him away and walked in the other direction.

His depression lifted. Right there, Chad committed his life to God. He vowed, *I'm going to follow you wherever that leads.*

Sure enough, his life changed. He married a Christian accountant named Tammi, and they moved to Minneapolis, where they attended a church that encouraged congregants to tell others about Jesus. He decided to do just that—but his efforts backfired.

He was getting ready to go on a four-hour car trip with his boss, a well-educated Hindu. *Okay, this is terrific,* Chad thought. *There's one Christian going out on this trip, and there'll be two Christians coming back.*

Instead, this sincere and articulate Hindu extolled the beauty and wonder of his religion so eloquently that he began influencing Chad. Since Chad had never really studied why he was a Christian, he became disoriented. "My head was spinning," he said.

That same week, a Mormon colleague shared her beliefs with Chad. A friend who had been studying with a cult challenged Chad's understanding of the Trinity. Another engineer who was part of a fringe sect attacked Chad's beliefs. At a meeting of a public speaking organization, Chad heard a woman give a passionate speech about the New Age movement and how everyone is part of Mother Gaia, this glorious flower of a universe.

"I was so confused," Chad said. "I didn't know what to believe anymore. I began rethinking that vision I had. Maybe it was from Allah or Brahman or some other divine reality. My faith drained away, and I became an agnostic."

He began to seek answers. On business trips to Minnesota, he would stop at a local branch of L'Abri Fellowship, started by Christian thinkers Francis and Edith Schaeffer. Instead of pushing their Christian beliefs, the people there gently encouraged Chad to carefully analyze differing worldviews. *Which is reasonable? Which is logical? Which is livable? Which one had the best evidence on its side?*

"I started at square one by asking the question, 'What is truth?'" Chad said. "I ended up researching worldviews for a year and a half. At the end, the conclusion was clear: Christianity is the most reasonable, the most livable, the best supported evidentially, and it matched my own personal experiences of God. I recommitted my life to Christ."

So exhilarating was his spiritual investigation that Chad left his engineering career to study theology and philosophy. Today, he is a widely published scholar—which is what brought me to Mishawaka, Indiana, where Chad is chair of the religion and philosophy department at Bethel University.

I wanted to know—with so many different religious beliefs in the world, why should people trust Christianity? In other words, *which* God is real?

INTERVIEW WITH

Chad V. Meister, PhD

With his incisive mind, gentle humor, and warm personality, Meister is among the most popular professors at Bethel, where he began teaching in 1998. He received his doctorate with honors from Marquette University. He also has been a visiting research scholar at the Oxford Centre for Hindu Studies—ironic in light of the conversation with his Hindu boss that once helped derail his faith.

Meister has authored, coauthored, or edited more than twenty books, including *Philosophy of Religion*; *Evil: A Guide for the Perplexed*; and *Debating Christian Theism*. He and Charles Taliaferro are general editors of a six-volume series called *The History of Evil*.

However, I was there to discuss Meister's first book, *Building Belief: Constructing Faith from the Ground Up*, released in 2006.[1] The story behind this book involves, well, me.

When Meister was a seminary student, he attended a church where I was a teaching pastor and became the volunteer leader of the church's apologetics ministry.

One Sunday after giving a sermon on the resurrection, I was greeting visitors while Chad sat nearby. A man approached me and said, "I'm an atheist, but what you presented was interesting. I'd like to pursue more. Would you be able to meet with me this week?"

I told him that, unfortunately, I would be traveling for the next three weeks. "But that guy there—he'll meet with you," I said, gesturing toward Meister.

Meister perked up. "Sure, I'd love to meet with you," he told the skeptic.

The atheist agreed to come to Meister's apartment for dinner. In the meantime, Meister prayed about how he could help this doubter—and into Meister's mind popped what has become known as the apologetics pyramid, a visual depiction of how a quest for the truth about Christianity can be logically and systematically pursued.

An outgrowth of Meister's own spiritual journey, the pyramid assumes nothing extraordinary at the outset, starting with the broadest question and then narrowing the issues as you get toward the peak. Its goal isn't to provide absolute proof, but rather to show that the most reasonable understanding of the evidence is to conclude that Christianity is true.

The atheist came over for dinner. At 7:00 p.m., they ate. Then they worked through the pyramid. By 2:00 a.m., the doubter was a believer.

I wanted Meister to walk through the six layers of evidence that constitute his pyramid. Francis Schaeffer always urged Christians to begin with common ground, and so we started at the base of the pyramid, with the fundamental laws of logic and reality.

The Apologetics Pyramid

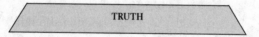

TRUTH

LEVEL 1: Truth—Why Can't Everyone Be Right?

I began by saying, "Pontius Pilate famously asked, 'What is truth?'[2] If you were asked that today, how would you respond?"

Meister cleared his throat. "Even before Pilate lived, the ancient Greeks thought carefully about this," he replied. "Plato said in his book *Sophist* that a true claim states things the way they are, and a false claim states things differently from the way they are.[3] His student Aristotle says something similar in *Metaphysics*.[4] And they were on to something.

"This is the correspondence theory of truth. A claim or proposition is true if it corresponds with a fact. If I make the claim, 'Your rental car is in the parking lot,' this would be true, because my statement corresponds with or matches reality. That would mean truth is absolute and universal."

"Seems like common sense," I said. "Of course, people try to exempt religion. They say religious truth isn't absolute but relative."

Meister wasn't buying it. "If I said, 'My truth is that your rental car isn't in the parking lot,' that wouldn't be accurate just because I say it's my truth; instead, that claim would be false. It doesn't match reality. Opinions and beliefs are subjective and personal, but facts aren't. Besides, there's a logical problem with relativism."

"What's that?"

"To say there are no absolutes is to make an absolute claim. It's self-refuting," he said. "Think of it this way. If a member of the Flat Earth Society disagreed that the Earth was round, you wouldn't say, 'Well, truth is relative. His belief in a flat Earth is his truth—it works for him or it coheres with his other beliefs.' No, you'd say, 'He's flat-out wrong.'"

"But," I interjected, "some say religion shouldn't be understood as being true or false, since we don't have a God's-eye view of things. They say a religious claim can become true as it informs the lives of those who believe it."

"All major religions make truth claims that are absolute," said Meister. "And they fundamentally contradict each other. They can't all be true because they assert opposite things— for example, the Bible says Jesus is the Messiah who gave his life as a sacrifice for sin. Other religions deny this claim. Both can't be true. That's the law of noncontradiction.[5] To say all religious claims are true may sound magnanimous, but it's logically absurd. Our task is to discover what's true and what isn't."

"Still, isn't it intolerant to say truth is absolute?"

"Truth can't be bigoted, but people certainly can be— whether they're Christians, atheists, Hindus, or Muslims. Truth is truth, but how we communicate it can be narrow-minded and arrogant. We need to follow the examples of Jesus and Gandhi, who taught in humble though passionate ways."

> "Truth isn't relative—that is, determined by what we believe—but truth is whatever is consistent with reality."

The foundation of the pyramid was established. Truth isn't relative—that is, determined by what we believe—but truth is whatever is consistent with reality. Our job is to figure out what's true by continuing to climb the pyramid.

Said theologian John Stackhouse, "Religion is fundamentally about truth: trying to figure out what is real and how best to represent it."[6]

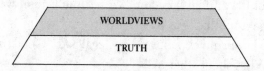

WORLDVIEWS

TRUTH

LEVEL 2: Worldviews—The Clash of the Three Isms

The next layer of the pyramid examines the three major worldviews.

"A worldview is a collection of beliefs and ideas about the central issues of life. It's the lens through which we view the world, whether consciously chosen or not," Meister explained. "Broadly speaking, every religion or ideology can be found within one of three categories—*theism*, *atheism*, or *pantheism*. But, of course, their core assumptions contradict each other and therefore only one of them can be true."

"What grid do you use to analyze them?" I asked.

"There are five fundamentals," he said. "First, is there a God, and what is God like? Second, what is ultimate reality? Third, how is knowledge obtained? Fourth, where is the basis of morality and value found? And fifth, who are we as human beings?"

"Okay," I said, "let's ripple through the three *isms*."

"First, there's *theism*, or belief in a personal God separate from the world," Meister said. "For the major theistic religions—Judaism, Christianity, and Islam—there is one God, creator of all, who is all-knowing, all-powerful, all-present, and all-good.

"The ultimate reality in theism is God, who is beyond the physical realm of existence. We acquire knowledge through our five senses and other means, including the revelation in Scripture. The basis of morality is God. Right, wrong, good, evil—they're all based on the nature of the infinite, personal God who created everything. Finally, what does it mean to be human? We're not on par with God, though we're on a higher plane than the rest of the animal kingdom. We're unique, and we have an immaterial soul that lives on in eternity."

I was jotting notes on my yellow legal pad. "Good summary," I said. "What about atheism?"

"*Atheism* means disbelief in God or the gods. What's the universal reality? As astronomer Carl Sagan put it, 'The universe is all there ever was, is, or will be.'[7] There's no supernatural domain or existence beyond this physical world. How do we acquire knowledge? Since the physical world is all that exists, any knowledge we have must be about it and it alone. We're limited to empirical knowledge, with the scientific method being the gold standard."

"What about morality?" I asked.

"Generally, atheists don't consider morality to be objectively true. Instead, they typically say it emerged through evolution. In other words, humans—or our genes—invented the idea of morality because it improved our chances for survival, so morality can vary from place to place and time to time. Now, some atheists are uncomfortable with that. One prominent atheist said morality doesn't come from God or evolution, but that 'it just is.'[8] Frankly, that doesn't really explain much.

"Finally, on the question of humankind, atheism says we're electromechanical machines—animals that have grown in complexity over the eons thanks to evolution. As biologist Richard Dawkins says, 'We are . . . robot vehicles blindly programmed to preserve the selfish molecules known as genes.'[9] There's no soul or immaterial aspect to people. We live, we die, we decay—that's all there is."

"How about pantheism?"

"*Pantheism* doesn't have a single form. There are both philosophical and religious aspects of it. Generally speaking, there are no ultimate distinctions in the universe—all is changeless, all is one, and all is God, or Brahman in Hinduism. In short, God is one with the universe.

"As for the ultimate reality, it's God—indistinguishable and indescribable. All distinctions are *maya*, or illusions. Animals, plants, insects, rocks, you, me—everything is one and the same fundamental reality. For pantheists of this sort, knowledge is acquired not through rational inquiry but through meditation and other practices intended to empty the mind. Chanting and various other techniques are used for altering consciousness and experiencing a unity with all that is.

"Also, objective good and evil are illusory. The pantheist Mary Baker Eddy, who founded Christian Science, said, 'Evil is but an illusion, and it has no real basis. Evil is a false belief.'[10]

"Finally, who are humans? For pantheists, we are God; we are spiritual divinity; we are one with the universe. But unfortunately we're under universal illusion, and as a result we don't realize our divine nature. Thus, our goal is to recognize this truth and win release from this illusion so we can see and experience the God we really are."

I let all this soak in. "Three worldviews—all contradictory to each other," I said. "How can anyone determine which is true?"

"Ah," said Meister with a grin, "we need to press onward."

TESTING ATHEISM AND PANTHEISM

Meister proposed two tests for which worldview is most plausible: logic and livability. A worldview is false if its core beliefs are internally contradictory or incoherent, and a worldview should be rejected if it cannot consistently be lived out.

"Let's start with atheism," I said. "Is there any objection that invalidates it?"

"Well, there's the logical problem of good," Meister replied.

"The problem of good? Are you saying atheists can't live decent lives?"

"Not at all. I'm saying that if morality is a survival mechanism, then it's a mere 'illusion fobbed off on us by our genes,' as atheist philosophers Michael Ruse and Edward Wilson admit.[11] So it's no more rational to believe in morality than Santa Claus. Even if morality isn't rooted in genetics but is just a social construct, then again it's subjective and relative, not absolute and universal.

"And if there is no objective morality, the atheist can't logically affirm that there are such things as objective good, evil, right, or wrong. An atheist can't even really claim that the murder of innocent children is objectively morally evil. They could say they're offended by it, but that's a preference; they can't consistently affirm it's really wrong.

"If this view of morality were actually lived out, chaos would ensue. As the atheist Jean-Paul Sartre said, 'Everything is indeed permitted if God does not exist.'[12] While some atheists have attempted to establish a kind of universal right and wrong, these arguments are also problematic."

"Crystalize your argument a bit more," I said.

"Okay. First, if objective moral values exist, then atheistic materialism must be false. Yet objective moral values *do* exist—and we all know it. Therefore, atheistic materialism must be false. On top of that, atheism fails the livability test.

"Frankly, atheists can't consistently live out the view that morality is merely illusory or relative. Is the statement 'torturing babies for fun is evil' objectively true, or is it just an opinion? If someone claims that doing this is okay, nobody would accept that. Why? Because we know it is really and truly wrong. Remember what the notorious serial killer Ted Bundy said."[13]

"What?"

"He said that given his enlightened view of the world, there is no God, no transcendent reality—we're just molecules in motion. He said there's no such thing as objective morality. We can decide for ourselves what to do because morality is personal and relative. Fortunately, few people really live that way. Even if someone claims they don't believe in moral absolutes, they act as though they do."

"Your conclusion, then, is that atheism isn't plausible," I said.

"That's right."

"What about pantheism?"

"Pantheists have a problem with right and wrong as well," he said.

He told me about having a spaghetti dinner with a pantheist, who told him, "Everything is God and everything is one. There are no distinctions." Meister replied, "But if there are no distinctions, then there is ultimately no right and wrong, no distinction between cruelty and noncruelty, or between good and evil."

With that, he took the pot of boiling water from the stove and held it over her head, pretending he was going to spill it on her. "Are you *sure* there's no distinction between right and wrong, cruelty and noncruelty?" he teased.

She acknowledged the gesture with a smile, saying, "Well, I guess there *does* seem to be a distinction between right and wrong!"

"Of course, pantheists can *say* there's no distinction between good and evil and that suffering is just an illusion, but they can't really live that way," Meister continued. "People live as though there *are* moral absolutes.

"Besides," he added, "pantheism seems to be logically incoherent. In pantheism, I am God and ultimately impersonal. I am the changeless All. Yet I'm encouraged to discover this fact about myself. Through meditation, I need to realize I am one with the Divine. But there's a problem."

"What's that?"

"First, under pantheism we are one with God. Second, God is the changeless All. Third, we—God—need to move beyond our ignorance and become enlightened by realizing our own divinity. Those statements are logically incoherent."

"How so?"

"To come to know something is to change from a state of ignorance to a state of enlightenment, and I can't be changeless and at the same time change in order to realize that I am changeless.

"Also," he added, "the universe is supposed to be impersonal—but I'm a person with hopes, dreams, thoughts, and feelings, all of which pantheists say are illusions. Somehow the universe coughs up illusory and deceived people, which are really nonpersons, and now they need to get back to the impersonal self that they really are. But how can impersonal me be deceived into believing that I am a personal being who needs to recognize my true, impersonal nature? How can something impersonal be deceived, anyway? Makes no sense."

I knew how pantheists would respond. "Wouldn't they say you need to get beyond rationality and open up to a mystical awareness of your unity with the cosmos?" I asked.

Meister's look soured. "To argue against reason is to use

reason in an attempt to deny reason—again, incoherent. Let's face it, if you want to be logical and consistent in your views, pantheism isn't the worldview you want."

WHAT ABOUT THEISM?

All of this left an obvious question: Does the existence of evil and suffering invalidate theism? Isn't it a contradiction to say there's a God who is powerful and loving, yet evil exists in the world he created?

"That's a serious problem. I don't pretend it isn't," Meister replied. "But it's not unique to theism. All worldviews wrestle with the issue of evil and suffering. However, I don't believe it's a contradiction for theism; in fact, I'd say Christians have the most plausible response."

"In what way?"

"For one thing, it's at least logically plausible to say that if there's a God, he gave people free will."

He collected his thoughts and then resumed. "I remember hearing about a large robotic device that crushed a worker. But the robot wasn't charged with a crime. Why? It wasn't culpable. There was no intentionality. It lacked free will. So it seems the very notion of moral responsibility and the ability to do good requires freedom. Even love requires the freedom to choose *not* to love—which is why robots can't fall in love. They can only do what they're programmed to do.

"God could have created a world where people were like robots, but then we could never experience the highest value in the universe, which is love. We couldn't truly be doing good and moral actions. And where there's freedom, this necessarily entails the freedom to turn against the good. That's a plausible explanation for why we have moral evil in the world."

Meister described how he once got a note from a woman at

church who was very effective at helping others who struggled with pain from their past. She disclosed to him how she herself had gone through a traumatic experience while growing up.

A few weeks earlier, Meister and his wife had baked a cake. Meister decided to taste every ingredient individually. Baking powder—*disgusting*. Raw eggs—*ugh*. Vanilla extract—*yuck*. But once they were mixed together and baked, the result was a flavorful chocolate cake.

"I shared that with the woman, and she was in tears," Meister recalled. "She realized God didn't want those bad things to happen to her. He didn't cause them. And yet in his omniscience and omnipotence, he is able to take even the bad stuff that happens and turn her into a beautiful person with a big heart for helping those who suffer.

"Now, we can resist God and become hardened against him, but that's not what he wants. Sometimes it takes trials and tribulations to make us into mature, spiritual human beings. The Bible talks about how hardship develops character and perseverance.[14] We all know that if we raise a child in a totally sheltered way, they won't fully mature."

"You're saying that creating a mature individual must necessarily involve some hardship?" I asked.

"Yes, that's plausible. There's no contradiction in God existing and evil existing if God has a good and sufficient reason for allowing them to exist. As I've shown, it's at least logically possible that God does have such reasons.

"Actually, Augustine wrote an entire book on how freedom allows for the possibility of the free agent choosing evil over good.[15] He argued that it's a good thing God gave us freedom, but with this freedom came the danger that people would use this good gift for the wrong reasons—even malicious ones. And this is what happened—humankind turned against its maker.

"But we can see why God might allow evil to exist. A serious difficulty or even a tragedy can cause people to acknowledge God and their need for salvation. As C. S. Lewis famously said, 'God whispers to us in our pleasures, speaks in our conscious, but shouts in our pains; [evil] is His megaphone to rouse a deaf world.'"[16]

> "It's a good thing God gave us freedom, but with this freedom came the danger that people would use this good gift for the wrong reasons."

I said, "Your bottom line, then, is that while pantheism and atheism are disqualified because of logical contradictions, incoherence, and unlivable claims, theism survives."

"Correct," came his response. "We're just scratching the surface here. But my conclusion is that, given all of this, it seems to me that theism in general—and Christianity in particular—is the most plausible worldview."

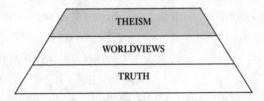

LEVEL 3: Theism—The Fingerprints of God

I was interested in Meister's assessment of the positive evidence for theism, so I offered him a challenge: "Give me three affirmative reasons that theism is true." Initially, he responded with two of the same arguments that have already been presented in this book.

"First, there's the fine-tuning of the universe," he said. "Second, the beginning of the universe points powerfully toward a creator." Then Meister raised a third reason for believing in God—the so-called moral argument, which he had referenced earlier when critiquing atheism. He spelled it out in its most basic form.

"If there are objective moral values, then God exists," he said. "Objective moral values are precepts that are universally binding on all people at all times and places, whether they follow them or not. And we know that objective moral values *do* exist—for example, it's objectively evil to torture a baby for fun. Therefore, God exists."

Again, Meister was not saying an atheist can't have moral values or live a basically ethical life. He was talking about *objective* moral values—for instance, to call the Holocaust objectively wrong is to say it was wrong even though the Nazis thought it was right. And it would be wrong even if the Nazis had won World War II and succeeded in brainwashing or exterminating everyone who disagreed with them. If there is no God, then moral values aren't objective in that way.[17]

William Lane Craig had used that Holocaust example in an earlier interview I conducted with him. I'll never forget how he spelled out the moral argument for theism on that day.

"If there is no God, moral values are merely the product of sociobiological evolution," Craig told me. "In fact, that's what many atheists think. According to atheist philosopher Michael Ruse, 'Morality is a biological adaptation no less than are hands and feet and teeth,' and morality is 'just an aid to survival and reproduction . . . and any deeper meaning is illusory.'[18]

"Or if there is no God, then morality is just a matter of personal taste, akin to statements like, 'Broccoli tastes good,'" Craig continued. "Well, it tastes good to some people but bad to others. There isn't any objective truth about that; it's a subjective matter of taste. And to say that killing innocent children is wrong would just be an expression of taste, like saying, 'I don't like the killing of innocent children.'

"Like Ruse and atheist Bertrand Russell, I don't see any reason to think that in the absence of God, the morality evolved by *Homo sapiens* is objective. After all, if there is no God, then what's so special about human beings? They're just accidental by-products of nature.

"In the atheistic view, some actions like rape may not be socially advantageous, and therefore this behavior has become taboo in the course of human development. But that doesn't prove that rape is really wrong. In fact, it's conceivable that rape could have evolved to something that's advantageous for the survival of the species. Thus, without God there is no absolute right and wrong that imposes itself on our conscience.

"However, we all know deep down that, in fact, objective moral values *do* exist. All we have to do to see that is to simply ask ourselves, *Is torturing a child for fun really a morally neutral act?* I'm persuaded you'd say, *No, that's not morally neutral; it's really wrong to do that.* And you'll say that in full cognizance of the Darwinian theory of evolution and all the rest.

"Actions like rape and child abuse aren't just behaviors that happen to be socially unacceptable; they are clearly moral abominations. They are objectively wrong. And such things as love, equality, and self-sacrifice really are good in an objective sense. We all know these things deep down. And since these objective moral values cannot exist without God, and they unquestionably do exist, it follows logically and inescapably that God exists."[19]

Scholars consider this line of reasoning to be particularly persuasive. "The moral argument is, in my estimation, the most powerful argument for God, and I have seen plenty of intellectual and spiritual seekers find God because of it," said philosopher Paul Copan.[20]

After summarizing all three arguments for God, Meister concluded, "For these and many other reasons, Lee, I'm convinced that theism is the most plausible worldview—by a long shot."

That did indeed seem logical. But which species of theism rings true? That brought us to the next level of the pyramid.

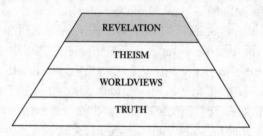

LEVEL 4: Revelation—Has God Spoken to Humankind?

Every major religion believes its scriptures are authoritative and divinely inspired. Christians see no conflict between their Bible and the Jewish scriptures contained in the Old Testament, since Christians regard their faith as being the fulfillment of Judaism.

However, there are irreconcilable differences between the Bible and other sacred texts. For example, the Qur'an explicitly contradicts biblical teaching about the Trinity, the death and resurrection of Jesus, and Jesus as God's unique Son. Consequently, if it's plausible to believe that the Bible is reliable, that would rule out the claims in the Qur'an that contradict those in the Bible.

I wanted to focus on the New Testament because it contains the starkest contrast with Jewish and Islamic beliefs. Meister proposed three tests for whether it's plausible to believe the New Testament can be trusted.

"First, there's the bibliographical test," he said. "This refers to whether we can trust the transmission of the text through history. It's no exaggeration to say the evidence for the New Testament text is staggering. We have more than 5,800 ancient Greek manuscripts and fragments, some of which date back to less than a hundred years after the originals. That swamps other ancient writings. While this information doesn't prove the New Testament is true, it does offer good reason to believe we have a reasonably accurate representation of what was originally written."

I spoke up. "Yet there are a lot of variances between the copies."

"True, but the vast majority are minor spelling differences, and no cardinal doctrine of Christianity is at stake," he replied.[21]

"Next," Meister continued, "there's internal evidence. Several New Testament documents refer to their authors *being* eyewitnesses to the events, *mentioning* eyewitnesses, or *interviewing* eyewitnesses. For example, the author of Luke's gospel talked with eyewitnesses and notes that he 'carefully investigated everything' to establish 'the certainty' of what occurred.[22] Peter says he was personally an eyewitness to the events he described.[23] Paul notes there are hundreds of witnesses to what he claimed about Jesus and his resurrection.[24] No other religious text has this level of eyewitness authentication. That gives the New Testament special credibility.

"Then there's external evidence, which looks at whether outside sources provide any corroboration. Over and over, archaeological discoveries have confirmed—and never disproven—core New Testament references. Plus, there are ancient writings outside the Bible that corroborate the basic outline of Jesus' life."[25]

"Are you saying, then, that the Bible's reliability has been proven?"

"All I'm trying to establish is that it's plausible to believe in the reliability of the Bible. I know I don't have to convince you, Lee—you've written hundreds of pages on this topic in your books. I'm merely saying any reasonable person would be justified in rendering the verdict that the Bible is essentially trustworthy."

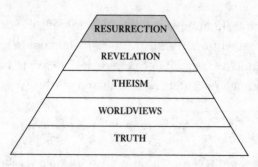

RESURRECTION

REVELATION

THEISM

WORLDVIEWS

TRUTH

LEVEL 5: Resurrection—Did Jesus Rise from the Grave?

The final category of evidence for Christianity, said Meister, is the resurrection of Jesus, which vindicated his claim to being the Messiah and God's unique Son.[26] When asked for historical data to support the resurrection, Meister raised the same "minimal facts" that historian Michael Licona discussed in an earlier chapter of this book.

"Many books have been written to refute the naturalistic explanations that skeptics have put forward," Meister told me. "The historical facts, in my opinion, are convincing—Jesus rose from the grave and, in doing so, demonstrated his divine nature.

"And this clinches Christianity as the worldview that makes the most sense to me. It's plausible and it's livable. As the apologetics pyramid demonstrates, Christianity is built on a solid foundation that can be trusted. In fact, through the years, a lot of people who started out as doubters have become believers after studying the evidence."

I slipped up my hand. "Including me," I said.

In fact, I remember years ago studying the life of a lawyer who was listed in the *Guinness Book of World Records* as the world's most successful defense attorney. He won more murder trials in a row than anyone in history. He was knighted twice by Queen Elizabeth and served as a justice on his country's highest court.

Sir Lionel Luckhoo was a skeptic toward the resurrection

until he applied his monumental legal skills to the historical record and reached this verdict: "I say unequivocally that the evidence for the resurrection of Jesus Christ is so overwhelming that it compels acceptance by proof which leaves absolutely no room for doubt."[27]

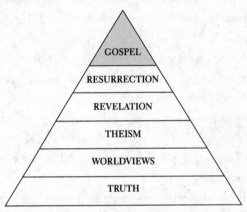

LEVEL 6: The Gospel—Opening the Door of Heaven

That brought us to the summit of the pyramid, which is the good news of the gospel. Logic and evidence had narrowed the credible choices down to one option: Jesus and his freely offered gift of forgiveness and eternal life. He said in Luke 4:43, "I must proclaim the good news of the kingdom of God . . . because that is why I was sent."

What is the good news? That Jesus is the Messiah who was unjustly killed, was resurrected in triumph over death, ascended to the Father, and is coming back to rule. Indeed, his death and resurrection were *for us*. He died to pay the penalty we deserved for our sins and rose to open the gates of heaven for all who come to him in repentance and faith.

It's an amazing truth. The God we sinned against loved us enough to sacrifice the life of his only Son, adopt us as his children, and invite us to spend eternity with him.

Meister told me about a movie he had seen about Camelot. "The idea is that you have this amazing kingdom where the king loves his people and the people love and serve the king. He provides for them and cares so much for them. That's the notion of a kingdom—a kingdom is the place where the good king rules.

"And Jesus opens God's kingdom to us. The kingdom of God is where God rules in a perfect way—he loves his people, provides for them, cares for them—and we gratefully love and serve and worship him in return. He invites everybody to enter—and in his kingdom, we are transformed.

> *"The God we sinned against loved us enough to sacrifice the life of his only Son, adopt us as his children, and invite us to spend eternity with him."*

"The Bible says the fruit of the spirit—love, joy, peace, patience, kindness, goodness, faithful, gentleness, and self-control—are manifestations of a life surrendered to the king.[28] The more we surrender, the more we experience what life was meant to be. It's the life we've always wanted. It's everything we desire. We can enter God's kingdom now and experience it forever."

Heaven is not a mirage like Camelot. It's life forever in the kingdom of a loving and powerful God who rules in truth and grace. The credibility of Christianity, demonstrated by Chad Meister's apologetics pyramid, gives us confidence that its version of the afterlife is the only one that passes the tests of logic and evidence.

Still, a couple of roadblocks stand in the way for many people. The first of those objections is this: If God is real, then why would he allow pain and suffering in our world? For many spiritual seekers, this question is the biggest sticking point in their journey toward God. Meister touched on this issue, but there is so much more to explore—which we'll do in the next chapter.

CHAPTER 7

CHALLENGE #1: IF GOD IS REAL, WHY IS THERE SUFFERING?

The fact of suffering undoubtedly constitutes the single greatest challenge to the Christian faith, and has been in every generation. Its distribution and degree appear to be entirely random and therefore unfair. Sensitive spirits ask if it can possibly be reconciled with God's justice and love.

Theologian John Stott, *The Cross of Christ*

When I was an idealistic young reporter fresh out of journalism school, one of my first assignments at the *Chicago Tribune* was to write a thirty-part series in which I would profile destitute families living in the city. Having been raised in the well-to-do suburbs, I quickly found myself immersed for the first time in Chicago's underbelly of deprivation and desperation.

The result: I settled deeper into my atheism. Surely there was no way to reconcile this world of poverty and despair with the existence of a just and loving deity.

Hardships, betrayal, illness, injuries, heartbreak—everyone suffers to some degree. Heart disease claimed my father when he should have had many years left. I watched my mother slowly succumb to cancer. I kept vigil at a neonatal intensive care unit as my newborn daughter fought for her life. I'm sure you could tell similar stories of personal anguish.

Too often the innocent are victimized. "If only villains got broken backs or cancers, if only cheaters and crooks got Parkinson's disease, we should see a sort of celestial justice in the universe," wrote agnostic-turned-Christian Sheldon Vanauken. "But, as it is, a sweet-tempered child lies dying of a brain tumor; a happy young wife sees her husband and child killed before her eyes by a drunken driver; and . . . we soundlessly scream at the stars, 'Why? Why?'"[1]

This isn't merely an intellectual issue; it's an intensely personal matter that can tie our emotions into knots and leave us with spiritual vertigo—disoriented, frightened, and angry. One writer referred to the problem of pain as "the question mark turned like a fishhook in the human heart."[2]

> "The problem of pain is 'the question mark turned like a fishhook in the human heart.'"

In fact, it's the single biggest obstacle for spiritual seekers. I commissioned a national survey with this inquiry: "If you could ask God only one question and you knew he would give you an answer right now, what would you ask?"[3] By a long shot, the top response was this one: "Why is there pain and suffering in the world?"[4] This is, in short, the heart's cry of humanity.

As you've read the affirmative case for the God of Christianity in the preceding chapters, perhaps this objection is your main impediment to deciding whether God is real. However, does the presence of suffering necessarily mean the absence of God?

To explore the matter, I placed a call to Boston College to make an appointment with the author of *Making Sense Out of Suffering*—a book whose title summed up exactly what I was seeking to do.

Peter John Kreeft, PhD

Peter Kreeft is a first-rate philosopher, with a doctorate from Fordham University, postgraduate studies at Yale University, and several decades of experience as a professor at Villanova University and Boston College. Yet he's no stuffy academic. He has a winsome and engaging manner, often wearing a bemused grin as he finds himself unable to restrain himself from cracking jokes about even the most sacrosanct subject.

A Catholic widely read by Protestants, Kreeft has written or coauthored more than eighty books, including *Love Is Stronger Than Death*, *A Refutation of Moral Relativism*, and *Handbook of Christian Apologetics*.

What drew me to Kreeft was his insightful book about suffering in which he skillfully weaves a journey of discovery through Socrates, Plato, and Aristotle; through Augustine, Kierkegaard, and Dostoevsky; through *Star Trek*, *The Velveteen Rabbit*, and *Hamlet*; and through Moses, Job, and Jeremiah. All along the way, there are clues that eventually, ultimately, finally, converge on Jesus and the tears of God.

I figured there was no better approach than to hit Kreeft head-on with evangelist-turned-agnostic Charles Templeton's blunt objections to Christianity that I mentioned in the introduction to this book.

A Bear, a Trap, a Hunter, and God

Confronting Kreeft with the same emotional intensity that Templeton had displayed to me, I described the *Life* magazine photo of an anguished mother clutching her dead infant in drought-ravaged Africa and then quoted this former pulpit partner of renowned evangelist Billy Graham:

> I thought, *Is it possible to believe that there is a loving or caring creator when all this woman needed was* rain? How could a loving God do this to that woman? Who runs the rain? I don't; you don't. He does—or that's what I thought. But when I saw that photograph, I immediately knew it is not possible for this to happen and for there to be a loving God. There was no way.[1]

I looked up from my notes. "How in the world would you respond to Templeton?"

Kreeft cleared his throat. "First of all," he began, "I'd focus on his words 'it is not possible.' Even David Hume, one of history's most famous skeptics, said it's just *barely* possible that God exists. That's at least a somewhat reasonable position—to say that there's at least a small possibility. But to say there's *no* possibility that a loving God who knows far more than we do, including about our future, could possibly tolerate such evil as Templeton sees in Africa—well, that strikes me as intellectually arrogant."

"Really?" I asked. "How so?"

"How can a mere finite human be sure that infinite wisdom would not tolerate certain short-range evils in order for longer-range goods we couldn't foresee?" he asked.

"Elaborate a bit."

"Look at it this way," he said. "Would you agree that the difference between us and God is greater than the difference between us and, say, a bear?"

I nodded.

"Okay, then, imagine a bear in a trap and a hunter who, out of sympathy, wants to liberate him. He tries to win the bear's confidence, but he can't do it, so he has to shoot the bear full of drugs. The bear, however, thinks this is an attack and that the hunter is trying to kill him. He doesn't realize this action comes from compassion.

"Then in order to get the bear out of the trap, the hunter has to push him further into the trap to release the tension on the spring. If the bear were semiconscious at that point, he would be even more convinced that the hunter was his enemy who was out to cause him suffering and pain. But the bear would be wrong. The bear reaches this incorrect conclusion because he's not a human being.

"Now," he concluded, "how can anyone be certain this isn't an analogy for the relationship between us and God? I believe God does the same to us sometimes, and we can't comprehend why he does it, any more than the bear can understand the motivations of the hunter. As the bear could have trusted the hunter, so we can trust God."

Faith and Prejudice

I paused to ponder Kreeft's point, but he continued before I could reply.

"However," he said, "I certainly don't want to demean Templeton. He's responding in a very honest and heartfelt way to the fact that something counts against God. Only in a world where faith is difficult can faith exist. I don't have faith in two plus two equals four or in the noonday sun. Those are beyond question. But Scripture describes God as a hidden God. You have to make an effort of faith to find him. There are clues you can follow.

"If that weren't so, if there were something more or less than clues, it's difficult for me to understand how we could really be free to make a choice about him. If we had absolute proof instead of clues, then you could no more deny God than you could deny the sun. If we had no evidence at all, you could never get there. God gives us just enough evidence so that those who want him can have him. Those who want to follow the clues will.

"The Bible says, 'Seek and you will find.'[2] It doesn't say *everybody* will find him; it doesn't say *nobody* will find him. *Some* will find. Who? Those who seek. Those whose hearts are set on finding him and who follow the clues."

I jumped in. "Wait a minute—a moment ago you admitted 'something counts against God'—that evil and suffering *are* evidence against him. Aren't you conceding, that evil disproves God's existence?"

"No, no," he insisted, shaking his head. "First of all, evidence is not necessarily certain or conclusive. I'm saying that in this world there is evidence against and evidence for God. Augustine put it very simply: 'If there is no God, why is there so much good? If there is a God, why is there so much evil?'

"There's no question that the existence of evil is one argument against God, but in one of my books I summarize twenty arguments that point persuasively in the other direction—in favor of the existence of God.[3] Atheists must answer all twenty arguments; theists must only answer one. However, each of us gets to cast a vote."

Evil as Evidence for God

Then Kreeft added this counterintuitive remark: "Besides, the evidence of evil and suffering can go both ways—it can actually be used in *favor* of God."

I sat up straight. "How," I asked, "is *that* possible?"

"Consider this. If Templeton is right in responding to these events with outrage, it presupposes that there really is a difference between good and evil. The fact that he's using the standard of good to judge evil—the fact that he's saying, quite rightly, that this horrible suffering isn't what ought to be—means that he has a notion of what ought to be, that this notion corresponds to something real, and that there is, therefore, a reality called the Supreme Good. Well, that's another name for God."

Warily, I summarized Kreeft's point. "You mean that unintentionally Templeton may be testifying to the reality of God because by recognizing evil he's assuming there's an objective standard on which it's based?"

"Right. If I give one student a grade of 90 and another a grade of 80, the presupposition is that 100 is a real standard. And my point is this: if there is no God, where did we get the standard of goodness by which we judge evil as evil?

"What's more, as C. S. Lewis said, 'If the universe is so bad . . . how on earth did human beings ever come to attribute it to the activity of a wise and good Creator?'[4] In other words, the very presence of these ideas in our minds—that is, the idea of evil, thus of goodness and of God as the origin and standard of goodness—needs to be accounted for."

An interesting counterpunch, I mused. "Then atheism," I said, "is an inadequate answer to the problem of evil?"

"It's an easy answer—maybe, if I may use the word, a *cheap* answer," he said. "Atheism is cheap on people. How is it possible that more than 90 percent of all the human beings who have ever lived—usually in far more painful circumstances than we—could believe in God? The objective evidence, just looking at the balance of pleasure and suffering in the world, would not seem to justify believing in an absolutely good God. Yet this has been almost universally believed. Are they all crazy? Well, I suppose you can believe that if you're a bit of an elitist.

"Also, atheism robs death of meaning, and if death has no meaning, how can life ultimately have meaning? Atheism cheapens everything it touches. Look at the results of Communism, the most powerful form of atheism on earth. And in the end, when the atheist dies and encounters God instead of the nothingness they had predicted, they'll recognize that atheism was a cheap answer because it refused the only thing that's not cheap—the God of infinite value."

A Problem of Logic

Kreeft had made some interesting initial points, but we had been dancing around the subject a bit. It was time to cut to the core.

"Christians believe in five things," I said. "First, God exists; second, God is all-good; third, God is all-powerful; fourth, God is all-wise; and fifth, evil exists. How can all of those statements be true at the same time?"

"It seems you have to drop one of those beliefs," replied Kreeft. "If God is all-powerful, he can do anything. If God is all-good, he wants only good. If God is all-wise, he knows what is good. So if all of those beliefs are true—and Christians believe they are—then it would seem that the consequence is that no evil can exist."

"But evil *does* exist," I said. "Therefore, isn't it logical to assume that such a God doesn't exist?"

"No, I'd say one of those beliefs about him must be false, or we're not understanding it in the right way."

It was time to find out. I invited Kreeft to examine these three divine attributes—God being all-powerful, all-good, and all-knowing—in light of the existence of evil.

ATTRIBUTE #1: God Is All-Powerful

"When we say that God is all-powerful, we mean he can do everything that is meaningful, everything that is possible, everything that makes any sense at all," Kreeft said. "God cannot make himself cease to exist. He cannot make good evil."

"So," I said, "there are some things he can't do."

"Precisely *because* he is all-powerful, he can't do some things. He can't make mistakes. Only weak and stupid beings make mistakes. One such mistake would be to try to create a self-contradiction, like two plus two equals five or a round square.

"Now, the classic defense of God against the problem of evil is that it's not logically possible to have free will and no possibility of moral evil. In other words, once God chose to create human beings with free will, it was up to them rather than to God as to whether there was sin or not. That's what free will means. Built into the situation of God deciding to create human beings is the chance of evil and, consequently, the suffering that results."

"Then God created evil."

"No, he created the *possibility* of evil; people actualized that potentiality. The source of evil is not God's power, but rather mankind's freedom. Even an all-powerful God could not have created a world in which people had genuine freedom and yet there was no potential for sin, because our freedom includes the possibility of sin within its own meaning. It's a self-contradiction—a meaningless nothing—to have a world where there's real choice while at the same time no possibility of choosing evil. To ask why God didn't create such a world is like asking why God didn't create colorless color or round squares."

"Then why didn't God create a world without human freedom?"

"Because that would have been a world without humans. Would it have been a place without suffering? Yes. But it also would have been a world without love, which is the highest value in the universe. That highest good never could have been experienced. Real love—our love of God and our love of each other—must involve a choice. But with the granting of that choice comes the possibility that people would choose instead to hate."

"But look at Genesis," I said. "God did create a world where people were free and yet there was no sin."

"That's precisely what he did," Kreeft said. "After creation, God declared that the world was 'good.' People were free to choose to love God or turn away from him. However, such a world is necessarily a place where sin is freely possible—and, indeed, that potentiality for sin was actualized not by God but by people. The blame, ultimately, lies with us. He did his part perfectly; we're the ones who messed up."

ATTRIBUTE #2: God Is All-Knowing

I asked Kreeft to move on to the next divine quality—God's omniscience.

"If God is all-wise, he knows not only the present but also the future. And he knows not only present good and evil but also future good and evil. If his wisdom vastly exceeds ours, as the hunter's exceeds the bear's, it is at least possible—contrary to Templeton's analysis—that a loving God could deliberately tolerate horrible things like starvation because he foresees that in the long run, more people will be better and happier than if he miraculously intervened. That's at least intellectually possible."

"Sounds like a cop-out."

"Okay, then, let's put it to the test," Kreeft replied. "You see, God has specifically shown us very clearly how this can work. He has demonstrated how the very worst thing that has ever happened in the history of the world ended up resulting in the very best thing that has ever happened in the history of the world."

"What do you mean?"

"I'm referring to deicide, the death of God himself on the cross," he said. "At the time, nobody saw how anything good could ever result from this tragedy. And yet God foresaw that the result would be the opening of heaven to human beings. So the worst tragedy in history brought about the most glorious event in history. And if it happened there—if the ultimate evil can result in the ultimate good—it can happen elsewhere, even in our own individual lives. Here God lifts the curtain and lets us see it. Elsewhere he simply says, 'Trust me.'"

ATTRIBUTE #3: God Is All-Good

That left us with God's attribute of goodness.

"*Good* is a tricky word," Kreeft began, "because even in human affairs there's such a wide range of meaning. But the difference between us and God is certainly greater than the difference between us and animals, and since good varies enormously between us and animals, it must vary even more enormously between us and God."

"Granted," I said. "But if I did nothing while my child got run over by a truck, I wouldn't be good in any sense of the word. Yet God sits by and refuses to perform miracles to take us out of danger. Why isn't *he* bad?"

"It looks like he is," he said. "But the fact that God deliberately allows certain things—which if we allowed them would turn us into monsters—doesn't necessarily count against God."

"You'll have to explain that."

"Let me give you an analogy in human relationships," he replied. "If I said to my brother, who's about my age, 'I could bail you out of a problem, but I won't,' I would probably be irresponsible and perhaps wicked. But we do that with our children all the time. We don't do their homework for them. We don't put a bubble around them and protect them from every hurt.

"I remember when one of my daughters was about four or five years old and she was trying to thread a needle. It was very difficult for her. Every time she tried, she hit herself in the finger and a couple of times she bled. I was watching her, but she didn't see me. She just kept trying and trying.

"My first instinct was to go and do it for her because I saw she was bleeding. But wisely I held back because I said to myself, *She can do it*. After about five minutes, she finally did it. I came out of hiding and she said, 'Daddy, Daddy—look what I did!' She was so proud she had threaded the needle that she had forgotten about the pain.

"That time, the pain was a good thing for her. I was wise enough to have foreseen it was good for her. Now, certainly God is much wiser than I was with my daughter. So it's at least possible that God is wise enough to foresee that we need some pain for reasons that we may not understand but that he foresees as being necessary toward some eventual good. Therefore, he's not being evil by allowing that pain to exist.

"Dentists, athletic trainers, teachers, parents—they all know that sometimes to be good is *not* to be kind. Certainly there are times when God allows suffering and deprives us of the lesser good of pleasure in order to help us toward the greater good of moral and spiritual education.

"We know that moral character gets formed through hardship, through overcoming obstacles, through enduring despite difficulties. Courage, for example, would be impossible in a world without pain. The apostle Paul testified to this refining quality of suffering when he wrote that 'suffering produces perseverance; perseverance, character; and character, hope.'[5]

"Let's face it, we learn from the mistakes we make and the suffering they bring. The universe is a soul-making machine, and part of that process is learning, maturing, and growing through difficult and challenging and painful experiences. The point of our lives in this world isn't comfort, but rather training and preparation for eternity. Scripture tells us that even Jesus 'learned obedience through suffering'[6]—and if that was true for him, why wouldn't it be even more true for us?"

> "The universe is a soul-making machine, and part of that process is learning, maturing, and growing through difficult and challenging and painful experiences."

Kreeft let the question hang in the air for a moment before continuing. "Suppose we didn't have any suffering at all. Suppose we had drugs for every pain, free entertainment, free love—everything but pain. No Shakespeare, no Beethoven, no Boston Red Sox, no death—no meaning. Impossibly spoiled little brats—that's what we'd become.

"In fact, pretend you're God and try to create a better world in your imagination. Try to create Utopia. But think through the consequences of everything you try to improve. Every time you use force to prevent evil, you take away freedom. To prevent all evil, you must remove all freedom and reduce people to puppets, which means they would then lack the ability to freely choose love.

"You may end up creating a world of precision that an engineer might like—*maybe*. But one thing's for sure: you'll lose the kind of world that a Father would want."

The Megaphone of Pain

Clue by clue, Kreeft was shedding more light on the mystery of suffering. But each new insight seemed to spawn new questions.

"Evil people get away with hurting others all the time. Certainly God can't consider that fair," I said. "Why doesn't he intervene?"

"People *aren't* getting away with it," Kreeft replied. "Justice delayed is not necessarily justice denied. There will come a day when God will settle accounts and people will be held responsible for the evil they've perpetrated and the suffering they've caused. Criticizing God for not doing it right now is like reading half a novel and criticizing the author for not resolving the plot. God will bring accountability at the right time—in fact, the Bible says one reason he's delaying is that some people are still following the clues and have yet to find him.[7] He's actually delaying the consummation of history out of his great love for them."

"But in the meantime, doesn't the sheer amount of suffering in the world bother you?" I asked. "Couldn't God curtail at least some of the more horrific evil?"

"It's true that there are some instances where quantity does become quality. Take, for example, boiling water. Once a temperature of 212 degrees is reached, you get a new state—gas—and gas laws rather than liquid laws apply. But suffering isn't like that. At what point does suffering disprove the existence of God? No such point can be shown. Besides, because we're not God, we can't say how much suffering is needed."

"You said a moment ago that some pain might be necessary. That indicates there is a meaning to suffering," I said. "If so, what is it?"

"One purpose of suffering in history has been that it leads to repentance," he answered. "Only after suffering, only after disaster, did Old Testament Israel, do nations, do individual people turn back to God. Let's face it, we learn the hard way. To quote C. S. Lewis, 'God whispers to us in our pleasures, speaks in our conscience, but shouts in our pains. It is his megaphone to rouse a deaf world.'[8] And, of course, repentance leads to something wonderful—to blessedness, since God is the source of all joy and all life. The outcome is good—in fact, better than good.

"Simply put, I believe that suffering is compatible with God's love if it is medicinal, remedial, and necessary—that is, if we are very sick and desperately need a cure. And that's our situation. Jesus said, 'It is not the healthy who need a doctor, but the sick.... I have not come to call the righteous, but sinners.'"[9]

"But good people suffer just as much—or sometimes more—than the bad," I pointed out. "How is that fair?"

"Well, the answer to that is that there are no good people," Kreeft replied.

"What about that old saying, 'God don't make no junk'?"

"Yes, we're ontologically good—we still bear God's image—but *morally* we're not. His image in us has been tarnished. The prophet Jeremiah said that 'from the least to the greatest, all are greedy for gain,'[10] and the prophet Isaiah said, 'All of us have become like one who is unclean, and all our righteous acts are like filthy rags.'[11] Our good deeds are stained with self-interest and our demands for justice are mixed with lust for vengeance. Ironically, it's the best people who most readily recognize and admit their own shortcomings and sin.

"We are good stuff gone bad, a defaced masterpiece, a rebellious child. Lewis pointed out that we're not just imperfect people who need growth; we're also rebels who need to lay down our arms.[12] Pain and suffering are frequently the means by which we become motivated to finally surrender to God and seek the cure of Christ.

"Pain and suffering are frequently the means by which we become motivated to finally surrender to God and seek the cure of Christ."

"That's what we need most desperately. That's what will

bring us the supreme joy of knowing Jesus. Any suffering, the great Christians from history will tell you, is worth that result."

Bearing the Pain

I sat back in my chair and reflected on what Kreeft had said so far. The clues seemed to be leading somewhere.

I decided to ask him about a quote from Augustine, who said, "Since God is the highest good, he would not allow any evil to exist in his works unless his omnipotence and goodness were such as to bring good even out of evil."[13] After reading him those words, I said, "Does that mean suffering and evil contain the potential for good?"

"Yes, I believe all suffering contains at least the opportunity for good," came his response, "but not everyone actualizes that potential. Not all of us learn and benefit from suffering; that's where free will comes in.

"But just about every human being can reflect on their past and say, 'I learned from that hardship. I didn't think I would at the time, but I'm a bigger and better person for having endured it and persevered.' Even people without religious faith are aware of that dimension of suffering. And if we can bring good out of evil even without bringing God into the picture, you can imagine how much more, with God's help, evil can work out for the greater good."

Still, I wondered, if God loves people, how could he emotionally tolerate the ongoing onslaught of pain and suffering? Wouldn't it overwhelm him?

I pulled out Charles Templeton's book and read Kreeft this quote: "Jesus said, 'Are not two sparrows sold for a penny, and not one of them is forgotten before God; and are you not of more value than many sparrows?'[14] But if God grieves over the death of one sparrow, how could even his eternal spirit bear the sickness, suffering, and death of the multiplied millions of men, women, children, animals, birds, and other sensate creatures?"[15]

"I think Mr. Templeton is anthropomorphizing God by saying, 'I couldn't imagine how any intelligent being could bear this,'" Kreeft said. "And, yes, he's right—we *can't* imagine it. But we can believe it. God does, in fact, weep over every sparrow and grieve over every evil and every suffering. So the suffering that Christ endured on the cross is literally unimaginable. It's not just what you and I would have experienced in our own finite human agony, physical and mental, but all the sufferings of the world were there.

"Let's go back to Templeton's photo of the starving woman in Africa—all she needed was rain. *Where is God?* He was entering into her agony. Not just her physical agony, but her moral agony. *Where is God? Why doesn't he send the rain?* God's answer is the incarnation. He himself entered into all that agony, he himself bore all of the pain of this world—and that's unimaginable and shattering and even more impressive than the divine power of creating the world in the first place.

"Just imagine every single pain in the history of the world, all rolled together into a ball, eaten by God, digested, fully tasted, eternally. In the act of creating the world, God not only said, 'Let there be pretty little bunny rabbits and flowers and sunsets,' but also 'Let there be blood and guts and the buzzing flies around the cross.' In a sense, Templeton is right. God is intimately involved in the act of creating a world of suffering. He didn't do it—we did it—and yet he did say, 'Let this world be.'

"And if he did that and then just sat back and said, 'Well, it's your fault after all'—although he'd be perfectly justified in doing that—I don't see how we could love him. The fact that he went beyond justice and quite incredibly took all the suffering upon himself makes him so winsome that the answer to suffering is—"

Kreeft's eyes darted around the room as he searched for the right words. "The answer," he said, "is how could you not love this Being who went the extra mile, who practiced more than he preached, who entered into our world, who suffered our pains, who offers himself to us in the midst of our sorrows? What more could he do?"

I said, "In effect, then, the answer to Templeton's question about how God could bear all that suffering is—he did."

"*He did!*" Kreeft declared. "God's answer to the problem of suffering is that he came right down into it. Many Christians try to get God off the hook for suffering; God put himself on the hook, so to speak—on the cross.

"And therefore the practical conclusion is that if we want to be with God, we have to be with suffering, we have to not avoid the cross, either in thought or in fact. We must go where he is, and the cross is one of the places where he is. And when he sends us the sunrises, we thank him for the sunrises; when he sends us sunsets and deaths and sufferings and crosses, we thank him for that."

I bristled. "Is it possible, really, to thank God for the pain that befalls us?"

"Yes. In heaven we will do exactly that. We will say to God, 'Thank you so much for this little pain I didn't understand at the time and that little pain I didn't understand at the time. I now see that these were the most precious things in my life.'

"Even if I don't find myself emotionally capable of doing that right now, even if I cannot honestly say to God in the middle of pain, 'God, thank you for this pain,' but have to say instead, 'Deliver me from evil,' that's perfectly right and perfectly honest—yet I believe that's not the last word. The last words of the Lord's Prayer aren't 'deliver us from evil'; the last words are 'yours is the kingdom and the power and the glory forever.'

"I do think that any fairly mature Christian can look back on their life and identify some moment of suffering that made them much closer to God than they had ever thought possible. Before this happened, they would have said, 'I don't really see how this can accomplish any good at all,' but after they emerge from the suffering, they say, 'That's amazing. I learned something I never thought I could have learned. I didn't think that my weak and rebellious will was capable of such strength, but God, through his grace, gave me the strength for each moment.' If it weren't for suffering, it wouldn't have been possible.

"The closeness to God, not just the feeling of being close to God but the ontological real closeness to God, the similarity to God, the conformity to God, the God-likeness of the soul, emerges from suffering with remarkable efficiency."

"You mentioned heaven," I said. "And the Bible does talk about our sufferings in this world being light and momentary compared to what God's followers will experience in heaven.[16] How does the heaven part play into this whole story?"

"Saint Teresa of Ávila said that in light of heaven, the worst suffering on earth, a life full of the most atrocious tortures on earth, will be seen to be no more serious than one night in a bad inn.[17] That's a challenging or even an outrageous statement! But she didn't speak from the kind of insulated bubble that so many of us live in; she spoke from a life full of suffering.

"The apostle Paul uses another outrageous word in a similar context when he's comparing earthly pleasures with the pleasure of knowing Christ. He said the privileges of Roman citizenship, of being a Pharisee of the Pharisees, of being highly educated— all this, as compared to knowing Christ, is 'dung.'[18] That's a very bold word!

"Similarly, compared with knowing God eternally, compared to the intimacy with God that Scripture calls a spiritual marriage, nothing else counts. If the way to that is through torture, well, torture is nothing compared with that. Yes, it's enormous in itself, but compared to that, it's nothing.

"So the answer to Templeton is, yes, you're perfectly right in saying that this photograph of the African woman is outrageous. This lack of rain, this starvation, is indeed outrageous in itself. And in one sense, the answer is not to figure it out; one answer is to look into the face of God and compare these two things.

"On the one side of the scale, this torture, or all the tortures of the world; on the other side of the scale, the face of God—the God available to all who seek him in the midst of their pain. The good of God, the joy of God, is going to infinitely outweigh all of the sufferings—and even the joys—of this world."

The Power of God's Presence

I was glad that Kreeft had brought the conversation back around to the woman from Templeton's photograph, since she personalized the issue of suffering. "If she were here right now," I said to Kreeft, "what would you say to her?"

"Nothing."

"*Nothing?*"

"Not at first anyway. I'd let her talk to me. The founder of an organization for the severely multiply impaired says that he works with the disabled for a very selfish reason: they teach him something much more valuable than he could ever teach them— namely, who he is. That sounds sentimental, but it's true.

"One of my four children is moderately disabled, and I've learned more from her than from the other three. I've learned that I'm disabled and that we're *all* disabled, and listening to her helps me to understand myself.

"So the first thing we must do with this woman is listen to her. Be aware of her. See her pain. Feel her pain. We live in a relative bubble of comfort, and we look at pain as observers, viewing it as a philosophical puzzle or theological problem. That's the wrong way to look at pain. The thing to do with pain is to enter it, be one with her, and then you learn something from it.

"In fact, it's significant that most objections to the existence of God from the problem of suffering come from outside observers who are quite comfortable, whereas those who actually suffer are, as often as not, made into stronger believers by their suffering."

That's a phenomenon many writers have noted. After wide-ranging research into the topic of suffering, Philip Yancey wrote, "As I visited people whose pain far exceeded my own . . . I was surprised by its effects. Suffering seemed as likely to reinforce faith as to sow agnosticism."[19]

"Let's go back to the woman," I said. "You indicated that we should listen and react to her, which sounds like a good thing. But there must be more."

"Yes," he said. "We would want to be Jesus to her, to minister to her, to love her, to comfort her, to embrace her, to weep with her. Our love—a reflection of God's love—should spur us to help her and others who are hurting."

Kreeft gestured toward the hallway. "On my door there's a cartoon of two turtles. One says, 'Sometimes I'd like to ask why he allows poverty, famine, and injustice when he could do something about it.' The other turtle says, 'I'm afraid God might ask me the same question.' Those who have Jesus' heart toward hurting people need to live out their faith by alleviating suffering where they can, by making a difference, by embodying his love in practical ways."

"That cartoon reminds me of the way God likes to turn questions around," I commented.

"Yes, he's constantly doing that. This happened to Job. Job

was wondering who God was, because it looked as if God was a cosmic sadist. At the end of the book of Job, the all-time classic on the problem of suffering, God finally shows up with the answer—and the answer is a question.

"He says to Job, 'Who are you? Are you God? Did you write this script? Were you there when I laid the foundations of the earth?' And Job realizes the answer is no. Then he's satisfied. Why? *Because he sees God!* God doesn't write him a book. He could have written the best book on the problem of evil ever written. Instead, he shows himself to Job."

"And that satisfied him—"

"Yes! It *has* to—that's what's going to satisfy us forever in heaven. I think Job gets a foretaste of heaven at the end of this book that bears his name because he meets God. If it had been only words that God gave him, it would have meant that Job could keep the dialogue going and ask God another question and God would give a good answer and Job would ask another question the next day and the next day, because Job was a very demanding philosopher. This would go on and on. What could make it end? *God's presence!*

"God didn't let Job suffer because he lacked love, but rather because he *did* love, in order to bring Job to the point of encountering God face-to-face, which is humanity's supreme happiness. Job's suffering hollowed out a big space inside him so that God and joy could fill it.

"As we look at human relationships, what we see is that lovers don't want explanations, but rather presence. And what God is, essentially, is *presence*—the doctrine of the Trinity says God is three persons who are present to each other in perfect knowledge and perfect love. That's why God is infinite joy.

"And insofar as we can participate in that presence, we too have infinite joy. So that's what Job has—even on his dung heap, even before he gets any of his worldly goods back—once he sees God face-to-face."

Every Tear, His Tear

The clues were converging, and I could sense an increasing passion and conviction in Kreeft's voice. I wanted to see more of his heart—and I wouldn't be disappointed.

"The answer, then, to suffering," I said in trying to sum up where we've come, "is not an answer at all."

"Correct," he said, leaning forward. "It's the Answerer. It's Jesus himself. It's not a bunch of words; it's *the* Word. It's not a tightly woven philosophical argument; it's a person. *The* person. The answer to suffering cannot just be an abstract idea because this isn't an abstract issue; it's a personal issue. It requires a personal response. The answer must be *someone*, not just something, because the issue involves someone—*God, where are you?*"

That question almost echoed in his small office. It demanded a response. To Kreeft, there is one—a very real one. A living One.

> "The answer, then, to suffering, is not an answer at all. It's the Answerer. It's Jesus himself. It's not a bunch of words; it's the Word."

"Jesus is there, sitting beside us in the lowest places of our lives," he said. "Are we broken? He was broken, like pieces of bread from the loaf, for us. Are we despised? He was despised and rejected by men. Do we cry out that we can't take any more? He was a man of sorrows and acquainted with grief. Do people betray us? He was sold out himself. Are our tenderest relationships broken? He too loved and was rejected. Do people turn from us? He was one from whom they hid their faces as though he were a leper.

"Does he descend into the hells of each one of us? Yes, he

does. From the depths of a Nazi death camp, Corrie ten Boom wrote, 'No matter how deep our darkness, he is deeper still.'[20] Jesus not only rose from the dead; he changed the meaning of death and therefore of all the little deaths—the sufferings that anticipate death and constitute all the aspects of it.

"He is gassed in Auschwitz. He is sneered at in Soweto. He is mocked in Northern Ireland. He is enslaved in the Sudan. He's the one we love to hate, yet to us he has chosen to return love. Every tear we shed becomes his tear. He may not wipe them away yet, but he will."

He paused, his confident tone downshifting. "In the end, God has only given us partial explanations," he said slowly, a shrug in his voice. "Maybe that's because he saw that a better explanation wouldn't have been good for us. I don't know why. As a philosopher, I'm obviously curious. Humanly, I wish he had given us more information."

With that, he looked fully into my face.

"But he knew that Jesus was more than an explanation," he said firmly. "He's what we really need. If your friend is sick and dying, the most important thing they want is not an explanation; they want you to sit with them. They're terrified of being alone more than anything else. So God has not left us alone."

Kreeft leaned back in his chair. There was only one more thing he wanted me to know.

"And for that," he said, "*I love him.*"

Drawing Good from Evil

Granted, the existence of suffering is a powerful objection to faith. I've wrestled with this issue down through the years, and undoubtedly you have too. However, I don't believe this challenge is sufficient to overcome all of the affirmative evidence that a loving God does indeed exist—especially now that Kreeft's analysis has relieved some of the sting from the objection.

While I certainly wish I knew more—and I'm grateful that someday, in eternity, I will—the sticking point of pain and suffering wasn't enough, in the end, to derail my belief that God is real.

And here's a surprising twist. Apparently Charles Templeton came to a similar conclusion. There's good evidence that this outspoken critic of faith, who once authored the caustic book *Farewell to God*, came to embrace God before he passed from this world.

In his hospital bed shortly before his death, he called out to his wife, "Madeleine, do you see them? Do you *hear* them? The angels! They're calling my name! I'm going home!"[21]

An article in the *Toronto Star* elaborated. "Suddenly, Madeleine said, he became very agitated, looking intensely toward the ceiling of the room, his eyes 'shining more blue than I'd ever seen before.' He cried out: 'Look at them, look at them! They're so beautiful. They're waiting for me. Oh, their eyes, their eyes are so beautiful!' Then, with great joy in his voice, he said, 'I'm coming!'"[22]

What was happening? Templeton's close friend, Salvation Army officer Beverly Ivany, is convinced she knows. "I really believed he finally made peace, in his own very private way, with God," she said. "And that he *was* going home to be with Jesus."[23]

CHAPTER 8

CHALLENGE #2:
IF GOD IS REAL, WHY
IS HE SO HIDDEN?

*Along with the problem of evil, the problem
of divine hiddenness has become one of the
most prominent arguments for atheism.*

**Philosopher Travis Dumsday, "C. S. Lewis on the
Problem of Divine Hiddenness,"** *International
Journal for Philosophy of Religion*

Jon Steingard compared the deconstruction of his Christian
faith to pulling on the threads of a sweater. One day, he
simply discovered that "there was no more sweater left."

The popular Christian musician stunned young evangelicals
in 2020 when he announced on Instagram that he had lost his
belief in God. However, he was careful to stress that he hadn't
become an atheist.

"I certainly couldn't say for certain that God isn't there," he
said. "I would prefer it if he was." He said he was open to having
his heart changed in the future. But for now, after a long period
of contemplation (aided by some "helpful" hallucinogenic

drugs), this pastor's son and frontman for the rock band Hawk Nelson said he was stepping away from his Christian faith.

"I'm open to the idea of there being God and I'm also open to the idea of Christianity being true," he said. "It's just whenever I come back to contemplating that and wondering if I can come back to a place I believe that, I'm consistently bumping up into the same problem—*where is he?*"[1]

Steingard was articulating a popular objection to Christianity, often called the problem of divine hiddenness. In 1897, Robert Anderson wrote *The Silence of God*, in which he talked about how God's hiddenness "tries faith, and hardens unfaith into open infidelity."[2] Indeed, Friedrich Nietzsche cited the silence of God in his embrace of atheism. "A god who is all-knowing and all-powerful and who does not even make sure that his creatures understand his intention—could that be a god of goodness?" he asked.[3]

While nearly four in ten Americans report having a miraculous encounter they can only attribute to God, that means a majority *don't* have that sort of experience.[4] Even many devoted believers wonder why God isn't more readily apparent to them in their personal devotions or amid times of struggle. In other words, if you've ever felt the absence of God when you were desperate for his presence, then frankly you're not alone.

"The biggest reason I'm an atheist is because of crickets—because of divine hiddenness, because . . . I spent a long time sincerely trying to get God to answer anything," said Baptist-turned-skeptic Matthew Dillahunty. "If there is a God who wants a relationship, remaining hidden is in direct conflict with that."[5]

In recent years, Oxford-educated philosopher J. L. Schellenberg's writings have raised the hiddenness objection to heightened prominence. Said philosophy professor Daniel Wiley,

"The challenge of divine hiddenness has become one of the greatest advocates for skepticism in modern philosophical debate."[6]

This argument has several permutations. Essentially, said philosopher Travis Dumsday, skeptics ask why God doesn't make his existence much more obvious so that no rational person could doubt that he's real. That is, if God were truly loving and wanted a relationship with humankind, he would make certain that every person who is not actively resisting God would always have a rationally secure belief in him.

"But as a matter of fact, lots of people fail to believe in God, often through no fault of their own," said Dumsday. Therefore, says the argument, the all-loving God of Christianity doesn't really exist after all. Here's one formulation of the argument, according to the *Stanford Encyclopedia of Philosophy*:

1. There are people who are capable of relating personally to God but who, through no fault of their own, fail to believe.
2. If there is a personal God who is unsurpassingly great, then there are no such people.
3. So, there is no such God.[7]

As for Steingard, he said his own son will never doubt that his father was there, "because I am present in his life. And it seems to me that God could be present in our lives in the same way, in a more practical, conversational way . . . [like] the relationship I have with my son. I don't see why that's not possible."

In effect, this puts responsibility for a person's disbelief squarely on God's shoulders. Asked Steingard, "If my son grew up to question my very existence, is that because he has done something wrong—or I have?"

A provocative question indeed. To investigate, I reached out to a respected and widely published author whose entire career has been devoted to responding to troublesome questions about faith.

INTERVIEW WITH

Kenneth Richard Samples, MA

Rocked by the suicide of his brother Frank, Kenneth Samples began to seek answers to deep questions. Frank had plummeted into despair after struggling with drug addiction and incarceration, and Ken started wondering, *What do I have in my life that's really meaningful?*

His spiritual curiosity had already been piqued when his sister gave him a copy of *Mere Christianity* by C. S. Lewis. Later he had a vivid dream in which he encountered a Christlike figure with scars and bruises on his face. "When he spoke—I kid you not—it was like *thunder*," Samples told me. This resulted in an insatiable urge to study the Bible and attend church.

He became a committed Christian and immediately gravitated toward apologetics. He earned an undergraduate degree in history from Concordia University and then a master's degree in theological studies from Biola University.

After working alongside legendary countercult apologist Walter Martin, Samples now serves as senior research scholar for Reasons to Believe, a nonprofit that focuses on science and faith. For more than twenty years, he has taught at Biola and lectured at universities around the country. His books include *Without a Doubt: Answering the 20 Toughest Faith Questions* and *Christianity Cross-Examined: Is It Rational, Relevant, and Good?*

Seated at a desk and wearing his gray hair cut short, Samples spoke in a sincere tone with an even cadence, unruffled by questions that might challenge his faith. After all, there are virtually no objections to Christianity that he hasn't addressed over his career.

God's Silence through the Centuries

I began by referencing several theists through history who struggled with the apparent silence of God and yet didn't abandon their faith. For example, the Hebrew psalmist cried out, "My God, my God, why have you forsaken me? . . . I cry out by day, but you do not answer, by night, but I find no rest."[1] The prophet Isaiah wrote, "Truly you are a God who has been hiding himself."[2]

"An important component of ancient Israel's worship was the engagement of divine absence," said Old Testament scholar Joel Burnett.[3] He added that in ancient Israel, "the sense of divine absence [and the sorrow and suffering that goes along with it] is regarded as a normal part of human experience."[4] Nevertheless, observed Michael Rea of the University of Notre Dame, none of the biblical texts that wrestle with divine silence ever question the *reality* of God.[5]

I turned to Samples. "Why do you think that many theists have struggled with the so-called hiddenness of God and yet never jettisoned their belief in him?" I asked.

"I would start by defining *faith*—it's a confident trust in a reliable source," he began. "That means faith is not trust in *any* source or *every* source, but we put our faith in something that's reliable. By that definition, faith has a rational component to it."

He paused, then continued. "These individuals put their trust in the one true God, someone they determined to be reliable and trustworthy. It was a faith that made sense and was fully rational. Of course, as C. S. Lewis said, you have to feed your faith.[6] I believe they did that and ended up building a robust and resilient faith that could withstand the times when they felt perplexed by the seeming absence of God."

"How did they feed their faith?"

"Through regular prayer, the study of Scripture, being part of a faith community, for example. And when you invest in your faith that way, it can sustain you even during those times when God seems distant.

"Sometimes when I talk to people who have walked away from faith, I ask them about their prayer life and their connection to a church, and there isn't anything there," he added. "Without that firm foundation, a person's faith can crumble during times when God seems particularly distant. I know in my own life that when God appears hidden, it's often at a time when I'm at a spiritual low."

A quote by Corrie ten Boom sprang to mind: "When a train goes through a tunnel and it gets dark, you don't throw away your ticket and jump off. You sit still and trust the engineer."[7] Her faith remained intact despite her painful circumstances during World War II because she knew that God could ultimately be trusted.

"Put Your House in Order"

I gestured toward Samples. "What about you personally—have you ever felt exasperated because God didn't make himself more apparent?"

"Well, the answer is yes," he said. "When I was forty-five years old, married with three children, I came home one day feeling sick. It turned out I had contracted a rare bacteria that resulted in a large lesion on my right lung and six brain abscess lesions. I remember the doctor telling me, 'What you have has a mortality rate of 80 percent.'"

My mouth dropped open. "I had no idea."

"Yeah, when the doctor gave me that percentage, it was like a cold breeze ran through my soul. I ended up going through a difficult period."

"I can only imagine."

"I remember being hospitalized and having lung surgery. Through it all, there certainly were times when God seemed present, and that was comforting. But then one night, my family and friends went home from the hospital and I couldn't sleep. I thought, *Lord, where are you? I'm in a tough spot.*"

"Did the silence of God threaten your faith?"

"Not in a serious way. As I began to think more clearly, I started to fall back on some things I had learned through the years."

"For instance?"

"I realized this experience of God's silence didn't invalidate the fact that I had encountered God before. And it certainly didn't rule out the solid argumentation that I had discovered about God's existence and the truth of Christianity. So, yeah, there were times when I thought, *Lord, where are you?* Admittedly, that can be scary. But when I fell back on the spiritual practices that I had nurtured through the years—prayer and worship, for example—the dark thoughts dissipated. Just reading the gospels raised my spirits."

"Were you concerned you might die?"

"I remember the doctor saying to me, 'Hey, put your house

in order.' I started by asking myself, *What do I really believe about life after death?* That prompted me to go through all of the evidence for the resurrection that I had researched through the years."

"Was that helpful?"

"No question, it really buoyed me. I realized that the evidence was sound when I first came across it, it remained sound, and I trusted that it would continue to be sound into the future."

"In the end, did this experience make you more sympathetic to people who wrestle with the silence of God?"

"Absolutely," he replied. "I can relate to what they're going through. And yet at the same time, can we really say that God has been hidden when the second person of the Trinity took on a human nature and entered into our world? I remember the theologian J. I. Packer saying that the incarnation is greater than anything in literature. I've found that just the practice of bringing that to mind has been an encouragement to me."

The Pitcher and the Catcher

One reason I sought out Samples was that he had written an article on the hiddenness of God in which he used an intriguing analogy from baseball.[8] As a former catcher who once aspired to the Major Leagues, Samples drew on his athletic background to look into the charge that God's hiddenness actually disproves his existence.

The atheist argument basically says that if there were a loving God, he would make himself so clearly known to humankind that no rational person could doubt his existence. But there are people who are open to believing in God and yet aren't convinced he's real. Therefore, this shows that a loving God doesn't actually exist.

Using the baseball metaphor, Samples likened God to the

pitcher and people to the catcher. Is there a problem with the pitcher—in other words, is God responsible for failing to send adequate evidence of his existence to humankind? Or is there a problem with the catcher—are there reasons why people aren't receiving the evidence of God's existence?

"Where do you think the problem lies?" I asked. "With God or with us?"

"From a biblical view, I would argue that there's a stronger case for the failure resting with the receiver rather than the sender," came Samples's reply. "At the forefront of Jewish and Christian religion is the idea that God has revealed himself. He does that through two books—the book of nature and the Bible. It seems that the book of nature buttresses the book of Scripture, and that the book of Scripture explains the book of nature."

"Define what you mean by the book of nature."

"The universe is like a repository of knowledge, so it's similar to a book. It doesn't have pages, of course, but you can get information or knowledge from it. We call this general revelation."

"And what is nature's essential message?"

"In the Old Testament, Psalm 19 reads, 'The heavens declare the glory of God; the skies proclaim the work of his hands. Day after day they pour forth speech; night after night they reveal knowledge.' In the Hebrew, this text indicates that the universe is continually pointing toward God's existence. It's perpetual; it hasn't stopped; it's going on today; and it will continue tomorrow. We can see that the heavens are glorious and complex, and this points toward a creator."

"What about the New Testament?"

"Romans 1:20 says that from the evidence of nature, we can discern the invisible qualities of God—for example, his power and divine nature. In fact, the verse says God's existence can be *clearly* seen by everyone, so that we are *without excuse*. This is a very powerful passage. And in Romans 2, we see that we have a conscience, which is held captive before a moral God."

He went on, "The problem comes because we're sinners. Our natural tendency is to rebel against God and to suppress the truth. The Greek here reveals that this suppression is like a pedal—we push it down, and the awareness of God pops it up, but we keep pushing it down again. So I would say that the problem is our own moral and spiritual obtuseness. One of the pernicious effects of sin is that it blinds people from seeing their spiritual and moral failings and their accountability before God."

I put up my hand to stop him. "However, atheists would say there are people who are truly open to believing in God. They seem neutral. They're willing to believe, yet they don't."

"But," interrupted Samples, "the Bible's insights into our human nature tell us that no one is really neutral. Nobody is totally without bias. We all have predispositions and presuppositions. As a sinner, apart from God's grace, our natural tendency is to deflect our moral responsibility before God. We don't want to be held accountable by him, so we suppress the truth about his existence.

"Our inclination is to turn the other way from him. It's not just that we're blind; it's our *willful* blindness. Consequently, I would challenge the idea that anyone is in a neutral position. We're not as detached and coolly objective as some intellectuals and atheists would like to think."

C-L-E-A-R Evidence for God

I asked, "Do you believe there's sufficient evidence of God's existence for the world to know that he's real?"

"I certainly do. There are cogent reasons for believing God exists and that Jesus is his unique Son. For example, we have the evidence from cosmology and the fine-tuning of the universe, and these arguments have been bolstered by modern science. And the moral argument is powerful. I can't dodge the fact that I have broken God's commandments and need God's forgiveness. We live in a moral universe—where did that come from? And then there's the historical evidence for the resurrection, which points to Jesus' divinity."

"How do you characterize the case for God?"

"It's cumulative, or as philosophers say, it's based on abductive reasoning. We see our world and ask what is the best explanation for it? I use letters from the word CLEAR to summarize it."

I gestured for him to unpack that assertion. "The C is for cosmos—we have a fine-tuned universe that had a beginning, and this points toward a creator," he said. "The L is for life—the Christian story has uncanny insights into our lives, our challenges, our longings, and our neediness. The E is for ethics—we live in an ethical world. There are universal moral laws and commands. Where do they come from? Evolution can't account for that. The A is for abstractions. These are invisible ideas. We can't have science without mathematics. We can't have philosophy without logic. Again, where do these come from? And the R is for religion—we all seem to be oriented toward religion, and Christianity provides a strong case that Jesus is the God we need."

I reflected for a moment before responding. "The Bible says if we seek God, we'll find him.[9] What about the person who says they've tried their best to sincerely seek God but haven't found him yet?"

"I would repeat the words of Jesus: keep seeking, asking, and knocking.[10] Just because you haven't found faith yet doesn't mean you never will," he said. "But I might also ask, 'What are your presuppositions? What would God have to do in order for you to accept him? What would you consider to be real evidence? Are there any subterranean reasons why you secretly don't want to find him?'

"And," he continued, "I'd quote French philosopher Blaise Pascal's advice to some of his friends: If you can't seem to have faith, why don't you do what people who have faith do? Why don't you pray? If there's no God, it's not going to hurt you. Why don't you open the Bible and read what religious people read? Why don't you go to church and see what's going on there? When you are around people who believe, who pray, and who are reading Scripture, who knows what benefits you might derive?"

Wrestling with God's Silence

Philosopher William Lane Craig has pointed out that God doesn't just want people to *know* he exists; rather, he wants people to come to him in a saving relationship and to love, trust, obey, and follow him. The Bible says that even the demons know that God exists, but they shudder rather than submit to him.[11] So even if God were to put a neon sign in the sky that read, "Jesus saves," on what basis should we believe that this would lead to greater love for God?

Said Craig, "We just don't really have any way of knowing that in a world of free creatures in which God's existence is as plain as the nose on your face, the number or the percentage of people who come to love him and experience his salvation is any greater than in the actual world."[12]

I read that quotation to Samples. "What's your reaction?" I asked.

"It's a persuasive point. We have to come to God on *his* terms, not ours. That means humility rather than pride; it means repentance rather than sinfulness; it means confession and submission. I wonder how many people who say they're open to God will only really come to him if they can do it on their own terms. Frankly, they want God to come to them rather than them coming to him."

I pointed out that there have been times in history when God has made his existence glaringly obvious, such as when he guided the Israelites through the wilderness as a pillar of cloud during the day and fire by night[13] and when he parted the Red Sea[14]—and yet even that didn't produce lasting heart change in people. Israel still fell into apostasy.

"Why should we think if he made his existence even more obvious today that people would react any differently?" I asked.

"That's a good point. To have faith, the mind has to obtain knowledge, but the will has to be engaged and the heart needs to trust. It's one thing to know some historical facts about Jesus; it's quite another to receive him as our forgiver and leader and to make a commitment of the will to follow him."

I said, "So when people ask why God couldn't make himself even more obvious, I guess we could reply, 'There have been times when he did that, and, frankly, people still walked the other way. Why should we think circumstances would be different today?'"

Samples nodded. "That's right. Our own Bible tells us that. We may think we'd react differently, but there's no assurance we would. Human nature is pretty consistent."

I turned in a different direction. "Maybe," I said, "the apparent silence of God can have some positive effects on us. For example, it may spur us into delving more deeply into Scripture, into praying with more fervency, and into pursuing God, as the psalmist says, 'as the deer pants for streams of water.'"[15]

"There's something to that," came his response. "I love recreation and vacations, but the things that have really changed my life for the positive are almost always the trials, difficulties, and problems I've encountered. Our struggles can lead us to deeper study and more honest and heartfelt prayers. Even when I've experienced challenges to my faith, it has caused me to look for God even harder. Romans 8:28 assures us that 'in all things God works for the good of those who love him, who have been called according to his purpose.'"

I opened my Bible and flipped to the book of Hebrews. "Interestingly, Hebrews 5:8 says even Jesus learned obedience through suffering. Why should we be any different?"

"Yes, Jesus suffered greatly, and we are his disciples. It's not something we may want to experience, but it comes with the territory. And the good news is that God can cause good to emerge from our struggles—a more profound faith, a more devout faith, a better tested faith, a faith that has been purified by the fire of doubt."

The Power of Self-Deception

I glanced at my notes. "We've covered a lot of territory," I said. "How would you summarize where we've come so far?"

Samples leaned forward. "God has provided sufficient evidence of his existence, but the problem lies with us. Humans have misused their freedom to rebel against God and—apart from receiving God's saving grace—they naturally suppress the truth of God and their moral responsibility before him. So biblically speaking, the denial of God's existence isn't because of God's absence or hiddenness, but rather it stems from a moral and spiritual obtuseness that has resulted from our fallen nature and spiritually resistant condition."[16]

I was reminded of writings by philosopher Douglas Groothuis, who talked about how self-deception can unwittingly blind people to the otherwise compelling evidence that God is real.

Wrote Groothuis, "The atheist or skeptic, having been exposed to general revelation sufficient to know there is a God, develops a false belief that God does not exist, since if God existed, one would need to humble oneself, be thankful, and worship God. Pride forbids this, and pride (or autonomy) is the essence of all sin."[17]

> *"The denial of God's existence isn't because of God's absence or hiddenness, but rather it stems from a moral and spiritual obtuseness that has resulted from our fallen nature and spiritually resistant condition."*

King David wrote about this in the Psalms: "In his pride the wicked man does not seek him; in all his thoughts there is no room for God."[18]

In analyzing the Bible's teachings, Rea said it's possible to conclude that "what passes for non-belief is really a kind of self-deception. Being an atheist is sort of like being an alcoholic in denial. You want so badly not to see the truth that you suppress it and convince yourself that things are how you want them to be. . . . Self-deception is a real phenomenon, and there is nothing implausible about the idea that people would prefer—indeed, would want very badly—for there to be no God."[19]

He cited the example of atheist philosopher Thomas Nagel, who conceded: "It is not just that I do not believe in God, and, naturally, hope that I'm right in my belief. It's that I hope there is no God! I do not want there to be a God. I do not want the universe to be like that."[20]

Groothuis said it was self-deception that led him down the path toward atheism as a young man, when he was exposed to the writings of Karl Marx, Sigmund Freud, and Nietzsche. "I wanted there to be no God, so I could be a god in a godless world," Groothuis said. "Often, it is we who are hiding from God and not God who is hiding from us."[21]

In the end, it was the book of nature that changed everything for Groothuis. "When I beheld the natural beauty of Colorado (particularly the Rocky Mountains), I felt defeated," he said. "I had a strong sense that God existed, despite my attempts at atheism."

The result: "My atheism ended up in a glorious defeat, because God cut through my self-deception and disclosed to me his saving truth and gracious love."[22]

Problems with the Pitcher?

There was one more facet of divine hiddenness that I wanted to explore. I returned to the analogy of the pitcher and catcher in baseball. "Another way of looking at this issue is to say that there's a catastrophic failure on the part of the sender, or pitcher—in other words, a problem with God himself," I said to Samples.

"Part of the problem with this idea is that we tend to anthropomorphize God and view him as just being a magnified version of us," Samples said. "But he's far more otherworldly than that. That means our encounters with God are going to involve some degree of mystery. We have to consider the possibility that he has reasons for his apparent silence that we just can't comprehend."

He added, "Christianity is a reasonable faith, but let's not forget it's still faith. The philosopher Michael Rea says it's possible there are things about God that make him appear silent, but it's not necessarily because something's wrong with him. Our own finitude might be at fault."[23]

I picked up a copy of my book *The Case for Faith* and flipped to a quote from philosopher J. P. Moreland: "God maintains a delicate balance between keeping his existence sufficiently evident so people will know he's there and yet hiding his presence enough so that people who want to choose to ignore him can do it. This way, their choice of destiny is really free."[24]

I read Moreland's words to Samples and then asked, "If God were to show himself more openly, could this have a negative impact on us? Might we be effectively coerced into submission? After all, the prophet Isaiah was totally undone when he caught a glimpse of God's glory."[25]

Samples replied by quoting Blaise Pascal: "There is enough light for those who desire only to see, and enough darkness for those of a contrary disposition."[26]

"That means for people who aren't really serious about encountering him, perhaps God chooses to be distant. For those who are sincerely looking for him, he might make himself more evident," Samples said. "Granted, Christians differ in their understanding of our freedom of the will, but nevertheless, I think there's some truth to this idea. It makes sense that God would modulate his existence in order to preserve people's volition and to allow them to consider seeking him."

In addressing this topic, Michael Rea used the analogy of the richest man in the world coming into the dating scene. "Wouldn't it be natural for him to want to be with someone who would love him for himself rather than for his resources?" Rea wrote. "Yet wouldn't it also be natural for him to worry that even the most virtuous of prospective dating partners would find it difficult to avoid having her judgment clouded by the prospect of living in unimaginable wealth? The worry wouldn't be that there would be anything coercive about his impressive circumstances; rather, it's that a certain kind of genuineness in a person's response to him is made vastly more difficult by those circumstances."

Now, said Rea, think of God. "God's resources and intrinsic nature are so incredibly impressive as to be not only overwhelmingly and unimaginably beautiful but also overwhelmingly and unimaginably *terrifying*. Viewed in this light, it is easy to suppose that God *must* hide from us if he wants to allow us to develop the right sort of non-self-interested love for him."[27]

Samples joined in with a key point. "Keep in mind," he said, "that God is omniscient. If that's true, can't we assume that he would know the right degree of revelation of himself so that the maximum number of people will come into a saving relationship with him?"

I pondered the observation. "That makes sense," I said.

Meeting God Face-to-Face

I wanted to end my discussion with Samples by returning to the anecdote I used to launch this topic—the story of Jon Steingard, the rock musician who said he lost his faith because of the hiddenness of God.

I pointed out that in a videotaped interview, Christian apologist Frank Turek said to Steingard, "I think the arguments we have for God are not negated by divine hiddenness. Because God is hidden doesn't mean that all the arguments don't work then." In reply, Steingard said, "Yeah, I agree with that."

"Isn't that the bottom line?" I said to Samples. "There are several arguments and lines of evidence that point to God's existence and the truth of Christianity, and the so-called silence of God doesn't wipe those away. They still stand. Isn't that something we need to keep in mind as we explore whether God is real?"

"No question about it," he said. "When I was going through that life-threatening health crisis, I would have loved to have had a close personal encounter with God—to have him tangibly appear to me, to have him hold my hand, to have him embrace me and reassure me. Who wouldn't? But that didn't happen.

"But what *did* happen," he continued, "is that I was able

to fall back on all the reasons for the existence of God that I had encountered in my years of study. God may at times appear hidden and he may seem silent, but that doesn't rule out these theistic arguments that have been around for centuries. And those things encouraged and sustained me when I was sick."

"Have you ever thought about what would have happened if you had died?" I asked.

Samples smiled. "That's the ironic part. If I had, then the hiddenness of God would have been solved for me forever, because Scripture tells me I would have encountered God face-to-face. Now, that may well be a metaphor, but it points to an encouraging truth: when a follower of Jesus passes from this world, they enter into an eternal existence where there's intimacy with God on a breathtaking level.

"We will enjoy him and revel in him and worship him and serve him forever in a joyful and exhilarating place called heaven. We'll experience him in a profoundly personal way. I've been longing for that my whole life—and because God is real, I have confidence it will come to pass."

> *"When a follower of Jesus passes from this world, they enter into an eternal existence where there's intimacy with God on a breathtaking level."*

Samples sighed. "And that, Lee, gives the hiddenness of God a whole different perspective."

CONCLUSION

Your Encounter with the Real God

*Heaven is a fairy story for people
who are afraid of the dark.*

**Theoretical physicist Stephen Hawking,
exclusive interview with *The Guardian***

*Atheism is a fairy story for those
who are afraid of the light.*

**Oxford mathematician John Lennox, address
at the National Parliamentary Prayer Breakfast
in London, England, June 25, 2013**

When Mary Jo Sharp was graduating from a public high school in Oregon, her music teacher surprised her by handing her a Bible. "When you go off to college, you're going to have hard questions," he said. "I hope you'll turn to this."

It turned out he was right. Raised in a thoroughly secular environment, Sharp did begin to ask pointed questions about the deeper meaning of life—and she found herself taken aback by the weighty and historical nature of the Bible. By her sophomore year in college, she had become a follower of Jesus.

But the hypocrisy she encountered among some Christians threatened to derail her faith. "What I found in the church was a bunch of superficially polite people who were very much lacking in personal introspection and self-discipline, theological depth, philosophical intelligence, and sacrificially loving friendships," she said.

She learned that this wasn't the place to process the issues that continued to plague her about her faith. "Whenever I would ask a difficult question about belief, I was quickly brushed aside or the subject was changed," she said. "Not surprisingly, I began to earnestly question my belief in God within the first decade of becoming a Christian."

Maybe, she mused, she had embraced her faith prematurely. "Perhaps my desire for an experience of beauty and goodness left me too open to finding something to fill a void," she said. "Perhaps I had believed before I understood what I was doing."

She began an exhaustive study of both Christianity and atheism—and, again, there were surprises. "When I decided to explore the arguments for atheism, I think I unrealistically expected the arguments to be smarter, sleeker, sexier. I also expected atheists to be more thoughtful, less authoritarian, and generally more relaxed in attitude," she said.

That's not what she found. "The atheist evangelists I encountered, specifically online, were haughty, arrogant, and belligerently dogmatic in their beliefs. Instead of actually arguing about the evidence, these people were more interested in making me look foolish or stupid while conversely making themselves appear thoughtful, studied, and sure."

As she delved deeper into the evidence that undergirded Christianity, she found herself increasingly impressed by the historical data for the resurrection of Jesus, as well as by the way objective moral values pointed toward a creator. In the end, she determined that the various arguments in favor of Christianity made the best sense of the universe in which she lived.

And the case for atheism? "As I explored the atheist argu-ments, they were not convincing, nor did they have any grounding for substantive and meaningful hope," she concluded. "I couldn't go back to atheism after studying the arguments for and against God's existence. It would have been intellectually dishonest."[1]

Sharp is an example of someone who made the effort to sift through the evidence with an open mind and come to a firm conclusion that truly satisfied her soul. Today, she helps others wrestle with faith issues as a professor of apologetics at Houston Christian University, where she teaches under the motto "Exploring the truth with love and logic."

"Why Would One Not Believe?"

"Has the jury reached a verdict?"

These words from the presiding judge mark the penultimate moment in a criminal or civil trial. After perhaps weeks or even months of testimony, exhibits, arguments, and instructions, the jurors return to the courtroom to announce their decision. The parties in the case hold their breath. Courtroom observers lean forward. Reporters grab a pen. Then comes the jury's decision— guilt or innocence has been determined.

Here's my question for you. After pondering the evidence for whether God is real, have you reached a personal verdict? Have the testimonies you've read, the facts you've digested, and the arguments you've considered led you to a conclusion about whether God is the product of legend, mythology, or wishful thinking—or is he a divine reality who can change your life and eternity?

Some may say a pragmatic approach is best. Oxford-trained anthropologist T. M. Luhrmann played with this idea in her book *When God Talks*.

If you could believe in God, why wouldn't you? There is good evidence that those who believe in a loving God have happier lives. Loneliness is bad for people in many different ways . . . and we know that people who believe in God are less lonely. We know that God is experienced in the brain as a social relationship. (Put someone in the scanner and ask them about God, and the same region of the brain lights up as when you ask them about a friend.) We know that those who go to church live longer and in greater health. . . . This God loves unconditionally; he forgives freely; he brings joy. Why would one not believe?[2]

Of course, nobody seriously advocates investing faith in something that's untrue just because some positive benefits might accrue. Said Oxford mathematics professor John Lennox, "Faith is not a leap in the dark; it's the exact opposite. It's a commitment based on evidence."[3]

I believe the preceding pages have laid out a persuasive case that Christianity is firmly rooted in reality. Think back for a few moments about the evidence and arguments we've investigated.

1. The Cosmos Requires a Creator

Virtually all scientists now agree that the universe and physical time itself had a beginning at some point in the past. This has led to what's known as the *kalam* cosmological argument, which says that whatever begins to exist has a cause; the universe began to exist; therefore, the universe has a cause behind it.

As Bill Craig mentioned in chapter 1, the famous atheist Kai Nielsen once said, "Suppose you suddenly hear a loud bang . . . and you ask me, 'What made that bang,' and I reply, 'Nothing, it just happened.' You would not accept that."[4] To which Craig responded that if there is obviously a cause for a little bang, doesn't it also make sense that there would be a cause for a big bang?[5]

Once-agnostic astronomer Robert Jastrow conceded that the essential elements of Christianity and modern cosmology are the same. "The chain of events leading to man commenced suddenly and sharply, at a definite moment in time, in a flash of light and energy," he said.[6]

Cosmologist Alexander Vilenkin of Tufts University is adamant. "With the proof now in place, cosmologists can no longer hide behind the possibility of a past-eternal universe," he said. "There is no escape: they have to face the problem of a cosmic beginning."[7]

What's "the problem"? For materialists who rule out the supernatural, the problem is that a beginning of the universe calls out for a cause being behind it—and, frankly, the best explanation for that cause is a personal creator, especially when combined with the next category of evidence.

2. The Universe Needs a Fine-Tuner

One of the most exciting discoveries of modern science is that the numbers that govern the operation of the universe are calibrated with mind-boggling precision so that life can exist. That is, the physics of the universe are finely tuned on a razor's edge in a way that defies the explanation that it's merely the result of chance. Rather, it's evidence for a creator. Combining the evidence for the universe's creation with the fine-tuning of the cosmos enables us to make several logical inferences about the creator's identity.

As physicist Michael Strauss told me, the creator must be transcendent, because he exists apart from his creation; he must be immaterial or spirit, because he existed before the physical world; he must be timeless or eternal, since he existed before physical time was created; he must be powerful, given the immense energy of the big bang; he must be smart, given the precision of the creation event; he must be personal, because a decision had to be made to create; he must be creative, given the beauty and complexity of the universe and life itself; he must be caring, because he so purposefully crafted a habitat for us; and the scientific principle of Occam's razor says there would be just one creator.[8]

All of those qualities—*transcendent, spirit, eternal, powerful, smart, personal, creative, caring, unique*—just so happen to match the description of the God of Christianity. In fact, Strauss said that since there is just one creator, that rules out polytheism, which claims there are many gods. Since the creator is separate from his creation, that rules out pantheism, which says everything is god. Since the universe is not cyclical, this violates the tenets of Eastern religions, and the big bang contradicts ancient religious assumptions that the universe is static.[9]

Skeptics have suggested that perhaps there is an infinite number of other universes, and if you were to spin the dials of physics in enough of them, sooner or later one universe would hit the cosmic lottery for life to exist—and that's us. But scientists have discounted this idea because it's untestable and lacks any physical corroboration.

Theoretical physicist Sabine Hossenfelder, an agnostic, branded this theory "a waste of time" from a scientific perspective.[10] Said Strauss, "If you want to believe in one of the multiverse theories, you basically need blind faith."[11]

A blunt assessment was offered by Harvard-trained astrophysicist John A. O'Keefe of NASA, considered "the godfather of modern astrogeology" and a recipient of the Goddard Space Flight Center's highest award. "If the universe had not been made with the most exacting precision we could never have come into existence," he said. "It is my view that these circumstances indicate the universe was created for man to live in."[12]

3. Our DNA Demands a Designer

Stephen C. Meyer, who earned his doctorate in origin-of-life biology at Cambridge University, pointed out that our DNA contains a vast storehouse of specific information. In fact, it comes in the form of a four-letter chemical alphabet that spells out the precise assembly instructions for all of the proteins out of which our bodies are made.

Meyer was able to rule out chance or blind evolutionary forces as explanations for this phenomenon; instead, he said that whenever we see information, there is *always* an intelligence behind it. "I believe the presence of information in the cell is best explained by the activity of an intelligent agent," he told me.[13]

Science writer George Sim Johnson made this observation: "Human DNA contains more organized information than the *Encyclopedia Britannica*. If the full text of the encyclopedia were to arrive in computer code from outer space, most people would regard this as proof of the existence of extraterrestrial intelligence. But when seen in nature, it is explained as the workings of random forces."[14]

Fazale Rana, who earned his doctorate in chemistry with an emphasis on biochemistry, agrees that the information content of DNA points toward God. "The harmony between the Bible's account of the origin of life and nature's record provides powerful evidence for the validity of the Christian faith," he said.[15]

4. Easter Showed That Jesus Is God

In a variety of ways, directly and indirectly, Jesus made transcendent, messianic, and divine claims about himself. Anyone, of course, can assert that they're God. However, if Jesus claimed to be divine, died, and then rose from the dead on the third day— well, that's pretty convincing evidence that he's telling the truth.

The idea that the resurrection is merely a spiritual metaphor, which somehow points to a vague rebirth of hope, is inconsistent with the historical record. N. T. Wright, former bishop of Durham in the Church of England and author of more than eighty books about Jesus, has made it clear that when the New Testament speaks of Jesus' resurrection, it's "talking about something that *actually* happened."

He added, "In the first century, the word for resurrection, the Greek word *anastasis*, was never about a vague sense of possibility or the rebirth of hope or anything like that. It was always about people who had been bodily dead now discovered to be bodily alive."[16]

What is the historical evidence for the resurrection? First, Jesus was truly dead after being executed. Even the *Journal of the American Medical Association*—a secular, peer-reviewed, scientific publication—carried an investigation into the crucifixion of Jesus that concluded, "Clearly, the weight of historical and medical evidence indicates that Jesus was dead [even] before the wound to his side was inflicted."[17]

Second, we have a report of the resurrection of Jesus, including names of eyewitnesses and groups of eyewitnesses— including five hundred people at once—that has been dated back by scholars to within *months* of his death. That kind of immediacy effectively rules out the possibility that the resurrection was the product of legendary development over time.

Third, even the opponents of Jesus implicitly admitted that his tomb was empty on the first Easter morning.

Fourth, we have nine ancient sources, inside and outside the New Testament, confirming and corroborating the conviction of the disciples that they encountered the risen Christ. That's an avalanche of historical data!

How strong is the evidence? Sir Lionel Luckhoo, once identified by the *Guinness Book of Records* as the most successful defense attorney in the world, spent years investigating the resurrection and reached this verdict: "I say unequivocally that the evidence for the resurrection of Jesus Christ is so overwhelming that it compels acceptance by proof which leaves absolutely no room for doubt."[18]

5. Experiencing God

Throughout history, people have reported having dramatic and transformative personal experiences they can only explain as coming from God. These include extraordinary dreams in which there is corroboration, such as people being told something verifiable in their dream that they otherwise could not have known.

Some of the most astounding experiences come in the form of miraculous answers to prayer. For example, a peer-reviewed medical journal published the case study of a woman who had been blind for more than a dozen years from an incurable condition. One night, her husband prayed, "O God! You can restore . . . eyesight tonight, Lord. I know you can do it! And I pray you will do it tonight." With that, his wife opened her eyes and saw her husband for the first time—and her eyesight has remained intact for nearly fifty years.[19]

Then there's the case I personally investigated, in which Barbara Snyder, on her deathbed from multiple sclerosis—curled up like a pretzel, virtually blind, kept alive by a breathing tube—heard the voice of God saying, "Get up, my child, and walk!" She did—and she was totally and instantaneously healed. Two of her physicians were so astounded by this miracle that they wrote about it in books. Barbara later married a pastor, and they subsequently ministered for decades at a small Wesleyan church in Virginia.[20]

In 2015, I commissioned a national survey disclosing that nearly two out of five US adults—and 78 percent of evangelical Christians—said they had at least one incident in their life that can only be attributed to a miracle of God.[21]

Philosopher Douglas Groothuis is among the scholars who believe that certain religious experiences can provide "considerable evidence for the existence of a personal and relational being who is the ground of these experiences."[22]

6. Which God Is Real?

Philosopher Chad Meister created an innovative apologetics pyramid that provides a visual illustration for how a systematic case can be made for Christianity, reasoning through the topics of truth, worldviews, theism, revelation, resurrection, and the gospel. Using logic, he was able to eliminate atheism and pantheism as being invalid worldviews, landing instead on theism— and finally on Christianity—as being the best-supported option.

Meister presented the so-called moral argument for God's existence. First, if there are objective moral values, then God exists. Objective moral values are precepts that are universally binding on all people at all times, whether they follow them or not. (Atheists generally deny that there's universal morality.) Second, we know that objective moral values *do* exist—for example, it's objectively evil to torture a baby for fun. Therefore, God exists.

"The moral argument is, in my estimation, the most powerful argument for God, and I have seen plenty of intellectual and spiritual seekers find God because of it," philosopher Paul Copan of Palm Beach Atlantic University said to me.[23]

Grappling with Objections

There are, of course, weighty questions that need to be considered. Peter Kreeft and Kenneth Samples provided insightful analysis of two of the biggest objections that skeptics raise—the existence of suffering in the world and God's apparent hiddenness. In the end, neither of those obstacles were able to overcome the other evidence that persuasively points toward the veracity of Christianity. In fact, I found the same was true for the eight top objections to Christianity that I investigated for my book *The Case for Faith.*[24]

When I was an atheist, I realized I would need to do more than raise random objections in order to cripple Christianity; I would have to come up with a nontheistic alternative that would better accommodate all of the facts I just listed. Yet atheism cannot credibly account for the big bang, the fine-tuning of the cosmos, the biological information inside our cells, the reality of objective moral values, and the historical data for Jesus' resurrection. The only hypothesis that explains them all is that there's a divine creator whose unique Son is Jesus of Nazareth.

There are, of course, numerous other lines of argument that buttress the case for God. In his book *Confident Faith*, apologist Mark Mittelberg goes through twenty arrows of evidence that point toward God being real and Christianity being true.[25] Philosopher Peter Kreeft and coauthor Ronald K. Tacelli lay out twenty arguments for God's existence in their book *Handbook of Christian Apologetics.*[26]

For example, secular scientists have failed to come up with any credible mechanism to account for how consciousness could have evolved naturalistically in humans. Consciousness, of course, is the locus of our introspection, volition, emotions, desires, memories, perceptions, and beliefs.

"How did evolution convert the water of biological tissue into the wine of consciousness?" asked philosopher Colin McGinn. "Consciousness seems like a radical novelty in the universe, not prefigured by the after-effects of the Big Bang, so how did it contrive to spring into being from what preceded it?"[27]

Even Darwinist philosopher Michael Ruse candidly conceded that "there is no scientific answer" to the consciousness issue.[28]

On the other hand, human consciousness makes sense if God is real. Cambridge-trained neuroscientist Sharon Dirckx told me, "The unembodied mind of God, which has always existed, gave rise to everything else. The Bible also says that human beings were made in God's image. Consequently, it makes sense to say that because God has a mind, we have a mind; because God thinks, we think; because God is conscious, so are we."[29]

Philosopher J. P. Moreland agrees. "Consciousness cannot be reduced merely to the physical brain," he told me in an interview. "This means the atheist creation story is inadequate and false. And yet there is an alternative explanation that makes sense of all the evidence: our consciousness came from a greater Consciousness."[30]

And, I would add, because God is a personal Being, not merely a collection of facts or the culmination of logical syllogisms, this means we can personally encounter him.

French philosopher Blaise Pascal put it powerfully in the seventeenth century: "The Christian's God does not consist merely of a God who is the author of mathematical truths, but the God of Abraham, Isaac, and Jacob. The God of the Christians is a God of love and consolation: he is a God who fills the soul and heart of those whom he possesses: he is a God who makes them inwardly aware of their wretchedness and his infinite mercy: who unites himself with them in the depths of their soul: who fills it with humility, joy, confidence, and love: who makes them incapable of having any other end but him."[31]

As compelling as the evidence for God might be, it's ultimately unsatisfying just to know a bunch of information *about* God; we need to personally meet and experience him. That's why the quest for the real God begins in the world of facts and evidence, logic and reasoning, philosophy and science, but it must not end there. If God is real, then the only appropriate ending is for us to have a personal relationship with him—one that has no ending.

"If the materialistic narrative is all there is, then we can throw meaning, purpose, and significance out the window," Dirckx said to me. "We're a blip on the landscape. The cosmos is billions of years old, and we appear in the last millisecond. We are utterly meaningless."

But if God is real, then this provides a firm foundation for our meaning. "We are created and loved by him. The reason all of us have a longing for eternity is that, indeed, we were made by God to live forever," Dirckx said. "God is relational, existing from eternity past as the Trinity. And so like him, we are relational beings. This means we can interact personally with God. He is someone to be encountered. He is a first-person experience, not a third-person observation."[32]

The Fallout from Atheism

When I was an atheist, I came to understand that disbelief in God is, in a sense, a metaphysical dead end, offering no transcendent meaning for life or hope for an existence beyond this world. Some skeptics have difficulty coping with this.

Said Staks Rosch in the *Huffington Post*, "Depression is a serious problem in the greater atheist community and far too often, that depression has led to suicide. This is something many of my fellow atheists often don't like to admit, but it is true."[33]

Research published in the *American Journal of Psychiatry* backs that up: "Religiously unaffiliated subjects had significantly more lifetime suicide attempts . . . than subjects who endorsed a religious affiliation. . . . Furthermore, subjects with no religious affiliation perceived fewer reasons for living."[34]

In contrast, Harvard University researchers released a study in 2020 documenting that attendance at religious services dramatically reduces death from suicide, drugs, and alcohol. Attending services at least once a week cut these so-called "deaths by despair" by 33 percent among men and a whopping 68 percent among women, compared to those who never attended services.[35]

My friend W. Mark Lanier, one of the most prominent attorneys in America and founder of the Lanier Theological Library in Houston, wrote a book called *Atheism on Trial* in which he summarized these implications of a worldview that denies the existence of God:

"1. Humans are sacks of chemicals, random remnants of cosmic stardust. 2. Parts of 'human' chemical sacks have electrical interactions called *thoughts*. 3. The electrical interactions in 'human' chemical sacks differ from the electric interactions in other animals. Deduction: There is nothing that exists that objectively sets 'right' and 'wrong.' Nothing in the universe dictates that some chemical/electrical interactions are inherently 'evil.' *Good, bad,* etc. are labels that stem from electrical interactions (thoughts) but are not based on anything beyond the ingrained electrical impulses of the 'human' chemical sacks. Implications: Some chemical sacks have electrical interactions that make them 'think' they are of more cosmic importance than another, but space dust is space dust."

Then Lanier contrasts that with a worldview based on a biblical God:

"1. Outside of the universe is an infinite, personal, and moral 'God' or Being responsible for the universe's existence. 2. Humans are unique among living beings, because people bear an imprint (image) of God, by being both moral and personal. 3. Humans exist to be in a personal relationship with God. 4. Humans do not measure up fully to God's morality, making a truly harmonious relationship impossible by itself. 5. Only God can provide a just mechanism to establish that personal relationship, all while maintaining and not compromising God's just and moral character. Deduction: 'Right' and 'wrong' have meaning, whether people accept it or not. They are defined by and rooted in the morality of God. Implications: People are not mere space dust. People have dignity and honor as beings bearing the image of God."[36]

University professor, bestselling author, and former agnostic Nancy R. Pearcey provided this perspective: "Christianity offers a genuine alternative to an empty, pointless cosmos. It says that we are not alone, that the universe is meaningful, that we do have intrinsic value, that sexuality has its own purpose or *telos*, that human community is real, and that there is objective truth, goodness, and beauty. Most of all, we are not the products of mindless chance but the creation of a loving Creator."[37]

What's particularly damning for atheism, in my view, is that it's insufficiently supported by the evidence of science, philosophy, and history. After spending two years investigating faith issues, I came to realize that to continue in my spiritual skepticism, these are the things I would need to believe:

- Nothing produces everything.
- Randomness produces fine-tuning.
- Non-life produces life.

- Chaos produces information.
- Unconsciousness produces consciousness.
- Non-reason produces reason.

What's more, I would need to ignore the compelling data that supports the resurrection of Jesus as being an actual event of history. Honestly, I didn't have enough faith to continue to be an atheist.

Conclusion: God Is Real

Ultimately, faith isn't about having perfect and complete answers to every possible spiritual issue. After all, we don't demand that level of conclusive proof in any other arena of life. The point is that we *do* have sufficient evidence about God on which to act. In the end, *that's* the issue.

Faith is about a choice, a step of the will, a decision to want to know God personally. It's humbly and vulnerably saying, "I believe. Please help me with my unbelief!"[38]

As the late philosopher Dallas Willard once told me, "It's the person who wants to know God that God reveals himself to."[39] Or as university professor Lynn Anderson said, "When you scratch below the surface, there's either a will to believe or there's a will not to believe. *That's* the core of it."[40]

> "Faith is about a choice, a step of the will, a decision to want to know God personally."

I was thankful I didn't have to throw out my intellect to become a Christian. But I *did* have to overcome my pride. I *did* have to drive a stake through the egoism and arrogance that threatened to hold me back. I *did* have to push past the self-interest and self-adulation that were keeping my heart shut tight from God.

To apply Willard's words to myself, the biggest issue was,

"What did I want?" Did I want to know God personally—to experience release from guilt, to live the way I was designed to live, to pursue his purposes for my life, to tap into his power for daily living, to commune with him in this life and for eternity in the next? If so, there was plenty of evidence on which to base a rational decision to say yes to him.

So that's what I did on the afternoon of November 8, 1981. In effect, I declared to God, "You win."

I wasn't sure what to do next until my wife pointed out a Bible verse that explained it with clarity. Says John 1:12, "Yet to all who did *receive* him, to those who *believed* in his name, he gave the right to *become* children of God" (italics added).

That verse embodies the formula of faith: Believe + Receive = Become. I *believed*, based on the evidence, that God is real and that Jesus is his unique Son, so I *received* his forgiveness through a heartfelt prayer in which I confessed my sinful behavior and turned to walk his path, and with that I *became* a child of God— for eternity.

Some people report having a rush of emotion at a moment like that. For me, it was different. *I felt the rush of reason.* And as a result, over time God transformed my character, morality, values, worldview, attitudes, priorities, and relationships—for the better.

So what's your conclusion? Which pathway is the evidence taking you down? Are you convinced God is real and that you can personally meet and experience him through Jesus? Or are you still in need of more evidence?

If you're uncertain about which direction to go, Welsh philosopher H. H. Price suggested what he called the Agnostic's Prayer: "O God, if there be a God, save my soul, if I have a soul." He called this "a devotional experiment," adding, "One must start somewhere, and how else is an intellectually honest man to start?"[41]

Actually, I'd suggest asking the God you're not sure exists to show himself to you through nature and Scripture—or any other way he chooses. You may want to repeat the twenty-word prayer I encouraged you to offer at the beginning of this journey: "God, if you open my eyes to who you really are, then I will open my life fully to you." Both the Old and New Testaments bring encouraging news—those who wholeheartedly seek God will find him.[42]

Once the evidence is in, remember that a good juror reaches a verdict. If you find in favor of God being real, then take the step I did by offering a heartfelt prayer of repentance and faith to receive his free gift of forgiveness and eternal life.

If you'll do this, the greatest adventure of your life will begin as you become a follower of the Nazarene who conquered death and the grave. Over time, you'll discover, as I have, that Jesus is the most glorious, the most beautiful, the most brilliant, the most loving, the most gracious, and the most forgiving Being in existence.

> "The greatest adventure of your life will begin as you become a follower of the Nazarene who conquered death and the grave."

He's kind, he's gentle, he's encouraging, he's patient, he's pure, he's joyful—and above all else, he's real. And he wants to adopt you as his son or daughter forever.

That, my friend, changes *everything*.

RECOMMENDED RESOURCES FOR FURTHER INVESTIGATION

Chapter 1: The Cosmos Requires a Creator

Craig, William Lane. *The* Kalam *Cosmological Argument*. Eugene, OR: Wipf and Stock, 2000.

———. *Reasonable Faith: Christian Truth and Apologetics*. Third edition. Wheaton, IL: Crossway, 2008.

Craig, William Lane, and Quentin Smith. *Theism, Atheism and Big Bang Cosmology*. New York: Oxford University Press, 1993.

Ross, Hugh. *Why the Universe Is the Way It Is*. Grand Rapids: Baker, 2008.

Strobel, Lee. *The Case for a Creator: A Journalist Investigates Scientific Evidence That Points toward God*. Grand Rapids: Zondervan, 2004.

Zweerink, Jeff. *Escaping the Beginning? Confronting Challenges to the Universe's Origin*. Covina, CA: Reasons to Believe, 2019.

Chapter 2: The Universe Needs a Fine-Tuner

Bussey, Peter. *Signposts to God: How Modern Physics and Astronomy Point the Way to Belief*. Downers Grove, IL: IVP Academic, 2016.

Dembski, William A. *Mere Creation: Science, Faith and Intelligent Design*. Downers Grove, IL: InterVarsity, 1998.

Denton, Michael. *The Miracle of Man: The Fine Tuning of Nature for Human Existence*. Seattle, WA: Discovery Institute, 2022.

Gonzalez, Guillermo, and Jay Wesley Richards. *The Privileged Planet: How Our Place in the Cosmos Is Designed for Discovery.* Washington, DC: Regnery, 2004.

Lewis, Geraint F., and Luke A. Barnes. *A Fortunate Universe: Life in a Finely Tuned Cosmos.* Cambridge, UK: Cambridge University Press, 2016.

Ross, Hugh. *Improbable Planet: How Earth Became Humanity's Home.* Grand Rapids: Baker, 2016.

———. *Designed to the Core.* Covina, CA: Reasons to Believe, 2022.

Strobel, Lee. *The Case for a Creator: A Journalist Investigates Scientific Evidence That Points toward God.* Grand Rapids: Zondervan, 2004.

Wallace, J. Warner. *God's Crime Scene: A Cold-Case Detective Examines the Evidence for a Divinely Created Universe.* Colorado Springs: Cook, 2015.

Ward, Peter, and Donald Brownlee. *Rare Earth: Why Complex Life Is Uncommon in the Universe.* New York: Copernicus, 2000.

Chapter 3: Our DNA Demands a Designer

Campbell, John Angus, and Stephen C. Meyer, eds. *Darwinism, Design, and Public Education.* East Lansing, MI: Michigan State University Press, 2003.

Laufmann, Steve, and Howard Glicksman. *Your Designed Body.* Seattle, WA: Discovery Institute, 2022.

Meyer, Stephen C. *Darwin's Doubt: The Explosive Origin of Animal Life and the Case for Intelligent Design.* New York: HarperOne, 2014.

———. *The Return of the God Hypothesis: Three Scientific Discoveries That Reveal the Mind behind the Universe.* New York: HarperOne, 2021.

———. *Signature in the Cell: DNA and the Evidence for Intelligent Design.* New York: HarperOne, 2010.

Ruse, Michael, and William Dembski. *Debating Design: From Darwin to DNA.* Cambridge, UK: Cambridge University Press, 2004.

Strobel, Lee. *The Case for a Creator: A Journalist Investigates Scientific Evidence That Points toward God.* Grand Rapids: Zondervan, 2004.

Woodward, Thomas. *Darwin Strikes Back: Defending the Science of Intelligent Design.* Grand Rapids: Baker, 2006.

Chapter 4: Easter Showed That Jesus Is God

Baggett, David, ed. *Did the Resurrection Happen? A Conversation with Gary Habermas and Antony Flew.* Downers Grove, IL: InterVarsity, 2009.

Copan, Paul, and Ronald K. Tacelli, eds. *Jesus' Resurrection: Fact or Figment? A Debate Between William Lane Craig and Gerd Lüdemann.* Downers Grove, IL: IVP Academic, 2000.

Craig, William Lane. *The Son Rises: Historical Evidence for the Resurrection of Jesus.* Eugene, OR: Wipf & Stock, 2000.

Habermas, Gary R., and Michael R. Licona. *The Case for the Resurrection of Jesus.* Grand Rapids: Kregel, 2004.

Johnston, Jeremiah. *Body of Proof.* Minneapolis: Bethany House, 2023.

Licona, Michael R. *The Resurrection of Jesus: A New Historiographical Approach.* Downers Grove, IL: IVP Academic, 2010.

Strobel, Lee. *The Case for Christ: A Journalist's Personal Investigation of the Evidence for Jesus.* Updated and Expanded Edition. Grand Rapids: Zondervan, 2016.

———. *In Defense of Jesus: Investigating Attacks on the Identity of Christ* (formerly *The Case for the Real Jesus*). Grand Rapids: Zondervan, 2016.

Swinburne, Richard. *The Resurrection of God Incarnate.* Oxford, UK: Clarendon, 2003.

Wallace, J. Warner. *Cold-Case Christianity: A Homicide Detective Investigates the Claims of the Gospel.* Colorado Springs: Cook, 2013.

Wright, N. T. *The Resurrection of the Son of God.* Minneapolis: Fortress, 2003.

Chapter 5: Experiencing God

Alston, William P. *Perceiving God: The Epistemology of Religious Experience.* Ithaca, NY: Cornell University Press, 1991.

Copan, Paul, and Paul K. Moser, eds. *The Rationality of Theism.* New York: Routledge, 2003.

Davis, Caroline Franks. *The Evidential Force of Religious Experience.* Oxford, UK: Clarendon, 1989.

Groothuis, Douglas. *Christian Apologetics: A Comprehensive Case for Biblical Faith.* Downers Grove, IL: IVP Academic, 2016.

Luhrmann, T. M. *When God Talks Back: Understanding the American Evangelical Relationship with God.* New York: Knopf, 2012.

Netland, Harold. *Religious Experience and the Knowledge of God: The Evidential Force of Divine Encounters.* Grand Rapids: Baker Academic, 2022.

Swinburne, Richard. *The Existence of God.* Second Edition. Oxford, UK: Clarendon, 2004.

Chapter 6: Which God Is Real?

On Truth

Beckwith, Francis, and Gregory Koukl. *Relativism: Feet Firmly Planted in Mid-Air.* Grand Rapids: Baker, 1998.

Groothuis, Douglas. *Truth Decay: Defending Christianity against the Challenges of Postmodernism.* Downers Grove, IL: InterVarsity, 2000.

On Worldviews

Lanier, W. Mark. *Religions on Trial: A Lawyer Examines Buddhism, Hinduism, Islam, and More*. Downers Grove, IL: InterVarsity, 2023.

Myers, Jeff, and David A. Noebel. *Understanding the Times: A Survey of Competing Worldviews*. Colorado Springs: Cook, 2015.

Nash, Ronald H. *Worldviews in Conflict: Choosing Christianity in a World of Ideas*. Grand Rapids: Zondervan, 1992.

Sire, James. *Naming the Elephant: Worldview as a Concept*. Downers Grove, IL: InterVarsity, 2004.

On Theism

Baggett, David, and Jerry Walls. *Good God: The Theistic Foundations of Morality*. New York: Oxford University Press, 2011.

Baggett, David, and Marybeth Baggett. *The Morals of the Story: Good News about a Good God*. Downers Grove, IL: IVP Academic, 2018.

Bowman, Robert M. Jr., and J. Ed Komoszewski. *Putting Jesus in His Place: The Case for the Deity of Christ*. Grand Rapids: Kregel, 2007.

Craig, William Lane. *Reasonable Faith: Christian Truth and Apologetics*. Third Edition. Wheaton, IL: Crossway, 2008.

Lanier, W. Mark. *Atheism on Trial: A Lawyer Examines the Case for Unbelief*. Downers Grove, IL: InterVarsity, 2022.

Samples, Ken. *Christianity Cross-Examined: Is it Rational, Relevant, and Good?* Covina, CA: Reasons to Believe, 2021.

Strobel, Lee. *The Case for a Creator: A Journalist Investigates Scientific Evidence That Points toward God*. Grand Rapids: Zondervan, 2004.

On Revelation

Blomberg, Craig L. *Can We Still Believe the Bible? An Evangelical Engagement with Contemporary Questions*. Grand Rapids: Brazos, 2014.

Cowan, Stephen B., and Terry L. Wilder. *In Defense of the Bible: A Comprehensive Apologetic for the Authority of Scripture.* Nashville: Broadman & Holman, 2013.

Köstenberger, Andreas J., Darrell L. Bock, and Josh D. Chatraw. *Truth in a Culture of Doubt: Engaging Skeptical Challenges to the Bible.* Nashville: B&H, 2014.

Morrow, Jonathan. *Questioning the Bible: 11 Major Challenges to the Bible's Authority.* Chicago: Moody, 2014.

Roberts, Mark D. *Can We Trust the Gospels? Investigating the Reliability of Matthew, Mark, Luke, and John.* Wheaton, IL: Crossway, 2007.

Williams, Peter J. *Can We Trust the Gospels?* Wheaton, IL: Crossway, 2018.

On Resurrection

Habermas, Gary R., and Michael R. Licona. *The Case for the Resurrection of Jesus.* Grand Rapids: Kregel, 2004.

Johnston, Jeremiah. *Body of Proof: The 7 Best Reasons to Believe in the Resurrection of Jesus—and Why It Matters Today.* Minneapolis: Bethany House, 2023.

Licona, Michael R. *The Resurrection of Jesus: A New Historiographical Approach.* Downers Grove, IL: InterVarsity, 2010.

Samples, Ken. *God Among Sages: Why Jesus Is Not Just Another Religious Leader.* Grand Rapids: Baker, 2017.

Strobel, Lee. *In Defense of Jesus: Investigating Attacks on the Identity of Christ.* Grand Rapids: Zondervan, 2007.

Wright, N. T. *The Resurrection of the Son of God.* Minneapolis: Fortress, 2003.

On the Gospel

McKnight, Scot. *The King Jesus Gospel: The Original Good News Revisited.* Revised Edition. Grand Rapids: Zondervan, 2016.

Mittelberg, Mark. *The Reason Why: Faith Makes Sense*. Carol
Stream, IL: Tyndale, 2011.

Strobel, Lee. *The Case for Grace: A Journalist Explores the Evidence
of Transformed Lives*. Grand Rapids: Zondervan, 2015.

Wright, N. T. *Simply Good News: Why the Gospel Is News and What
Makes It Good*. New York: HarperOne, 2015.

Chapter 7: Challenge #1: If God Is Real, Why Is There Suffering?

Dirckx, Sharon. *Why? Looking at God, Evil and Personal Suffering*.
Downers Grove, IL: IVP, 2021.

———. *Broken Planet: If There's a God, Then Why Are There Natural
Disasters and Diseases?* Downers Grove, IL: IVP, 2023.

Geisler, Norman. *If God, Why Evil? A New Way to Think about the
Question*. Minneapolis: Bethany House, 2011.

Jones, Clay. *Why Does God Allow Evil? Compelling Answers for Life's
Toughest Questions*. Eugene, OR: Harvest House, 2017.

Keller, Timothy. *Walking with God through Pain and Suffering*. New
York: Penguin, 2015.

Kreeft, Peter. *Making Sense Out of Suffering*. Ann Arbor, MI:
Servant, 1986.

Lewis, C. S. *The Problem of Pain*. Reprint Edition. New York:
HarperCollins, 2001.

Meister, Chad. *Evil: A Guide for the Perplexed*. Second Edition. New
York: Bloomsbury Academic, 2018.

Orr-Ewing, Amy. *Where is God in All the Suffering?* Charlotte, NC:
Good Book, 2020.

Palau, Luis. *Where Is God When Bad Things Happen? Finding Solace
in Times of Trouble*. New York: Doubleday, 1999.

Strobel, Lee. *The Case for Faith: A Journalist Investigates the Toughest
Objections to Christianity*. Updated and Expanded Edition.
Grand Rapids: Zondervan, 2021.

Wright, N. T. *Evil and the Justice of God.* Downers Grove, IL: InterVarsity, 2013.

Chapter 8: Challenge #2: If God Is Real, Why Is He So Hidden?

Burnett, Joel S. *Where Is God? Divine Absence in the Hebrew Bible.* Minneapolis, MN: Fortress, 2010.

Green, Adam, and Eleonore Stump, eds. *Hidden Divinity and Religious Belief: New Perspectives.* Cambridge, UK: Cambridge University Press, 2015.

Howard-Snyder, Daniel, and Paul K. Moser, eds. *Divine Hiddenness: New Essays.* Cambridge, UK: Cambridge University Press, 2001.

Rea, Michael C. *The Hiddenness of God.* Reprint Edition. Oxford, UK: Oxford University Press, 2021.

Samples, Kenneth Richard. *Christianity Cross-Examined: Is it Rational, Relevant, and Good?* Covina, CA: Reasons to Believe, 2021.

Schellenberg, J. L. *The Hiddenness Argument: Philosophy's New Challenge to Belief in God.* Reprint Edition. Oxford, UK: Oxford University Press, 2017.

GUIDE FOR REFLECTION AND GROUP DISCUSSION

To help with either your own reflection or your discussion with others, I put together the following questions that I hope will stimulate your thinking and conversation. This is not a Bible study. Rather, it's designed to aid you in further exploring the evidence, arguments, and perspectives presented in this book.

Regardless of where you find yourself on your spiritual journey, I hope this guide will help you analyze, understand, and personalize the points made by the experts I interviewed on the all-important topic, "Is God real?"

Introduction: Exploring Whether God Is Real

1. Using a scale with 0 representing ardent atheism, 5 representing the point of conversion, and 10 representing a life fully devoted to Jesus, what number best reflects your current status regarding Christianity? Why did you select that number? What would it take to prompt you to go to the next step?
2. More than two hundred times a second, around the clock, someone is asking an online search engine about God. What question would you ask about God if you knew he would give you an answer right now? Of all the possible questions in the universe, what motivated you to choose that one?
3. A survey showed that 44 percent of Americans are more open

to God today than before the COVID-19 pandemic. Is that true of you? Why or why not?

4. The book's introduction includes several brief accounts of people who have found or lost their faith in Christ. Which story did you most identify with? If you were to tell the story of your own spiritual journey in just one paragraph, what would you say?

5. Evolutionary biologist William Provine of Cornell University spelled out the implications to humankind if God is *not* real. Do you agree with his five points? How would the world look differently if we lived as though those five assertions were true?

6. Generation Z (those born between 1999 and 2015) is considered by some to be the first post-Christian generation in America. Why is the percentage of Christians lowest among this group and why do twice as many call themselves atheist as older adults? What societal or psychological factors might be at play?

7. Philosopher Douglas Groothuis said, "We all experience a deep sense of yearning or longing for something that the present natural world cannot fulfill—something transcendently glorious." Is that true for you? How so?

8. The introduction suggests that you say a prayer at the beginning of your quest to determine if God is real—something along the lines of, "God, if you open my eyes to who you really are, then I will open my life fully to you." Are you willing to do that? If not, what's holding you back? If you are open to praying it, how much confidence do you have that God will answer?

Chapter 1: The Cosmos Requires a Creator

1. As you look out at the vast array of stars in the sky on a dark night or examine the wonderous images of the cosmos captured by a space telescope, what emotions are evoked in you?

2. Astrophysicist C. J. Isham, described as Britain's greatest quantum gravity expert, said, "Perhaps the best argument . . . that the big bang supports theism is the obvious unease with which it is greeted by some atheist physicists." How might a scientist's worldview affect their willingness to follow the evidence where it leads?

3. How convincing is the first premise of the *kalam* cosmological argument—that whatever begins to exist has a cause behind it? Can you conceive of anything that has come into existence without some sort of cause? How well do you believe William Lane Craig responded to the possibility that the universe might have emerged, uncaused, from a sea of quantum energy?

4. The second premise of the *kalam* argument says that the universe began to exist. Do you think the evidence from mathematics and cosmology sufficiently supports the claim that the universe had a beginning at some point in the past? Why or why not?

5. The *kalam* argument says that if the two premises are true, then it's logical to conclude that the universe has a cause. Can you think of any alternative theory that would support another conclusion?

6. Craig explains several characteristics of the cause of the universe that can be deduced from the evidence: "A cause of space and time must be an uncaused, beginningless, timeless, spaceless, immaterial, personal being endowed with freedom of will and enormous power." How persuasive is his argument that the cause of the universe must be personal?

7. How do you assess the credibility of Bill Bryson's comment, "It seems impossible that you could get something from nothing, but the fact that once there was nothing and now there is a universe is evident proof that you can." Does this make sense to you? Why or why not?

Chapter 2: The Universe Needs a Fine-Tuner

1. According to an article in the *New York Times*, some physicists "feel it is their mission to find a mathematical explanation of nature that leaves nothing to chance or the whim of the creator." Physicist Robin Collins disagrees, saying, "We shouldn't shrink back from the God hypothesis if that's what the facts fit." Which position best reflects your attitude?

2. Collins said the evidence for the fine-tuning of the universe is widely regarded as "by far the most persuasive current argument for the existence of God." How do you personally assess the evidence? What facts seem most compelling?

3. Given the explanations by physicist Michael Strauss, do you think that the finely balanced parameters of physics could be the result of random happenstance? Why or why not?

4. Some scientists believe that an as-yet-undiscovered "Theory of Everything" could somehow require the parameters of physics to have exactly the values they do. Other scientists believe this would be even more evidence for a creator. Which position do you find most convincing and why?

5. Do you believe that ours is the only universe in existence, or can you imagine that some other universes also exist? What specific evidence prompts your belief? How do you assess the observation that even if multiple universes exist, an intelligently designed mechanism for creating them must exist?

6. Astronomer Hugh Ross points to several ways in which the ancient writings in the Bible reflect the findings of contemporary cosmology. He said, "Scripture speaks about the transcendent beginning of physical reality, including time itself (Genesis 1:1; John 1:3; Colossians 1:15–17; Hebrews 11:3); about continual cosmic expansion, or 'stretching out' (Job 9:8; Psalm 104:2; Isaiah 40:22, 45:12; Jeremiah 10:12); about

unchanging physical laws (Jeremiah 33:25), one of which is the pervasive law of decay (Ecclesiastes 1:3–11; Romans 8:20–22). These descriptions fly in the face of ancient, enduring, and prevailing assumptions about an eternal, static universe—until the twentieth century." How significant is Ross's observation?

7. The late John O'Keefe, a prominent pioneer in space research, said the evidence led him to conclude that "the universe was created for man to live in." Assume for a moment that he's right. What are three or four reasons why God might have been motivated to create the Earth and then populate it with creatures of his design, including humankind? What relevance do these reasons have for you personally?

8. Atheist Patrick Glynn cites the evidence from physics as providing one of the reasons why he came to believe in God. How persuasive must the evidence be for you to come to the same conclusion that God is real? How close does the evidence presented in the first two chapters—cosmology and physics—come to meeting that test?

Chapter 3: Our DNA Demands a Designer

1. Science writer George Sim Johnson made this observation: "Human DNA contains more organized information than the *Encyclopedia Britannica*. If the full text of the encyclopedia were to arrive in computer code from outer space, most people would regard this as proof of the existence of extraterrestrial intelligence. But when seen in nature, it is explained as the workings of random forces." What's your reaction to his reasoning?

2. If you were a teacher evaluating Stephen Meyer on how well he defended his thesis that DNA is best explained by an intelligent cause, what grade would you give him? What two or three reasons would you give in defending that grade?

3. While scientists are virtually unanimous in ruling out random chance for the origin of life, this theory is still prevalent in popular opinion. What's your assessment of the odds that life could have assembled by chance? Do you agree or disagree with Meyer's conclusion that believing in chance is like invoking a "naturalistic miracle"?

4. Bill Gates said that DNA is like a software program, only much more complex than anything we've ever devised. Based on the interview with Meyer, do you think this is a valid observation? Or is it a false analogy? What leads to your conclusion?

5. Meyer also critiqued two other scenarios—that natural selection or self-ordering tendencies could have been responsible for the origin of life. In light of his analysis, do you believe either of these possibilities has merit? Why or why not? What's your response to Meyer's assertion that only intelligent entities produce information—including the information spelled out in DNA's four-letter chemical alphabet?

6. Were you taught in school that life somehow emerged from a "prebiotic soup" of chemicals that supposedly existed on the primitive Earth? What was your reaction to the lack of evidence that this ever existed? Were you surprised? Dismayed? Perturbed? Why?

7. Biologist Michael Behe said that when he concludes that life is intelligently designed, some people "don't just disagree; many of them jump up and down and get red in the face." Why do you believe this issue generates so much controversy? Do you feel any kind of emotional investment in the matter? How so?

Chapter 4: Easter Showed That Jesus Is God

1. Theologians believe that without the resurrection of Jesus, there can be no Christianity. The apostle Paul wrote in

1 Corinthians 15:17 that if Jesus had not risen from the dead, "your faith is futile." Why is that? Why is the resurrection a nonnegotiable for Christians?

2. How would you respond to agnostic scholar Bart Ehrman's claim that "because historians can only establish what probably happened, and a miracle of this nature is highly improbable, the historian cannot say it probably occurred." Can historians legitimately investigate the resurrection? Historically speaking, what evidence would you look for? What facts from history would convince you that Jesus rose from the dead?

3. In making the case for Jesus' resurrection, historian Michael Licona used what his colleague Gary Habermas calls the "minimal facts approach." How would you describe that approach? Do you believe that credible conclusions can be reached by looking only at evidence that is strongly supported historically and that the vast majority of historians—including skeptics—accept as facts?

4. The first of the minimal facts is that Jesus was killed by crucifixion. Licona said Jesus' death on the cross is "as solid as anything in ancient history." After reading his evidence, how would you respond to someone who speculated that perhaps Jesus survived his crucifixion and was resuscitated by the cool, damp air of his tomb?

5. Licona's second fact is that the disciples believed that Jesus rose and appeared to them. He lists several historical sources in support of that conclusion. How would you evaluate the credibility of those sources? Did you find any of them unpersuasive? Which source did you find especially convincing?

6. Licona cites the conversion of the church persecutor Saul of Tarsus and the skeptic James, who was the half brother of Jesus, as evidence that they truly encountered the risen

Christ. However, people convert to other religions all the time. In your view, what makes these conversions particularly relevant? How much evidential weight do they carry? How would you answer William Lane Craig's question regarding the conversion of James: "What would it take to convince you that your brother is the Lord?"

7. Licona provides three reasons for believing the tomb of Jesus was empty: the Jerusalem factor, enemy attestation, and the criterion of embarrassment because women discovered the empty tomb. How would you rank these three points in terms of their persuasive power? Are they sufficient to convince you that Jesus' tomb was empty that first Easter morning? Why or why not?

8. Taken together, do you find the five minimal facts sufficient to establish that Jesus did indeed rise from the dead and thus prove he is the unique Son of God? In the end, which of the five facts carried the most weight for you? Why? What are some of the implications for the world if the resurrection is an actual event of history? What are some personal implications for your life?

Chapter 5: Experiencing God

1. Have you had an experience in your life that you can only attribute to the work of God? If so, describe the circumstances. How did this incident influence your faith?

2. What's your reaction to the "principle of credulity" proposed by Richard Swinburne and the "critical trust approach" of Harold Netland? Are they appropriate in determining whether religious experiences are real? Why or why not? Can you think of another test that should be used in evaluating these experiences?

3. It's understandable that a spiritual experience would have an impact on the individual who went through the event. But are you influenced by stories you hear about the experiences that other people went through? Do you tend to be skeptical or accepting of what they describe? Why?

4. Skeptics claim that religious experiences are the result of wish fulfillment. Does that make sense to you, or did you find Douglas Groothuis's assessment to be persuasive? How would you answer a skeptic who maintains that all religious experiences are somehow illegitimate?

5. How would you respond if a Mormon missionary encouraged you to read *The Book of Mormon* and see if you have a "burning in your breast"? What's the thinking behind your response?

6. The Bible contains assurances that followers of Christ will experience God in various ways—his comfort, his guidance, his calling on their life, his peace, and so forth. Describe times when you've benefited from these emotions. Are you confident they're from the Lord. Why?

7. Groothuis cautions that an experience from God isn't sufficient, by itself, to establish that God exists, but we should consider other avenues of evidence as well. Think about some of the evidence for God you've read so far in this book. What do you find most persuasive? The cosmological argument? The evidence of the universe's fine-tuning? The biological information found in every cell in our bodies? The historical data for the resurrection of Jesus? What makes this convincing to you?

Chapter 6: Which God Is Real?

1. As you began reading this chapter, how would you have classified yourself—as a hardcore skeptic, a moderate skeptic, a spiritually neutral person, a spiritual seeker, a believer in

Christ, or a strong and confident Christian? Did this chapter change where you fit along that continuum? In what way?

2. Chad Meister went through a period of doubting Christianity after he encountered credible people with conflicting beliefs. Have you ever doubted your faith? What happened? How did you process that experience? Did you come to any resolution?

3. Does Meister's apologetics pyramid make sense to you? Do you believe it covers the essential issues that need to be investigated? Which level of the pyramid was the most important for you and why?

4. Pontius Pilate famously asked, "What is truth?" How would you answer him? Is your answer different now than it would have been before you read the interview with Meister?

5. Meister gave three reasons for believing in God: the origin of the universe, the fine-tuning of the universe, and the existence of objective morality. In what ways do you find these arguments persuasive?

6. The Qur'an and the Bible make conflicting claims. How important is the *eyewitness* nature of the Christian claims? Is corroboration of Christianity from outside sources important to you? On a scale of one to ten, with one being absolute skepticism and ten being a belief that the Bible is trustworthy, where would you place yourself and why?

7. If Jesus was resurrected, it would be a miracle—but miracles are possible if God exists. Philosopher Richard Purtill described a miracle as an event brought about by the power of God that is a temporary exception to the ordinary course of nature for the purpose of showing that God has acted in history. Have you ever had an experience in your life that you can only describe as a miracle? If so, what happened? How did it affect you?

8. The top level of Meister's pyramid is the gospel. If someone asked you why Jesus died "for our sins," what would you say

to them? Does God's kingdom as Meister described it sound attractive to you? Are you confident at this point that God is real and that you will spend eternity with him? Please explain.

Chapter 7: Challenge #1: If God Is Real, Why Is There Suffering?

1. Have you personally encountered pain or suffering in your life that made you question the existence of a loving God? What were the circumstances? What emotions did you encounter? What are the various ways this had an impact on your spiritual outlook? Did you come to any resolution of this issue, or is this experience still an impediment in your faith journey?

2. Philosopher Peter Kreeft cites the biblical assurance that those who seek God will find him. Have you been sincerely seeking God? How so? What progress have you made? How confident are you that you will find God in the end?

3. Kreeft makes the startling comment that the existence of evil is evidence for God. How would you articulate his position on this? Do you find it credible? Why or why not?

4. Kreeft raises the question, "How is it possible that more than 90 percent of all the human beings who have ever lived—usually in far more painful circumstances than we—could believe in God?" How would you answer him?

5. I challenged Kreeft with a question about how Christians can believe that first, God exists; second, God is all-good; third, God is all-powerful; fourth, God is all-wise; and fifth, evil exists. I asked Kreeft how all of those statements could be true at the same time. How did he respond? Did you find his answers to be satisfactory? Where do you believe they fell short or succeeded?

6. Kreeft said God took the very worst thing that could ever happen in the universe—the death of the Son of God—and turned it into the very best thing that has ever happened in the universe—the opening of heaven to all who follow him. Do you find this helpful in considering the suffering in your life?

7. At one point, Kreeft made this observation: "The universe is a soul-making machine, and part of that process is learning, maturing, and growing through difficult and challenging and painful experiences. The point of our lives in this world isn't comfort, but rather training and preparation for eternity. Scripture tells us that even Jesus 'learned obedience through suffering'—and if that was true for him, why wouldn't it be even more true for us?" What is your response to his comment?

8. How did this interview impact your overall viewpoint about suffering? Kreeft pointed out that the existence of evil and pain doesn't negate the affirmative evidence that God is real. Do you believe that a person can logically conclude that God exists and still not have a fully satisfactory answer for why he allows suffering?

Chapter 8: Challenge #2: If God Is Real, Why Is He So Hidden?

1. Have you ever felt frustrated or exasperated because God has been silent when you've wanted to hear more personally from him? What were the circumstances?

2. Ken Samples uses the analogy of a baseball pitcher and catcher to analyze the issue of God's hiddenness. What was your initial thought? Is the silence of God the problem of the pitcher (him?), or the catcher (us)? Or both? Why do you think so?

3. In the past, there have been times when God has made his existence readily evident, such as when he parted the Red

Sea. Yet ancient Israel still fell back into apostasy. Do you think things would be any different if God made himself more apparent today? Why or why not?

4. The book of Romans says there is adequate evidence in nature for people to recognize that God exists, but we tend to suppress that truth and walk the other way. Do you believe that's true? Why do you think we have that tendency?

5. Might the apparent hiddenness of God actually have some positive effects on people? How so? Can you think of some circumstances in which this might be true?

6. Philosopher J. P. Moreland once told me, "God maintains a delicate balance between keeping his existence sufficiently evident so people will know he's there and yet hiding his presence enough so that people who want to choose to ignore him can do it. This way their choice of destiny is really free." What's your reaction to his statement?

7. Philosopher Michael Ray speculated that perhaps divine silence is an expression of God's preferred mode of interaction and that we shouldn't experience his silence as absence. Is that a cop-out, or do you think he makes a good point?

8. In God's omniscience, could it be that he knows exactly how much to make his presence known in order to bring the most people into a relationship with him? Why or why not?

Conclusion: Your Encounter with the Real God

1. Mary Jo Sharp experienced a crisis of faith when she met Christians who were hypocrites. Have you run into people who profess Christianity but act in ways Jesus would not endorse? How did you react? In what ways did this cause you to question your own beliefs? Have you found resolution to this issue?

2. Oxford-trained anthropologist T. N. Luhrmann talked about the positive effects that faith can have on our lives. How has your faith in God—or lack of it—affected your everyday life? Can you see a specific impact on your physical, emotional, or psychological health? How so?
3. The book's conclusion summarizes the affirmative evidence for Christianity that the book has covered. Which categories do you find the most compelling—the origin of the universe, fine-tuning of the cosmos, biological information, the resurrection, personal experiences with God, or the moral argument? Why are these the most significant for you?
4. Human consciousness is mentioned as another category of evidence that God is real. In what ways does consciousness support belief in a personal God? Do you find the existence of consciousness to be a compelling argument for God?
5. In my own spiritual journey, I came to realize that to continue in my atheism, I would need to believe that nothing produces everything, randomness produces fine-tuning, non-life produces life, chaos produces information, unconsciousness produces consciousness, and non-reason produces reason. Is that a fair assessment? Which of these would be the hardest for you to believe and why?
6. The late philosopher Dallas Willard once told me, "It's the person who wants to know God that God reveals himself to." Does that make sense to you? Applying Willard's words to yourself, what do *you* want? Do you have a will to believe or not? Describe your biggest spiritual desire.
7. John 1:12 contains a formula for faith: Believe + Receive = Become. If you don't yet believe that God is real and Jesus is his unique Son, why not pray the seeker's prayer: "God, if you open my eyes to who you really are, then I will open my life fully to you." What additional steps do you plan to take in

your quest for spiritual answers? How do you plan to continue pursuing the truth about God? (Two ideas: a book from the Recommended Resources list and a good local church.)

8. If you believe that God is real and Jesus is his Son who died for your sins, have you received his free gift of forgiveness and eternal life? If so, describe what happened. Was your experience more like a rush of emotion or a rush of reason? If you *haven't* taken that step, why not do it right now in a prayer of repentance and faith? What could you gain? If you take that step to receive God's grace, who will be the first person you tell and why?

ACKNOWLEDGMENTS

This book may have just one person listed as the author, but the project has actually been a unique team effort from the beginning. Mike Briggs and Angela Guzman from Zondervan noted the huge number of people who type the words *Is God real?* into online search engines and suggested I address this topic. The idea immediately resonated with me—and the end result is the book you're holding in your hands. Thanks to both of them for their insights and creativity!

As always, I'm indebted to the entire Zondervan crew, including Webster Younce, Paul Pastor, Dirk Buursma, Alicia Mey Kasen, and so many others in the editorial, marketing, sales, and production areas. I've done dozens of projects with Zondervan through the years, and it has been nothing but a pleasure to work with such a talented and committed team.

Thanks as well to my literary agent, Don Gates; my close friend and ministry partner Mark Mittelberg; and each of the scholars who allowed me to interview them. And, of course, my wife, Leslie, deserves a ton of credit for tolerating my quirky work hours and incessant travel.

Most of all, I'm grateful that God has given me another opportunity to tell the world about his love and grace. There's nothing I'd rather do than let everyone know that, yes, God *is* real—and you can know him personally, forever.

MEET LEE STROBEL

Atheist-turned-Christian Lee Strobel, the former award-winning legal editor of the *Chicago Tribune*, is a *New York Times* bestselling author of more than forty books and curricula that have sold fourteen million copies in total. He currently serves as founding director of the Lee Strobel Center for Evangelism and Applied Apologetics at Colorado Christian University.

Lee has been described in the *Washington Post* as "one of the evangelical community's most popular apologists." He was educated at the University of Missouri (Bachelor of Journalism degree) and Yale Law School (Master of Studies in Law degree). He was a journalist for fourteen years at *The Chicago Tribune* and other newspapers, winning Illinois's highest honors for both investigative reporting and public service journalism from United Press International.

After probing the evidence for Jesus for nearly two years, Lee became a Christian in 1981. He subsequently became a teaching pastor at three of America's largest churches and hosted the weekly national network TV program *Faith Under Fire*. In addition, he taught First Amendment law at Roosevelt University and was professor of Christian thought at Houston Baptist University.

In 2017, Lee's spiritual journey was depicted in an award-winning motion picture, *The Case for Christ*, which showed in theaters around the world. Lee won national awards for his books *The Case for Christ*, *The Case for Faith*, *The Case for a Creator*, and *The Case for Grace*. His most recent books are *The Case for Miracles* and *The Case for Heaven*. A documentary based on *The Case for Heaven* was shown in movie theaters nationwide in 2022.

Lee and Leslie have been married for more than fifty years. Their daughter, Alison Morrow, is a novelist and homeschooling expert, and their son, Kyle, earned a doctorate in theology and is a professor of spiritual theology at the Talbot School of Theology at Biola University. He has authored several academic and popular-level books.

NOTES

Introduction

1. See "Searching for God: How to Optimize Your Search Results for Biblical Accuracy," incmedia.org, https://incmedia.org /searching-for-god-how-to-optimize-your-search-results-for -biblical-accuracy, accessed June 24, 2023.
2. See Phillip E. Johnson, *Darwin on Trial*, 2nd ed. (Downers Grove, IL: InterVarsity, 1993), 126–27.
3. Cited in Lydia Saad and Zach Hrynowski, "How Many Americans Believe in God," Gallup, June 24, 2022, https://news .gallup.com/poll/268205/americans-believe-god.aspx.
4. Cited in David Kinnaman, "Rising Spiritual Openness in America," Barna Research, January 18, 2023, www.barna.com /research/rising-spiritual-openness.
5. Leonardo Blair, "Most Millennials Like Jesus and the Bible, but 30% Identify as LGBT: Study," *Christian Post*, November 4, 2021, www.christianpost.com/news/30-of-millennials-identify-as -lgbt.html. Millennials are identified in this study as those who were born between 1984–2002.
6. "Atheism Doubles among Generation Z," Barna Research, January 24, 2018, www.barna.com/research/atheism-doubles -among-generation-z.
7. See "Youth Behavior Survey: Data Summary and Trends Report, 2011–2021," Centers for Disease Control and Prevention, 2023, www.cdc.gov/healthyyouth/data/yrbs/pdf/YRBS_Data-Summary -Trends_Report2023_508.pdf, accessed June 24, 2023.
8. Greg Stier, "A Jesus Revolution Youth Group," Greg Stier.org, March 16, 2023, https://gregstier.org/a-Jesus-revolution-youth -group.
9. Stier, "Jesus Revolution."
10. Quoted in Adam MacInnis, "Study: Gen Z Wants to Know More about Jesus," *Christianity Today*, October 26, 2022, www

.christianitytoday.com/news/2022/october/gen-z-barna-research
-survey-christian-faith-jesus.html.

11. See John Blake, "Predictions about the Decline of Christianity in
America May Be Premature," CNN, April 8, 2023, www.cnn.com
/2023/04/08/us/christianity-decline-easter-blake-cec/index.html;
see also "Modeling the Future of Religion in America," Pew
Research Center, September 13, 2022, www.pewresearch.org
/religion/2022/09/13/modeling-the-future-of-religion-in-america.

12. Ricky Gervais, "Why I'm an Atheist," *Wall Street Journal*,
December 19, 2010, www.wsj.com/articles/BL-SEB-56643.

13. See Lee Strobel, *The Case for Miracles: A Journalist Investigates
Evidence for the Supernatural* (Grand Rapids: Zondervan, 2018),
39–46.

14. See Lee Strobel, *The Case for Faith: A Journalist Investigates
the Toughest Objections to Christianity*, rev. ed. (Grand Rapids:
Zondervan, 2021), 1–15, 297–98.

15. See Lee Strobel, *Finding the Real Jesus: A Guide for Curious
Christians and Skeptical Seekers* (Grand Rapids: Zondervan,
2008), 32–47. For an account of my full interview with Bruce
Metzger, who died in 2007, see Lee Strobel, *The Case for Christ:
A Journalist's Personal Investigation of the Evidence for Jesus*, rev.
ed. (Grand Rapids: Zondervan, 2016), 58–77.

16. Bart D. Ehrman, *God's Problem: How the Bible Fails to Answer
Our Most Important Question—Why We Suffer* (New York:
HarperOne, 2008), 3; see also Randy Alcorn, "A Case Study:
Bart Ehrman, a 'Christian' Who Lost His Faith," Eternal
Perspectives Ministry, April 15, 2020, www.epm.org/resources
/2020/Apr/15/case-study-bart-ehrman.

17. Alisa Childers, *Another Gospel? A Lifelong Christian Seeks Truth
in Response to Progressive Christianity* (Wheaton, IL: Tyndale
Elevate, 2020), 24.

18. Alisa Childers, "Why We Should Not Redeem
'Deconstruction,'" Gospel Coalition, February 18, 2022,
www.thegospelcoalition.org/article/redeem-reconstruction.

19. For some helpful insights into this phenomenon, see Joe Terrell, "Five Real Reasons Young People Are Deconstructing Their Faith," careynieuwhof.com, April 19, 2022, https://careynieuwhof .com/five-real-reasons-young-people-are-deconstructing-their -faith.

20. Sean McDowell and John Marriott, *Set Adrift: Deconstructing What You Believe without Sinking Your Faith* (Grand Rapids: Zondervan Reflective, 2023), xiv.

21. For the full story, see Strobel, *Case for Christ*.

22. Though I have a Master of Studies in Law (MSL) degree from Yale Law School, I am not an attorney. The MSL degree is for professionals who want to understand law but not practice it. For example, I wrote about law for the *Chicago Tribune*, authored a book on a landmark court case, and taught First Amendment law at Roosevelt University.

23. J. Warner Wallace, "How Jesus' Resurrection Changes Everything," *Decision*, April 1, 2021, https://decisionmagazine .com/j-warner-wallace-how-jesus-resurrection-changes -everything.

24. See J. Warner Wallace, *Cold-Case Christianity: A Homicide Detective Investigates the Claims of the Gospels* (Wheaton, IL: Cook, 2013); see also his *Person of Interest: Why Jesus Still Matters in a World That Rejects the Bible* (Grand Rapids: Zondervan Reflective, 2021).

25. See Lee Strobel, *The Case for Heaven: A Journalist Investigates Evidence for Life after Death* (Grand Rapids: Zondervan, 2021), 99–101.

26. Watch McWhirter tell his story ("Meth Addict to Worship Leader // My Testimony") on YouTube, www.youtube.com /watch?v=5MVGuez4VEk.

27. See Guillaume Bignon, *Confessions of a French Atheist: How God Hijacked My Quest to Disprove the Christian Faith* (Carol Stream, IL: Tyndale Momentum, 2022).

28. See Strobel, *Case for Christ*, 186–203.

29. Holly Ordway, *Not God's Type: A Rational Academic Finds a Radical Faith*, rev. ed. (Chicago: Moody, 2010).

30. See Lee Strobel, *The Case for Grace: A Journalist Explores the Evidence of Transformed Lives* (Grand Rapids: Zondervan, 2015), 107–22.

31. See Lee Strobel, *In Defense of Jesus: Investigating Attacks on the Identity of Christ* (Grand Rapids: Zondervan, 2007), 204–39.

32. See Thomas A. Tarrants, *Consumed by Hate, Redeemed by Love: How a Violent Klansman Became a Champion of Racial Reconciliation* (Nashville: Nelson, 2019).

33. Douglas Groothuis, *Christian Apologetics: A Comprehensive Case for Biblical Faith* (Downers Grove, IL: IVP Academic, 2011), 367–68.

34. Groothuis, *Christian Apologetics*, 368.

35. C. S. Lewis, *Mere Christianity* (1943; repr., New York: Macmillan, 1960), 120.

36. John Elek, "When Ronald McDonald Did Dirty Deeds," *The Guardian*, May 21, 2006, www.theguardian.com/books/2006/may/21/fiction.douglascoupland.

37. Douglas Coupland, *Life after God* (New York: Simon & Schuster, 1994), 359.

38. Hebrews 11:6.

39. John 4:14.

40. Cited in "Doubt and Faith: Top Reasons People Question Christianity," Barna Research, March 1, 2023, www.barna.com/research/doubt-faith.

Chapter 1: The Cosmos Requires a Creator

1. "Where Did Everything Come From?" *Discover* magazine, April 2002.

2. Genesis 1:1.

3. "And God said, 'Let there be light,' and there was light" (Genesis 1:3).

4. Bill Bryson, *A Short History of Nearly Everything* (New York: Broadway, 2003), 13.

5. Quoted in Robert Jastrow, *God and the Astronomers*, 2nd ed. (New York: Norton, 1992), 104.

6. All interviews in this book are edited for content, conciseness, and clarity.

Chapter 1: Interview with William Lane Craig, PhD, DTheol

1. Stuart C. Hackett, *The Resurrection of Theism*, 2nd ed. (Grand Rapids: Baker, 1982). Hackett died in 2012.

2. William Lane Craig and Quentin Smith, *Theism, Atheism, and Big Bang Cosmology* (Oxford, UK: Clarendon Press, 1993), 135.

3. Timothy Ferris, *The Whole Shebang: A State-of-the-Universe(s) Report* (New York: Touchstone, 1998), 265.

4. Brad Lemley and Larry Fink, "Guth's Grand Guess," *Discover*, April 2002, www.discovermagazine.com/the-sciences/guths -grand-guess.

5. I didn't intend to get into the biblical controversy over the age of the universe. My approach was to make the case for a Creator based on the conclusion of the vast majority of scientists that the universe is billions of years old.

6. Stephen Hawking and Roger Penrose, *The Nature of Space and Time* (Princeton, NJ: Princeton University Press, 1996), 20.

7. Kai Nielsen, *Reason and Practice: A Modern Introduction to Philosophy* (New York: Harper & Row, 1971), 48.

8. George H. Smith, *Atheism* (Amherst, NY: Prometheus, 1989), 239, italics in original.

9. For a summary of evidence for the resurrection, see Lee Strobel, *The Case for Easter: A Journalist Investigates the Evidence for the Resurrection* (Grand Rapids: Zondervan, 2004).

10. See William Lane Craig, "J. Howard Sobel on the Kalam Cosmological Argument," *Canadian Journal of Philosophy* 36

(2006): 565–84, www.reasonablefaith.org/writings/scholarly
-writings/the-existence-of-god/j.-howard-sobel-on-the-kalam
-cosmological-argument.

Chapter 2: The Universe Needs a Fine-Tuner

1. Geraint F. Lewis and Luke A. Barnes, *A Fortunate Universe: Life in a Finely Tuned Cosmos* (Cambridge, UK: Cambridge University Press, 2016), 291.
2. See "Christopher Hitchens Makes a Shocking Confession," YouTube, July 5, 2010, www.youtube.com/watch?v=E9TMwfkDwIY.
3. See Patrick Glynn, *God: The Evidence* (Rocklin, CA: Forum, 1997), 1–20.
4. Paul Davies, *The Mind of God: The Scientific Basis for a Rational World* (New York: Touchstone, 1992), 16, 232.

Chapter 2: Interview with Michael G. Strauss, PhD

1. William Lane Craig, *How Do We Know God Exists?* (Bellingham, WA: Lexham, 2022), 44.
2. Credit to Daniel Bakken, a Christian apologist who has a degree in physics.
3. Paul Davies, *The Edge of Infinity: Where the Universe Came From and How It Will End* (New York: Simon & Schuster, 1982), 90.
4. Hugh Ross, *The Creator and the Cosmos: How the Latest Scientific Discoveries Reveal God* (Colorado Springs: NavPress, 1995), 117.
5. Roger Penrose, *The Emperor's New Mind: Concerning Computers, Minds, and the Laws of Physics* (Oxford, UK: Oxford University Press, 1989), 344.
6. Paul Davies, *God and the New Physics* (New York: Simon & Schuster, 1983), 189.
7. Peter D. Ward and Donald Brownlee, *Rare Earth: Why Complex Life Is Uncommon in the Universe* (New York: Copernicus, 2000), 220; on the importance of plate tectonics, see pages 191–220.

8. See Hugh Ross, "Probability for Life on Earth," Reasons to Believe, April 1, 2004, www.reasons.org/articles/probability-for-life-on-earth; see also Hugh Ross, *Improbable Planet: How Earth Became Humanity's Home* (Grand Rapids: Baker, 2016).

9. Some planets being discovered by the James Webb Space Telescope are downright bizarre. For example, a Jupiter-like exoplanet called WASP-96b, located about 1,150 light years away from Earth, has such extreme heat and pressure that rock can condense in the air like water does on Earth, producing clouds made of sand (see Marina Koren, "There Is a Planet with Clouds Made of Sand," *The Atlantic*, July 19, 2022, www.theatlantic.com /science/archive/2022/07/james-webb-space-telescope-charts -exoplanets/670568).

10. See John D. Barrow and Frank J. Tipler, *The Anthropic Cosmological Principle* (Oxford, UK: Oxford University Press, 1996).

11. Lewis and Barnes, *Fortunate Universe*, 355.

12. Quoted in Lee Strobel, *The Case for Faith: A Journalist Investigates the Toughest Objections to Christianity*, rev. ed. (Grand Rapids: Zondervan, 2021), 78.

13. Quoted in Lee Strobel, *The Case for a Creator: A Journalist Investigates Scientific Evidence That Points toward God* (Grand Rapids: Zondervan, 2004), 136.

14. Quoted in Strobel, *Case for a Creator*, 137.

15. Lewis and Barnes, *Fortunate Universe*, endorsement in front of book.

16. John Horgan, "Cosmic Clowning: Stephen Hawking's 'New' Theory of Everything is the Same Old Crap," *Scientific American* blog post, September 13, 2010, https://blogs .scientificamerican.com/cross-check/cosmic-clowning-stephen -hawkings-new-theory-of-everything-is-the-same-old-crap.

17. Besides, Strauss added, even if it turned out the multiverse idea was true, it would actually support the case for a creator. Why? He explained, "Not only would the Borde-Guth-Vilenkin

theorem point toward a beginning that would need a creator, but the extra dimensions of string theory would require that any creator exist in multiple dimensions. That would mean he could easily perform miraculous acts in our four dimensions. In fact, a discovery of other universes or extra dimensions would, in some sense, increase the necessary magnitude of any creator. One could legitimately ask the question, 'How many universes would an infinite God create?'"

18. John Polkinghorne, *Science and Theology: An Introduction* (Minneapolis: Fortress, 1998), 38.

19. Richard Swinburne, *Is There a God?* (Oxford, UK: Oxford University Press, 1995), 68.

20. Quoted in Killian Fox, "Physicist Sabine Hossenfelder: 'There Are Quite a Few Areas Where Physics Blurs into Religion,'" *The Guardian*, November 26, 2022, www.theguardian.com/science /2022/nov/26/physicist-sabine-hossenfelder-there-are-quite-a-few -areas-where-physics-blurs-into-religion-multiverse.

21. Lewis and Barnes, *Fortunate Universe*, 241.

22. Lewis and Barnes, *Fortunate Universe*, 242.

23. John Leslie, *Universes* (New York: Routledge, 1989), 198.

24. Paul Copan, Tremper Longman III, Christopher L. Reese, and Michael G. Strauss, eds., *Dictionary of Christianity and Science* (Grand Rapids: Zondervan, 2017), 66.

25. "'For my thoughts are not your thoughts, neither are your ways my ways,' declares the LORD. 'As the heavens are higher than the earth, so are my ways higher than your ways and my thoughts than your thoughts'" (Isaiah 55:8–9).

Chapter 3: Our DNA Demands a Designer

1. Nicholas Wade, "A Revolution at 50; DNA Changed the World. Now What?" *New York Times*, February 25, 2003, www.nytimes .com/2003/02/25/science/a-revolution-at-50-dna-changed-the -world-now-what.html.

2. See Nancy Gibbs, "The Secret of Life," *Time*, February

17, 2003, https://content.time.com/time/subscriber/article
/0,33009,1004240,00.html.

3. Michael Denton, *Evolution: A Theory in Crisis*, 3rd ed.
   (Bethesda, MD: Adler & Adler, 2002), 334.

4. Denton, *Evolution*, 334.

5. Quoted in Larry Witham, *By Design: Science and the Search for
   God* (San Francisco: Encounter, 2003), 172.

Chapter 3: Interview with Stephen C. Meyer, PhD

1. Bernd-Olaf Küppers, *Information and the Origin of Life*
   (Cambridge, MA.: MIT Press, 1990), xviii.

2. Henry Quastler, *The Emergence of Biological Organization* (New
   Haven, CT: Yale University Press, 1964), 16.

3. Francis Darwin, *The Life and Letters of Charles Darwin* (New
   York: Appleton, 1887), 202.

4. See Denton, *Evolution*, 260.

5. Jim Brooks, *Origins of Life* (Hertfordshire, UK: Lion, 1985), 118.

6. Denton, *Evolution*, 261.

7. See Richard Dawkins, *Climbing Mount Improbable* (New York:
   Norton, 2016).

8. Theodosius G. Dobzhansky, "Discussion of G. Shramm's Paper,"
   in *The Origins of Prebiological Systems and of their Molecular
   Matrices*, ed. S. W. Fox (New York: Academic Press, 1965),
   309–15.

9. For a summary of other arguments against the "RNA first
   hypothesis," see "How Intelligent Is Intelligent Design: Stephen
   C. Meyer Replies," *First Things*, October 2000, www.firstthings
   .com/article/2000/10/how-intelligent-is-intelligent-design.

10. "Evolutionist Criticisms of the RNA World Conjecture:
    Quotable Quote by Cairns-Smith," Creation Ministries, https://
    creation.com/cairns-smith-detailed-criticisms-of-the-rna-world
    -hypothesis, accessed June 24, 2023.

11. Gerald F. Joyce, "RNA Evolution and the Origins of Life,"
    Nature 338 (March 1989): 217–24.

12. From an interview with Dean Kenyon in the documentary *Unlocking the Mystery of Life,* dir. Lad Allen (Ilustra Media and Focus on the Family, 2003). The documentary can be viewed on YouTube at www.youtube.com/watch?v=tzj8iXiVDT8.

13. See Michael Polanyi, "Life's Irreducible Structure: Live Mechanisms and Information in DNA Are Boundary Conditions with a Sequence of Boundaries above Them," *Science* 160, no. 3834 (June 1968): 1308–12.

14. Francis Crick, *Life Itself: Its Origin and Nature* (New York: Simon & Schuster, 1981), 88.

15. Robert Shapiro, *Origins: A Skeptic's Guide to the Creation of Life on Earth* (New York: Bantam, 1987), 189.

16. Fazale Rana, "Origin-of-Life Predictions Face Off: Evolution vs. Biblical Creation," Reasons to Believe, March 31, 2001, https://reasons.org/explore/publications/rtb-101/origin-of-life-predictions-face-off-evolution-vs-biblical-creation.

Chapter 4: Easter Showed That Jesus Is God

1. See Billy Hallowell, "Lee Strobel Details Conversation He Had with Hugh Hefner about God, Gospel," *Christian Post,* October 7, 2017, www.christianpost.com/news/lee-strobel-details-conversation-he-had-with-hugh-hefner-about-god-gospel.html.

2. 1 Corinthians 15:17.

3. For the ways Jesus made divine claims and fulfilled divine attributes, see Robert M. Bowman Jr. and J. Ed Komoszewski, *Putting Jesus in His Place: The Case for the Deity of Christ* (Grand Rapids: Kregel, 2007).

4. John 10:30.

5. The footnote for John 10:30 in the NET Bible says this verse reflects "a significant assertion with Trinitarian implications." According to the note, "the assertion is not that Jesus and the Father are one person, but one 'thing.' Identity of the two persons is not what is asserted, but essential unity (unity of essence)."

6. John 10:33.

7. John 19:7, italics added.

Chapter 4: Interview with Michael Licona, PhD

1. Gary R. Habermas and Michael R. Licona, *The Case for the Resurrection of Jesus* (Grand Rapids: Kregel, 2004), 1.

2. John Dominic Crossan, *Jesus: A Revolutionary Biography* (San Francisco: HarperSanFrancisco, 1991), 145.

3. James D. Tabor, *The Jesus Dynasty: The Hidden History of Jesus, His Royal Family, and the Birth of Christianity* (New York: Simon & Schuster, 2007), 230, italics in original.

4. Galatians 3:13, for example, connects Jesus' crucifixion with the Pentateuch, where the record reads that anyone who is hung on a tree is under God's curse (see Deuteronomy 21:23 ESV).

5. W. D. Edwards et al., "On the Physical Death of Jesus Christ," *Journal of the American Medical Association* 255, no. 11 (March 1986): 1455–63, https://jamanetwork.com/journals/jama/article-abstract/403315.

6. See: Acts 9:26–30; 15:1–35.

7. 1 Corinthians 15:3–7.

8. See Galatians 1:18.

9. Dean John Rodgers of Trinity Episcopal School for Ministry, quoted in Richard N. Ostling, "Who Was Jesus?" *Time*, August 15, 1988.

10. James D. G. Dunn, *Jesus Remembered*, vol. 1 of *Christianity in the Making* (Grand Rapids: Eerdmans, 2003), 825, italics in original.

11. "For example," Licona noted, "Paul says in Acts 13:36–38, in words very similar to what Peter reports in Acts 2, 'Now when David had served God's purpose in his own generation, he fell asleep; he was buried with his ancestors and his body decayed. But the one whom God raised from the dead did not see decay. Therefore, my friends, I want you to know that through Jesus the forgiveness of sins is proclaimed to you." Said Licona, "That's a

bold and forthright assertion. David's body decayed, but Jesus' didn't, because he was raised from the dead."

12. I said, "You'd admit, though, that the final verses in Mark, which describe the resurrection appearances, were not part of his original text." Licona replied, "Yes, I believe that's true. But still, Mark clearly knows of the resurrection appearances of Jesus. Mark predicts the resurrection in five places, and he reports the testimony of the angel to the resurrection, the empty tomb, and the imminent appearance of Jesus in Galilee. In fact, Mark's reference to Peter in Mark 16:7 may be the very same appearance reported in the creed I just mentioned. One more thing. Most scholars believe Mark is the earliest gospel, but we have an even earlier report about the resurrection—the 1 Corinthians 15 creed I mentioned. This clearly spells out various post-Easter appearances by Jesus—including his appearance to five hundred people."

13. See my interview with New Testament scholar Craig Blomberg in *The Case for Christ: A Journalist's Personal Investigation of the Evidence for Jesus*, rev. ed. (Grand Rapids: Zondervan, 2016), 35.

14. Said Licona, "As for Caesar Augustus, who is generally regarded as Rome's greatest emperor, there are five chief sources used by historians to write a history of his adulthood: a very brief funeral inscription, a source written between fifty and a hundred years after his death, and three sources written between a hundred and two hundred years after he died. So it's really remarkable that in the case of Jesus, we have four biographies that even liberals agree were written within thirty-five to sixty-five years after his execution."

15. 1 Clement 42:3 (translation by Gary Habermas and Michael Licona).

16. Polycarp's letter to the Philippians 9:2 (translation by Gary Habermas and Michael Licona).

17. Paula Fredriksen, *Jesus of Nazareth, King of the Jews* (New York: Vintage, 1999), 264.

18. See Acts 9; 22; 26; 1 Corinthians 9:1; 15:8.
19. See Mark 3:21, 31; 6:3–4; John 7:3–5.
20. Asked if there was any other evidence of the brothers' skepticism, Licona said, "At the crucifixion, to whom does Jesus entrust the care of his mother? Not to one of his half brothers, who would be the natural choice, but to John, who was a believer. Why on earth would he do that? I think the inference is very strong. If James or any of his brothers had been believers, they would have gotten the nod instead. So it's reasonable to conclude that none of them were believers, and Jesus was more concerned with his mother being entrusted into the hands of a spiritual brother."
21. "In fact," said Licona, "James may have been involved in passing along the 1 Corinthians 15 creed to Paul, in which case James would be personally endorsing what the creed reports about him."
22. See Acts 15:12–21; Galatians 1:19.
23. See Josephus (*Jewish Antiquities* 20:200); Hegesippus (quoted by Eusebius in *Ecclesiastical History* 2:23); Clement of Alexandria (quoted by Eusebius in *Ecclesiastical History* 2:1, 23).
24. Some skeptics have said the reason Jesus' tomb was empty was because his body was never in it. They say the Romans didn't allow for the burial of crucifixion victims and therefore Jesus' body was thrown in a pit for the dogs to consume. However, eminent New Testament scholar Craig Evans wrote, "It is simply erroneous to assert that the Romans did not permit the burial of the executed, including the crucified. The gospel narratives are completely in step with Jewish practice, which Roman authorities during peacetime respected" ("Getting the Burial Traditions and Evidences Right," in *How God Became Jesus: The Real Origins of Belief in Jesus' Divine Nature*, ed. Michael F. Bird et al. [Grand Rapids: Zondervan, 2014], 89). Also, atheist-detective-turned-Christian-apologist J. Warner Wallace pointed out that an ossuary containing the remains of a crucifixion victim was discovered in 1968, with part of an iron spike still in

his heel bone—evidence that at least some crucifixion victims were buried (see Lee Strobel, *The Case for Miracles: A Journalist Investigates Evidence for the Supernatural* [Grand Rapids: Zondervan, 2018], 189–210).

25. Acts 2:32.

26. William Ward, *Christianity: A Historical Religion?* (Valley Forge, PA: Judson, 1972), 93–94.

27. According to the late psychologist Gary Collins, a university professor for more than two decades, the author of two dozen books on psychology, and the president of a national association of psychologists and counselors, "Hallucinations are individual occurrences. By their very nature only one person can see a given hallucination at a time. They certainly aren't something which can be seen by a group of people. Neither is it possible that one person could somehow induce a hallucination in somebody else. Since a hallucination exists only in the subjective, personal sense, it is obvious that others cannot witness it" (quoted in Strobel, *Case for Christ*, 238).

28. In addition, I asked Licona if something more subtle could have been at play—groupthink, where suggestible people are influenced by others into believing they had seen something they didn't really see. Said Licona, "At best, this only would account for the belief of the disciples that they had seen the risen Jesus. It would not account for the empty tomb because then the body should still be in there. It would not account for the conversion of Paul because it's unlikely an opponent like him would be susceptible to groupthink. Same with the skeptic James."

29. Tryggve N. D. Mettinger, *The Riddle of Resurrection: "Dying and Rising Gods" in the Ancient Near East* (Stockholm: Almqvist & Wicksell, 2001), 221.

30. Mettinger, *Riddle of Resurrection*, 221.

31. Mettinger, *Riddle of Resurrection*, 221.

32. Marcus J. Borg and N. T. Wright, *The Meaning of Jesus: Two Visions* (San Francisco: HarperSanFrancisco, 1999), 124–25.

33. N. T. Wright, *The Resurrection of the Son of God* (Minneapolis: Fortress, 2003), 718.

Chapter 5: Experiencing God

1. See Lee Strobel and Mark Mittelberg, *The Unexpected Adventure: Taking Everyday Risks to Talk with People about Jesus* (Grand Rapids: Zondervan, 2009), 272–74.

2. See Mark Mittelberg, *Confident Faith: Building a Firm Foundation for Your Beliefs* (Carol Stream, IL: Tyndale, 2013), 155–57.

3. See Luke 14:15–24.

4. Nabeel Qureshi, *Seeking Allah, Finding Jesus: A Devout Muslim Encounters Christianity* (Grand Rapids: Zondervan, 2014). See Lee Strobel, *The Case for Miracles: A Journalist Investigates Evidence for the Supernatural* (Grand Rapids: Zondervan, 2018), 139–41.

5. Cited in Tom Doyle, *Dreams and Visions: Is Jesus Awakening the Muslim World?* (Nashville: Nelson, 2012), 127.

6. Tyler Huckabee, "How M. I. A. Found Jesus," *Relevant*, September 21, 2022, https://relevantmagazine.com/magazine /how-m-i-a-found-jesus, italics in original.

7. Lee Strobel, "Does Science Support Miracles? New Study Documents a Blind Woman's Healing," *The Stream*, May 16, 2020, https://stream.org/does-science-support-miracles-new-study -documents-a-blind-womans-healing. See also Clarissa Romez et al., "Case Report of Instantaneous Resolution of Juvenile Macular Degeneration Blindness after Proximal Intercessory Prayer," *Explore* 17, no. 1 (January–February 2021), www .sciencedirect.com/science/article/pii/S1550830720300926. For another miracle documented in a medical journal, see Clarissa Romez et al., "Case Report of Gastroparesis Healing: 16 Years of a Chronic Syndrome Resolved after Proximal Intercessory

Prayer," *Complementary Therapies in Medicine* 43 (April 2019), https://doi.org/10.1016/j.ctim.2019.03.004.

8. A random representative sample of one thousand US adults completed this questionnaire. The sample error is +/-3.1 percentage points at the 95 percent confidence level. The response rate was 55 percent. The research was conducted in 2015.

9. Dallas Willard, *Hearing God: Developing a Conversational Relationship with God* (Downers Grove, IL: InterVarsity, 2012), 21.

10. T. M. Luhrmann, *When God Talks Back: Understanding the American Evangelical Relationship with God* (New York: Knopf, 2012), xi, xv.

11. Luhrmann, *When God Talks Back*, xx. The study found that 23 percent of Americans call themselves charismatic or Pentecostal, or they speak in tongues at least several times a year (Pew Research Center, 2006).

12. Quoted in Naomi Reese, "The Evidential Value of Religious Experience: An Interview with Harold Netland," *Worldview Bulletin*, March 16, 2022, https://worldviewbulletin.substack.com /p/the-evidential-value-of-religious.

13. Harold Netland, *Religious Experience and the Knowledge of God: The Evidential Force of Divine Encounters* (Grand Rapids: Baker Academic, 2022), 3.

14. Quoted in Randy Alcorn, "Can Cancer Be God's Servant?" Eternal Perspective Ministries, December 19, 2022, www.epm .org/blog/2022/Dec/19/cancer-servant, italics in original.

15. Douglas Groothuis, *Christian Apologetics: A Comprehensive Case for Biblical Faith* (Downers Grove, IL: IVP Academic, 2011), 388.

Chapter 5: Interview with Douglas Groothuis, PhD

1. See Strobel, *Case for Miracles*, 235–53.

2. See Douglas Groothuis, *Walking through Twilight: A Wife's Illness—A Philosopher's Lament* (Downers Grove, IL: InterVarsity, 2017).

3. "So God created mankind in his own image, in the image of God he created them; male and female he created them" (Genesis 1:27).

4. See Francis A. Schaeffer, *Escape from Reason* (Downers Grove, IL: IVP Classics, 2006), 37.

5. See Isaiah 6.

6. "The thief comes only to steal and kill and destroy. I came that they may have life and have it abundantly" (John 10:10 ESV).

7. See Galatians 5:22–23 (ESV).

8. "Dear friends, do not believe every spirit, but test the spirits to see whether they are from God, because many false prophets have gone out into the world" (1 John 4:1).

9. See Rudolf Otto, *The Idea of the Holy*, 2nd ed. (New York: Oxford University Press, 1958).

10. See Richard Swinburne, *The Existence of God*, 2nd ed. (New York: Oxford University Press 2004), 303.

11. See Swinburne, *Existence of God*, 322–24.

12. See Strobel, *Case for Miracles*, 146–48.

13. Sigmund Freud, *The Future of an Illusion* (Garden City, NY: Anchor, 1961), 49.

14. Hans Küng, *Does God Exist? An Answer for Today*, trans. Edward Quinn (1980; repr., Eugene, OR: Wipf and Stock, 2006), 301.

15. See Matthew 5:22.

16. See Paul Vitz, *Faith of the Fatherless: The Psychology of Atheism* (Dallas, TX: Spence, 1999).

17. Said C. S. Lewis, "When I was an atheist I had to try to persuade myself that most of the human race have always been wrong about the question that mattered to them most" (*Mere Christianity* [1943; repr., New York: Macmillan, 1960], 43).

Chapter 6: Interview with Chad V. Meister, PhD

1. Chad Meister, *Building Belief: Constructing Faith from the Ground Up* (Grand Rapids: Baker, 2006).

2. John 18:38.

3. See Edith Hamilton and Huntington Cairns, eds., *The Collected Dialogues of Plato* (Princeton, NJ: Princeton University Press, 1989), 262E-263D.

4. See Jonathan Barnes, ed., *The Complete Works of Aristotle*, rev. ed. (Princeton, NJ: Princeton University Press, 1984), 4.1011b25–27. Meister wrote, "Richard Kirkham notes that Plato, in the *Sophist*, is presenting a correspondence theory of truth—possibly correspondence as congruence—and that Aristotle is here presenting the earliest correspondence as correlation theory" (Meister, *Building Belief*, 201). See also Richard L. Kirkham, *Theories of Truth: A Critical Introduction* (Cambridge, MA: MIT Press, 1992), 119–40.

5. "The Law of non-contradiction is one of the basic laws in classical logic. It states that something cannot be both true and not true at the same time when dealing with the same context. For example, the chair in my living room, right now, cannot be made of wood and not made of wood at the same time" ("Law of Non-Contradiction," CARM, https://carm.org/dictionary/law-of-non-contradiction, accessed June 24, 2023).

6. John Stackhouse, *Humble Apologetics: Defending the Faith Today* (New York: Oxford University Press, 2002), 95.

7. Carl Sagan, in the Public Television Broadcasting series *Cosmos* (1980).

8. See William Lane Craig and Walter Sinnott-Armstrong, *God? A Debate between a Christian and an Atheist* (New York: Oxford University Press, 2004), 32–36.

9. See Richard Dawkins, *The Selfish Gene*, rev. ed. (New York: Oxford University Press, 2006), xxi.

10. Mary Baker Eddy, *Science and Health with Key to the Scriptures* (Boston: First Church of Christ, Scientist, 1934), 480.

11. Michael Ruse and Edward O. Wilson, "The Evolution of Ethics," in *Philosophy of Biology*, ed. David L. Hull and Michael Ruse (New York: Macmillan, 1989), 316.

12. Jean-Paul Sartre (1905–1980) made this comment in a lecture

given in 1946 (see Walter Kaufman, ed., *Existentialism from Dostoyevsky to Sartre* (New York: Plume, 1975).

13. See Stephen G. Michaud and Hugh Aynesworth, *Ted Bundy: Conversations with a Killer* (London, UK: Mirror Books, 2019).

14. "We know that suffering produces perseverance; perseverance, character; and character, hope" (Romans 5:3–4).

15. See Augustine, *On the Free Choice of the Will*, trans. Thomas Williams (Indianapolis: Hackett, 1993). Meister notes that Augustine (354–430) derived his argument from the *Enneads*, written by the Neoplatonic philosopher Plotinus (ca. 205–270 BC).

16. C. S. Lewis, *The Problem of Pain* (New York: Macmillan, 1962), 93.

17. William Lane Craig made this observation in Lee Strobel, *The Case for Faith: A Journalist Investigates the Toughest Objections to Christianity*, rev. ed. (Grand Rapids: Zondervan, 2021), 88.

18. Michael Ruse, *The Darwinian Paradigm: Essays on Its History, Philosophy, and Religious Implications* (New York: Routledge, 1989), 262, 269.

19. See Strobel, *Case for Faith*, 88–90.

20. Personal email to author, dated December 12, 2022. Copan is the Pledger Family Chair of Philosophy and Ethics and professor in the MA philosophy of religion program at Palm Beach Atlantic University in West Palm Beach, Florida.

21. See Lee Strobel, *In Defense of Jesus: Investigating Attacks on the Identity of Christ* (Grand Rapids: Zondervan, 2007), 68–105.

22. See Luke 1:1–4.

23. See 2 Peter 1:16.

24. See 1 Corinthians 15:3–8.

25. Historian Edwin Yamauchi told me that even if we didn't have the New Testament or any other Christian writings, we would know the following about Jesus from ancient non-Christian sources: "First, Jesus was a Jewish teacher; second, many people believed that he performed healings and exorcisms; third, some

people believed he was the Messiah; fourth, he was rejected by the Jewish leaders; fifth, he was crucified under Pontius Pilate in the reign of Tiberius; sixth, despite this shameful death, his followers, who believed he was still alive, spread beyond Palestine so that there were multitudes of them in Rome by AD 64; and seventh, all kinds of people from the cities and countryside—men and women, slave and free—worshiped him as God" (Lee Strobel, *The Case for Christ: A Journalist's Personal Investigation of the Evidence for Jesus*, rev. ed. [Grand Rapids: Zondervan, 2016], 93).

26. Jesus made this claim in John 10:30.
27. Quoted in Strobel, *Case for Christ*, 275.
28. See Galatians 5:22–23 ESV.

Chapter 7: Challenge #1: If God Is Real, Why Is There Suffering?

1. Sheldon Vanauken, foreword to Peter Kreeft, *Making Sense Out of Suffering* (Ann Arbor, MI: Servant, 1986), viii.
2. Philip Yancey, *Where Is God When It Hurts?*, rev. ed. (Grand Rapids: Zondervan, 1990), 21, quoting novelist Peter De Vries.
3. OmniPoll, conducted by the Barna Group (January 1999).
4. This was asked by 17 percent of those who offered a question.

Chapter 7: Interview with Peter John Kreeft, PhD

1. For my full interview with Charles Templeton, see Lee Strobel, *The Case for Faith: A Journalist Investigates the Toughest Objections to Christianity*, rev. ed. (Grand Rapids: Zondervan, 2021), 1–15.
2. Matthew 7:7.
3. See Peter Kreeft and Ronald K. Tacelli, *Handbook of Christian Apologetics: Hundreds of Answers to Crucial Questions* (Downers Grove, IL: IVP Academic, 1994), 48–88.
4. C. S. Lewis, *The Problem of Pain* (New York: Macmillan, 1962), 15.
5. Romans 5:3–4.

6. "Son though he was, he learned obedience from what he suffered" (Hebrews 5:8).

7. "The Lord is not slow in keeping his promise, as some understand slowness. Instead he is patient with you, not wanting anyone to perish, but everyone to come to repentance" (2 Peter 3:9).

8. Lewis, *Problem of Pain*, 93.

9. Matthew 9:12–13.

10. Jeremiah 6:13.

11. Isaiah 64:6.

12. See C. S. Lewis, *Mere Christianity* (1943; repr., New York: Macmillan, 1960), 59.

13. Augustine, *Enchiridion* xi.

14. See Matthew 10:29, 31 (Templeton's translation).

15. Charles Templeton, *Farewell to God: My Reasons for Rejecting the Christian Faith* (Toronto: McClelland & Stewart, 1996), 201.

16. See 2 Corinthians 4:17.

17. Adapted from Teresa of Ávila, *The Way of Perfection*, chap. 40, para. 9, Christian Classics Ethereal Library, https://ccel.org/ccel/teresa/way/way.i.xlvi.html.

18. "I count all things but loss for the excellency of the knowledge of Christ Jesus my Lord: for whom I have suffered the loss of all things, and do count them but dung, that I may win Christ" (Philippians 3:8 KJV).

19. Philip Yancey, *Where Is God When It Hurts?*, rev. ed. (Grand Rapids: Zondervan, 1990), 260.

20. Corrie ten Boom, *The Hiding Place* (1971; repr., Grand Rapids: Chosen, 2006), 227.

21. Quoted in Beverly Ivany, "The Pastor and the Agnostic," *Salvationist*, October 17, 2013, https://salvationist.ca/articles/2013/10/the-pastor-and-the-agnostic (italics in original).

22. Tom Harpur, "Charles Templeton," *Toronto Star*, June 24, 2001, 1.

23. Ivany, "Pastor and the Agnostic," italics in original; see Greg Laurie, *Billy Graham: The Man I Knew* (Washington, DC:

Salem, 2021), 159–70. Laurie, a noted pastor and evangelist, is confident that Templeton is in heaven: "I have no doubt that when Billy [Graham] died in 2018, his old and dear friend Charles Templeton was there sitting near the throne of God to welcome him to the Kingdom" (p. 170).

Chapter 8: Challenge #2: If God Is Real, Why Is He So Hidden?

1. Quoted in "How Is It My Fault If I Can't Feel God?" YouTube, August 27, 2022, www.youtube.com/watch?v=hE5Bu8TdFxQ; see also Jesse T. Jackson, "Former Christian Rocker Details Why He Left the Faith, Cites 'The State of Christian Culture in America,'" *ChurchLeaders*, July 29, 2022, https://churchleaders.com/news/430755-jon-steingard-details-why-he-left-the-faith-cites-the-state-of-christian-culture-in-america.html; Elyse Pham, "How Christian Singer's Life Has Changed Since Revealing He No Longer Believes in God," *The Today Show*, October 6, 2020, www.today.com/popculture/how-jon-steingard-s-life-has-changed-revealing-he-no-t192211.

2. Robert Anderson, *The Silence of God* (New York: Dodd, Mead, 1897), 63.

3. Friedrich Nietzsche, *Daybreak*, trans. R. J. Hollingdale (Cambridge, UK: Cambridge University Press, 1985), 52.

4. Based on a poll I commissioned through the Barna Group in 2015, asking a random sample of one thousand American adults if they ever had an experience they could only attribute to a miracle of God. The sample error is +/-3.1 percentage points at the 95 percent confidence level. The response rate was 55 percent.

5. Matthew Dillahunty, "Atheist Debates – Divine Hiddenness," YouTube, October 1, 2015, www.youtube.com/watch?v=TRB0TDq8tWE.

6. Daniel Wiley, "The God Who Reveals: A Response to J. L. Schellenberg's Hiddenness Argument," *Themelio* 44, no. 3

(August 2020), www.thegospelcoalition.org/themelios/article
/the-god-who-reveals-a-response-to-j-l-schellenbergs-hiddenness
-argument.

7. Daniel Howard-Snyder and Adam Green, "Hiddenness of God," *Stanford Encyclopedia of Philosophy*, Edward N. Zalta, ed., https://plato.stanford.edu/entries/divine-hiddenness, accessed June 24, 2023.

Chapter 8: Interview with Kenneth Richard Samples, MA

1. Psalm 22:1–2.
2. Isaiah 45:15.
3. Joel S. Burnett, *Where Is God? Divine Absence in the Hebrew Bible* (Minneapolis: Fortress, 2010), 149.
4. Burnett, *Where Is God?*, 117.
5. See Michael C. Rea, *The Hiddenness of God* (Oxford, UK: Oxford University Press, 2018), 6.
6. See C. S. Lewis, *Mere Christianity* (1943; repr., New York: Macmillan, 1960), 123–24.
7. Corrie ten Boom, *Jesus Is Victor* (Grand Rapids: Revell, 1985), 183.
8. Kenneth Samples, "Divine Hiddenness: A Sender or Receiver Problem?" *Worldview Bulletin*, December 30, 2022.
9. "You will seek me and find me when you seek me with all your heart" (Jeremiah 29:13); "[God] rewards those who earnestly seek him" (Hebrews 11:6).
10. "Ask and it will be given to you; seek and you will find; knock and the door will be opened to you" (Matthew 7:7).
11. "You believe that there is one God. Good! Even the demons believe that—and shudder" (James 2:19).
12. William Lane Craig, "Excursus on Natural Theology (Part 29): The Hiddenness of God," www.reasonablefaith.org/podcasts /defenders-podcast-series-3/s3-excursus-on-natural-theology /excursus-on-natural-theology-part-29, accessed June 24, 2023.

13. "By day the Lord went ahead of them in a pillar of cloud to guide them on their way and by night in a pillar of fire to give them light, so that they could travel by day or night" (Exodus 13:21).

14. See Exodus 14.

15. Psalm 42:1.

16. See Psalm 14:1; Romans 1:18–21; 5:12, 18–19.

17. Douglas Groothuis, *Christian Apologetics: A Comprehensive Case for Biblical Faith*, 2nd ed. (Downers Grove, IL: IVP Academic, 2022), 445.

18. Psalm 10:4.

19. See Michael Rea, "Divine Hiddenness, Divine Silence," in Louis P. Pojman and Michael C. Rea, *Philosophy of Religion: An Anthology*, 6th ed. (Stamford, CT: Cengage Learning, 2012), 266–75.

20. Thomas Nagel, *The Last Word* (New York: Oxford University Press, 1997), 130.

21. See Genesis 3:8.

22. Groothuis, *Christian Apologetics*, 446.

23. See Rea, "Divine Hiddenness, Divine Silence."

24. Strobel, *The Case for Faith: A Journalist Investigates the Toughest Objections to Christianity* (Grand Rapids: Zondervan, 2000), 201.

25. See Isaiah 6:5.

26. Blaise Pascal, *Pensées*, trans. and ed. Alban Krailsheimer (New York: Penguin, 1966), 149/430, 80.

27. See Rea, "Divine Hiddenness, Divine Silence," 271.

Conclusion

1. For more on Sharp's journey, see her *Why I Still Believe: A Former Atheist's Reckoning with the Bad Reputation Christians Give a Good God* (Grand Rapids: Zondervan, 2019).

2. T. M. Luhrmann, *When God Talks: Understanding the American Evangelical Relationship with God* (New York: Knopf, 2012), xvi.

3. Quoted in Dan Delzell, "A Christian Turned Atheist vs. Atheist Turned Christian," *Christian Post*, February 25, 2023, www .christianpost.com/voices/bart-ehrman-and-hugh-ross-provide -context.html.

4. Kai Nielsen, *Reason and Practice: A Modern Introduction to Philosophy* (New York: Harper & Row, 1981), 48.

5. See Lee Strobel, *The Case for Faith: A Journalist Investigates the Toughest Objections to Christianity* (Grand Rapids, Zondervan, 2000), 80.

6. Robert Jastrow, *God and the Astronomers*, 2nd ed. (New York: Norton, 1992), 14.

7. Alexander Vilenkin, *Many Worlds in One: The Search for Other Universes* (New York: Hill and Wang, 2006), 176.

8. See Lee Strobel, *The Case for Miracles: A Journalist Investigates Evidence for the Supernatural* (Grand Rapids: Zondervan, 2018), 186.

9. Strobel, *Case for Miracles*, 187.

10. Killian Fox, "Physicist Sabine Hossenfelder: 'There Are Quite a Few Areas Where Physics Blurs into Religion,'" *The Guardian*, November 26, 2022, www.theguardian.com/science/2022/nov/26 /physicist-sabine-hossenfelder-there-are-quite-a-few-areas-where -physics-blurs-into-religion-multiverse.

11. Strobel, *Case for Miracles*, 183.

12. Quoted in Jastrow, *God and the Astronomers*, 118.

13. Lee Strobel, *The Case for a Creator: A Journalist Investigates Evidence That Points toward God* (Grand Rapids: Zondervan, 2004), 225.

14. George Sim Johnson, "Did Darwin Get It Right?" *Wall Street Journal*, October 15, 1999.

15. Fazale Rana, "Origin-of-Life Predictions Face Off: Evolution vs. Biblical Creation," Reasons to Believe, March 31, 2001, https:// reasons.org/explore/publications/rtb-101/origin-of-life-predictions -face-off-evolution-vs-biblical-creation.

16. Quoted in Tish Harrison Warren, "Did Jesus Really Rise from

the Dead?" *New York Times*, April 9, 2023, www.nytimes.com /2023/04/09/opinion/jesus-rise-from-the-dead-easter.html.

17. William D. Edwards, Wesley J. Gabel, and Floyd E. Hosmer, "On the Physical Death of Jesus Christ," *Journal of the American Medical Association* 255, no. 11 (March 21, 1986): 1455–63, https://jamanetwork.com/journals/jama/article-abstract/403315.

18. Quoted in Lee Strobel, *The Case for Christ: A Journalist's Personal Investigation of the Evidence for Jesus*, rev. ed. (1998; repr., Grand Rapids: Zondervan, 2016), 277.

19. Lee Strobel, "Does Science Support Miracles? New Study Documents a Blind Woman's Healing," *The Stream*, May 16, 2020, https://stream.org/does-science-support-miracles-new-study -documents-a-blind-womans-healing; see also Clarissa Romez et al., "Case Report of Instantaneous Resolution of Juvenile Macular Degeneration Blindness after Proximal Intercessory Prayer," *Explore* 17, no. 1 (January–February 2021): 79–83, www .sciencedirect.com/science/article/pii/S1550830720300926.

20. For more on this story, see Lee Strobel, *Case for Miracles*, 101–5.

21. A random representative sample of one thousand US adults completed this questionnaire. The sample error is +/-3.1 percentage points at the 95 percent confidence level. The response rate was 55 percent. See Strobel, *Case for Miracles*, 29–31.

22. Douglas Groothuis, *Christian Apologetics: A Comprehensive Case for Biblical Faith*, 388.

23. Personal email to author, dated December 12, 2022.

24. Strobel, *Case for Faith*.

25. Mark Mittelberg, *Confident Faith: Building a Firm Foundation for Your Beliefs* (Wheaton, IL: Tyndale, 2013).

26. Peter Kreeft and Ronald K. Tacelli, *Handbook of Christian Apologetics: Hundreds of Answers to Crucial Questions* (Downers Grove, IL: IVP Academic, 1994), 47–88.

27. Colin McGinn, *The Mysterious Flame: Conscious Minds in a Material World* (New York: Basic Books, 1999), 13–14.

28. Michael Ruse, *Can a Darwinian Be a Christian? The Relationship between Science and Religion* (New York: Cambridge University Press, 2000), 78.

29. Lee Strobel, *The Case for Heaven: A Journalist Investigates Evidence for Life after Death* (Grand Rapids: Zondervan, 2021), 43.

30. Strobel, *Case for a Creator*, 270.

31. Blaise Pascal, *Pensées*, trans. W. F. Trotter (Overland Park, KS: Digireads, 2018), 121.

32. Strobel, *Case for Heaven*, 44.

33. Staks Rosch, "Atheism Has a Suicide Problem," *Huffington Post*, December 8, 2017, www.huffpost.com/entry/atheism-has-a-suicide-problem_b_5a2a902ee4b022ec613b812b.

34. Kanita Dervic et al., "Religious Affiliation and Suicide Attempt," *American Journal of Psychiatry* 161, no. 12 (December 2004), https://ajp.psychiatryonline.org/doi/full/10.1176/appi.ajp.161.12.2303.

35. Researchers tracked more than one hundred thousand nurses and other health-care professionals for seventeen years for the study. See Ying Chen et al., "Religious Service Attendance and Deaths Related to Drugs, Alcohol, and Suicide Among U.S. Health Care Professionals," *JAMA Psychiatry* 77, no. 7 (May 6, 2020), https://jamanetwork.com/journals/jamapsychiatry/fullarticle/2765488. Interestingly, research published by the *Sociology of Religion* journal found that "'while in-person religious service attendance was associated with better mental and physical health, virtual attendance was not significantly related to either outcome,' according to a summary published by *Religion Watch* at the Baylor Institute for Studies of Religion" (see Aaron Earls, "Does Online Church Attendance 'Count'?" Lifeway Research, March 28, 2023, https://research.lifeway.com/2023/03/28/does-online-church-attendance-count).

36. W. Mark Lanier, *Atheism on Trial: A Lawyer Examines the Case for Unbelief* (Downers Grove, IL: InterVarsity, 2022), 59.

37. Nancy R. Pearcey, *Love Thy Body: Answering Hard Questions about Life and Sexuality*, rev. ed. (Grand Rapids: Baker, 2019), 256.

38. See Mark 9:24.

39. Strobel, *Case for Faith*, 289.

40. Strobel, *Case for Faith*, 289.

41. H. H. Price, *Belief* (London: Allen & Unwin, 1969), 484. This book is based on the Gifford Lectures delivered at the University of Aberdeen in 1960.

42. "You will seek me and find me when you seek me with all your heart" (Jeremiah 29:13); "God . . . rewards those who earnestly seek him" (Hebrews 11:6).

From the Publisher

GREAT BOOKS

ARE EVEN BETTER WHEN THEY'RE SHARED!

Help other readers find this one:

- Post a review at your favorite online bookseller

- Post a picture on a social media account and share why you enjoyed it

- Send a note to a friend who would also love it—or better yet, give them a copy

Thanks for reading!